CHILDREN AND YOUNG PEOPLE'S PARTICIPATION IN CHILD PROTECTION

INTERNATIONAL POLICY EXCHANGE SERIES

*Published in collaboration with the
Center for International Policy Exchanges
University of Maryland*

Series Editors
Douglas J. Besharov
Neil Gilbert

*Decent Incomes for All:
Improving Policies in Europe*
Edited by Bea Cantillon, Tim Goedemé, and John Hills

*Social Exclusion in Cross National Perspective:
Actors, Actions, and Impacts from Above and Below*
Edited by Robert J. Chaskin, Bong Joo Lee, and Surinder Jaswal

The "Population Problem" in Pacific Asia
Stuart Gietel-Basten

United States Income, Wealth, Consumption, and Inequality
Edited by Diana Furchtgott-Roth

Europe's Income, Wealth, Consumption, and Inequality
Edited by Georg Fischer and Robert Strauss

The World Politics of Social Investment: Volume 1
Edited by Julian Garritzman, Bruno Palier, and Silja Hausermann

The World Politics of Social Investment: Volume 2
Edited by Julan Garritzman, Bruno Palier, and Silja Hausermann

*The Public/Private Sector Mix in the Financing and Delivery of Healthcare Services:
Some Impacts on Health Equity and the Quality of Healthcare Services*
Edited by Howard A. Palley

*Revitalizing Residential Care for Children and Youth:
Cross-National Trends and Challenges*
Edited by James K. Whittaker, Lisa Holmes, Jorge F. del Valle, and Sigrid James

*Work and the Social Safety Net:
Labor Activation in Europe and the United States*
Edited by Douglas J. Besharov and Douglas M. Call

European Social Policy and the COVID-19 Pandemic
Edited by Stefanie Börner and Martin Seeleib-Kaiser

SCHOOL of
PUBLIC POLICY

CHILDREN AND YOUNG PEOPLE'S PARTICIPATION IN CHILD PROTECTION

INTERNATIONAL RESEARCH AND PRACTICAL APPLICATIONS

Edited by

KATRIN KRIŽ AND MIMI PETERSEN

OXFORD
UNIVERSITY PRESS

Oxford University Press is a department of the University of Oxford. It furthers
the University's objective of excellence in research, scholarship, and education
by publishing worldwide. Oxford is a registered trade mark of Oxford University
Press in the UK and certain other countries.

Published in the United States of America by Oxford University Press
198 Madison Avenue, New York, NY 10016, United States of America.

© Oxford University Press 2023

All rights reserved. No part of this publication may be reproduced, stored in
a retrieval system, or transmitted, in any form or by any means, without the
prior permission in writing of Oxford University Press, or as expressly permitted
by law, by license, or under terms agreed with the appropriate reproduction
rights organization. Inquiries concerning reproduction outside the scope of the
above should be sent to the Rights Department, Oxford University Press, at the
address above.

You must not circulate this work in any other form
and you must impose this same condition on any acquirer.

Library of Congress Cataloging-in-Publication Data
Names: Križ, Katrin, editor. | Petersen, Mimi, editor.
Title: Children and young people's participation in child protection :
international research and practical applications / Katrin Križ and Mimi Petersen (editors).
Description: New York, NY : Oxford University Press, [2023] |
Series: International policy exchange series | Includes bibliographical references and index.
Identifiers: LCCN 2023004615 (print) | LCCN 2023004616 (ebook) |
ISBN 9780197622322 (hardback) | ISBN 9780197622346 (epub) |
ISBN 9780197622353
Subjects: LCSH: Child welfare—Citizen participation. | Youth in development. |
Youth—Political activity.
Classification: LCC HV713 .C39638 2023 (print) | LCC HV713 (ebook) |
DDC 362.7—dc23/eng/20230302
LC record available at https://lccn.loc.gov/2023004615
LC ebook record available at https://lccn.loc.gov/2023004616

DOI: 10.1093/oso/9780197622322.001.0001

Printed by Integrated Books International, United States of America

This book is dedicated to our children.

Contents

List of Illustrations ix
Foreword by Marit Skivenes xi
Acknowledgments xv
Contributor Affiliations xvii
Contributor Bios xix

1. Introduction 1
   Katrin Križ and Mimi Petersen

PART I: CHILDREN AND YOUNG PEOPLE AS CHANGE AGENTS

2. The Change Factory's Participation in Social Work Education in Norway 13
   Roar Sundby

3. Child-Directed Child Welfare Research and Development in Denmark 34
   Mimi Petersen

4. Care Leavers' Participation in Designing Child Welfare Services and Policy in Israel 63
   Talia Meital Schwartz-Tayri and Hadas Lotan

5. Children Claiming the Right to Live Without Violence in Nicaragua 85
   Harry Shier

PART II: PARTICIPATORY PROFESSIONAL PRACTICES

6. The Participation of LGBTQIA+ Children and Youth in Care in the Netherlands 107
   Rodrigo González Álvarez, Mijntje ten Brummelaar, Kevin R. O. van Mierlo, Gerald P. Mallon, and Mónica López López

7. Children's Participation in Foster Care in Germany 129
   Daniela Reimer

8. Creating and Crossing Age-Related Participation Boundaries in Child Protection in the United States (California) 156
   Megan Canfield, Emma Frushell, Jenna Gaudette, and Katrin Križ

9. Arts-Based Research With Children in Program Evaluation in Spain 182
   Nuria Fuentes-Peláez, Ainoa Mateos, M. Àngels Balsells, and María José Rodrigo

10. The "Making My Story" Project in Brazil 201
    Monica Vidiz, Lara Naddeo, and Debora Vigevani

PART III: CONCLUDING REMARKS

11. Concluding Remarks 229
    Katrin Križ and Mimi Petersen

Afterword 240
   Nigel Patrick Thomas

Index 245

List of Illustrations

Figures

3.1.	Child-centered social work	44
3.2.	Child-directed social work	44
3.3.	Project participants meeting with the president of Iceland in Reykjavik in 2017	48
3.4.	Project participants giving a presentation at the International Federation of Social Workers meeting in Reykjavik in 2017	49

Tables

3.1.	The Roskilde Project: Participants, Roles, Activities, and Duration	39
3.2.	Project Bella: Participants, Roles, Activities, and Duration	41
8.1.	Research Questions and Findings	164
9.1.	Examples of Drawings and Quotes From the Report	194

Foreword

Marit Skivenes

In this excellent book, Katrin Križ and Mimi Petersen provide us with a highly interesting international analysis of children's right to participation. This right is possibly the most controversial and difficult right in the United Nations Convention on the Rights of the Child (UNCRC). The difficulties with implementing and realizing children's participation rights are especially challenging, as several chapters in the book point out. I will use this opportunity to elaborate briefly on the rationale for why children should participate and why professionals (and others) find participation challenging. (I discuss this conundrum in more detail in Skivenes, 2018.)

There is no doubt that children have a legal right to participate. In addition to their legal right, there are five fundamental reasons children should participate:

1. It is a moral obligation to involve children and any individual in matters that concern them.
2. A decision about a child's best interests can only be made when the child who is affected by the decision is involved. Children must be allowed to be "authors" of their own lives because they know their needs, and they know when they are happy.
3. The quality of the decisions about children is improved by involving them because they have unique access to information about themselves, their wishes, and their values. They possess first-hand experience of what happened and how they experienced what occurred.
4. Involving children also means that children can learn and better understand situations, themselves, and their surroundings.
5. Practitioners can provide better services and solutions by involving children and thus improve the implementation of their decisions and intervention measures.

Drawing much of my empirical knowledge from studies of child protection decision-making, I would state that children's involvement cannot be a choice for the child protection services and courts. It is an obligation that decision makers are required to fulfill, as Part 2 of the UNCRC, Article 12 states: "The child shall in particular be provided the opportunity to be heard in any legal and administrative proceedings affecting the child" (United Nations, 1989, p. 4).

Disappointingly, research has shown that children's right to participate is often not realized when adults make decisions about their lives (see, e.g., Toros et al., 2018, and van Bijleveld et al., 2015, for reviews on this topic). Using child protection as a point of departure, I argue that there are six distinct reasons that decision makers in child protection do not allow children to participate:

1. Decision makers may wish to protect children from the pain and misery the children experience. They want to avoid harming the child and creating a situation that puts children in difficult loyalty conflicts. Decision makers perceive children as vulnerable and think that they should not contribute to their burden by inflicting additional negative experiences on children.
2. Decision makers are paternalistic and believe they possess the solutions and insights to ensure that children's best interests are safeguarded.
3. Many decision makers believe that children do not have sufficient ability and maturity to get involved or have reasonable perceptions about a case.
4. There may be a perception among decision makers that it does not matter whether the child participates in making the decision. If the risk of harm to the child is considered high, then decision makers may reason that they must do what is necessary regardless of what the child would say. Thus, they will not involve or hear the child.
5. Decision makers lack the competence and training in talking about difficult and sensitive issues with children and therefore avoid speaking with children and including them.
6. Much too often, there is a lack of solid structures in place for involving children in child protection. In addition to bureaucratic case management rules focused on securing due process for adults, child protection is an area that is characterized by high time pressure and often physical surroundings designed for adults, not children.

An overarching challenge for all adults lies in a cultural frame related to families and parent-child relations. Children are to be raised, guided, and educated. Within this frame, parents are superior in experience and moral and cognitive development. Children growing up to become adults and citizens in our society live in a cultural sphere of adultism, as this book elaborately shows its readers. Despite their training and clear instructions to let children participate, it is still difficult for professionals working with children to detach themselves from adultism, which is taken for granted. Barth and Olsen (2020) argue that we should view children as an oppressed group to increase awareness and implement measures for them. Although the implementation of children's right to participate is moving forward only slowly, many positive practices should be highlighted, which this book illustrates. One interesting illustration of a child perspective that I would like to use as a final word comes from a court decision about adoption from care in England. The court stated at the end of the judgment: "I have not written this [judgment] for the benefit of the adults but for Z [the baby] and wish to be sure it reaches her" (Family Court Sitting at Leeds, 2016).

References

Barth, R. P., & Olsen, A. N. (2020). Are children oppressed? The timely importance of answering this question. *Children & Youth Services Review, 110*, 104780. https://doi.org/10.1016/j.childyouth.2020.104780

Family Court Sitting at Leeds. (2016, September 5). Case No: LS15C00739.

Skivenes, M. (2018). Barneperspektiv i fokus [Child perspective in focus]. In A. Proff, G. Proff, G. Toresen, & I. Steinrem (Eds.), *Barnas Barnevern: Trygt, nyttig og samarbeidende for barn* [Children's child welfare: Safe, useful and cooperative for children] (pp. 12–17). Universitetsforlaget.

Toros, K., DiNitto, T. M., & Tiko, A. (2018). Family engagement in the child welfare system: A scoping review. *Children & Youth Family Services Review, 88*, 598–607. https://doi.org/10.1016/j.childyouth.2018.03.011

United Nations. (1989). *Convention on the rights of the child.* https://www.ohchr.org/Documents/ProfessionalInterest/crc.pdf

Van Bijleveld, G. G., Dedding, C. W., & Bunders-Aelen, J. F. (2015). Children's and young people's participation within child welfare and child protection services: A state-of-the-art review. *Child & Family Social Work, 20*(2), 129–138.

Acknowledgments

This book has been a long time in the making. The idea for it was born at a fortuitous meeting between two people from different parts of the world (Kati and Mimi) at the 2018 conference of the European Scientific Association on Residential and Family Care for Children and Adolescents (EUSARF) in Porto. We processed the idea and then contacted several of the chapter authors. The idea matured in 2019, and we established a good rapport with the authors and hoped to meet again for further discussions at the EUSARF conference in 2020. However, the coronavirus pandemic hit the world in early 2020, catapulting us all into a massive reorganization of our lives and work.

Despite the significant challenges and dilemmas, we persisted and finished this book. This feat would not have been possible without the supportive personal and professional networks of people surrounding us. All of you have believed in our work with steadfast commitment and infinite patience, communicating, writing, and contributing to creating this book in so many ways. Thank you for being who you are and for believing in us!

We owe tremendous gratitude to the practitioners and scholars who contributed to this book. A huge thanks goes to the chapter authors. You continued your contributions to the book and actively and patiently responded to our reviews and edits in 2020 and 2021.

We want to thank the children who have contributed to the projects described in many of the chapters through their direct and indirect input. You live and work in different parts of the world, speak various languages, face different living conditions, and have encountered various opportunities and obstacles. You have participated in your respective country's projects in different ways. Together, you have created a common voice for children and young people's right to participate. Your voices and impact have been a tremendous inspiration for researchers and practitioners.

In addition, a huge thanks to co-editor Kati (from Mimi) and Mimi (from Kati). Without your steadfast and joyful collaboration during the pandemic, we could not have finished this book.

Mimi: Thanks to Copenhagen University College, my workplace, for supporting me during the process of publishing this book.

Kati: I would like to thank Neeva Manandhar, my daughter, for showing me the power of joy, resilience, and positive thinking. I would like to thank Mark Ahern, my life partner, for his kindness, patience, sense of humor, and many forms of support. Lastly, I want to thank the Emmanuel College Faculty Development Fund for giving me the opportunity to engage in research with a team of talented young people with a passion for social justice.

Contributor Affiliations

M. Àngels Balsells, Department of Pedagogy, Faculty of Education, Psychology, and Social Work, University of Lleida, Spain

Megan Canfield, Departments of Sociology and International Studies, Emmanuel College, Boston, USA

Emma Frushell, Department of Sociology, Emmanuel College, Boston, USA

Nuria Fuentes-Peláez, Department of Research Methods and Diagnosis in Education, Faculty of Education, University of Barcelona, Spain

Jenna Gaudette, Department of Sociology, Emmanuel College, Boston, USA

Rodrigo González Álvarez, Faculty of Behavioral and Social Sciences, University of Groningen, the Netherlands

Katrin Križ, Department of Sociology, Emmanuel College, Boston, USA; University of Bergen, Norway

Mónica López López, Faculty of Behavioral and Social Sciences, University of Groningen, the Netherlands

Hadas Lotan, Israeli Council for Children in Care Research Division, Tel Aviv-Yaffa, Israel

Gerald P. Mallon, Silberman School of Social Work, Hunter College, New York, USA

Ainoa Mateos, Department of Research Methods and Diagnosis in Education, Faculty of Education, University of Barcelona, Spain

Lara Naddeo, Instituto Fazendo Historia, Sao Paulo, Brazil

Mimi Petersen, Department of Social Work, University College Copenhagen, Denmark

Daniela Reimer, Zurich University of Applied Sciences School of Social Work, Institute of Childhood, Youth and Family, Switzerland

María José Rodrigo, Department of Developmental and Educational Psychology, University of La Laguna, Spain

Talia Meital Schwartz-Tayri, Spitzer Department of Social Work, Ben-Gurion University of the Negev, Israel

Harry Shier, CESESMA, Nicaragua

Marit Skivenes, Centre for Research on Discretion and Paternalism, Department of Government, University of Bergen, Norway

Roar Sundby, Department of Social Work, Norwegian University of Science and Technology (NTNU), Trondheim, Norway

Mijntje ten Brummelaar, Cornerstones Youth Care and University of Groningen, the Netherlands

Nigel Patrick Thomas, Centre for Children and Young People's Participation, University of Central Lancashire, Preston, England

Kevin R. O. van Mierlo, Department of Political Science, University of Waterloo, Canada

Monica Vidiz, Instituto Fazendo Historia, Sao Paulo, Brazil

Debora Vigevani, Instituto Fazendo Historia, Sao Paulo, Brazil

Contributor Bios

M. Àngels Balsells is a Professor in the Department of Education, Psychology, and Social Work at the University of Lleida, Spain. She directs the Education and Adolescence Chair and the Doctoral School. Her research focuses on family reunification in the child protection system, positive parenting, and children and young people's participation. Her research contributes to creating scientific reference frameworks and transforming them into educational and social resources. She has managed the research unit Children's Rights and Education in partnership with the Spanish UNICEF Committee since 2010. She is a member of the expert group on positive parenting organized by the Spanish Ministry of Health, Social Services and Equality; the Spanish Federation of Municipalities and Provinces; and the Catalan and Lleida Observatories on Children's Rights. She is also part of the research group GRISIJ (Socio-educational Interventions in Childhood and Youth). ORCID ID: https://orcid.org/0000-0003-3283-8222

Megan Canfield double majored in Sociology with a concentration in Social Justice and Inequality and International Studies in Sustainability and Global Justice at Emmanuel College. While attending Emmanuel, Canfield worked as a research assistant with Katrin Križ for two years. She contributed to the chapter on the United States and assisted in language-editing chapters in this book.

Emma Frushell graduated with a degree in Sociology and Criminology from Emmanuel College in Boston, Massachusetts. As an undergraduate student, she worked as a research assistant in the Sociology Department, assisting in numerous research projects. Frushell also collaborated with Katrin Križ and Janese Free on a research project that analyzes the experiences of college students in the northeastern United States who work more than 20 hours a week during the academic year.

Nuria Fuentes-Peláez is a Professor at the Department of Research Methods and Diagnosis with the Faculty of Education at the University of Barcelona, Spain. She chairs the research group GRISIJ (Socio-educational Interventions in Childhood and Youth). She is a member of international academic networks on child protection, including the International Foster Care Research Network, and an expert member of the Catalan Observatory on Children's Rights and Barcelona's Welfare Council. Her research interests lie in child protection systems. She contributes to these research areas: children, youth, and families in foster care and adoption; family socio-educational group programs addressing families in vulnerable or risk situations; and collaborative research and participatory research methods with professionals, families, and children. Her publications span relevant and innovative group programs aimed at foster care, adoptive families, biological families, and families in vulnerable situations, as well as books, book chapters, and scientific articles. ORCID ID: https://orcid.org/0000-0003-0751-2140

Jenna Gaudette is a recent graduate from Emmanuel College in Boston, Massachusetts, with a bachelor's degree in Sociology. At Emmanuel, Gaudette worked as a research assistant with Katrin Križ and Janese Free.. Since graduating, Gaudette has worked as a Domestic Violence Advocate with United Services. She aspires to obtain a master's degree in Social Work.

Rodrigo González Álvarez is a Mexican queer cisgender PhD candidate at the Department of Pedagogical and Educational Sciences, Faculty of Behavioral and Social Sciences, at the University of Groningen, the Netherlands. González Álvarez obtained his Bachelor's in Psychology at the National Autonomous University of México (UNAM) and moved to the Netherlands to pursue graduate studies. Currently in the last year of his PhD program, González Álvarez studies the lives of LGBTQIA+ youth in out-of-home care within the Audre project. One of his main interests is their resilience, understood as a multisystemic complex process. He has presented his findings at several conferences and published them in academic journals. González Álvarez truly believes in the importance of using his personal and professional life to better the world and society. He finds meaning and energy in striving for social justice and creating a more equal, inclusive, and diverse world for everybody.

Katrin Križ is a Professor of Sociology at Emmanuel College in Boston, Massachusetts. She earned a PhD degree in Sociology at Brandeis University and a master's degree in International Development at Clark University, United States. Križ, who grew up in Austria, has taught at colleges and universities in the United States and Europe. Her research interests lie in children and young people targeted for oppression, migrant education, and child welfare policy and practice. She has published numerous articles and book chapters and two books: *Child Welfare Systems and Migrant Children: A Cross-Country Study of Policies and Practice* (Oxford University Press, 2015), edited with Marit Skivenes, Ravinder Barn, and Tarja Pösö, and *Protecting Children, Creating Citizens: Participatory Child Protection Practice in Norway and the United States* (Policy Press, 2020).

Mónica López López obtained her PhD degree in Psychology at the University of Oviedo, Spain. She is an Associate Professor at the Faculty of Behavioral and Social Sciences of the University of Groningen, the Netherlands. Her research interests include the disparities in child protection decisions, the participation of children and families in decision-making processes, and the experiences of LGBTQIA+ youth in care. López López serves as a board member of the European Scientific Association on Residential and Family Care for Children and Adolescents (EUSARF) and teaches decision-making in child protection at the international master's degree in Youth,

Society, and Policy. Recent publications include *Decision Making and Judgment in Child Welfare and Protection* (Oxford University Press, 2020) and *Working With LGBTQIA+ Youth in the Child Welfare System* (University of Groningen Press, 2021).

Hadas Lotan, BSW, is the coordinator of the Israeli Council for Children in Care Research Division. She graduated with excellence from the Ruppin Academic Center, School of Social Work, and is a graduate of the Policy Practice and Social Rights master's degree program at the Bob Shapell School of Social Work at Tel Aviv University. Her master's thesis analyzed the participation of disadvantaged youth in multilevel decision-making. She is currently involved in developing and guiding a policy advocacy forum for young people who aged out of care.

Gerald P. Mallon, DSW, is the Julia Lathrop Professor of Child Welfare and the Senior Associate Dean of Scholarship and Research at the Silberman School of Social Work at Hunter College in New York City. For more than 46 years, Mallon has been a child welfare practitioner, advocate, educator, and researcher. He was the first child welfare professional in the United States to research, write about, and develop programs for LGBTQIA+ youth in child welfare settings. He has written extensively about child welfare and child protection issues. He is the Senior Editor of the professional journal *Child Welfare* and the author or editor of more than 29 books. His most recent books include *Strategies for Child Welfare Professionals Working With Transgender and Gender Expansive Youth*, published by Jessica Kingsley Press and co-edited with Jama Shelton, and *Social Work Practice With Transgender and Gender Expansive Youth* (3rd edition), published by Routledge Press. Mallon earned his doctorate in Social Welfare from the Graduate Center at the City University of New York.

Ainoa Mateos is an Associate Professor at the Faculty of Education, University of Barcelona, where she earned a PhD degree in Education, awarded with special merit. She teaches and conducts research in the Research Methods and Diagnosis Department and coordinates the internships for the degree in Social Education. Since 2006, her research has focused on protecting children and on family- and gender-based violence as a member of the research group GRISIJ (Socio-educational Interventions in Childhood and Youth). Her publications include books, book chapters, and scientific articles about socio-educational programs for biological families, vulnerable families, and youth and the prevention of gender-based violence. ORCID ID: https://orcid.org/0000-0002-1159-9966

Lara Naddeo majored in Psychology at the Pontificia Universidade Católica, Sao Paulo, Brazil, and earned a master's degree in Psychosocial Intervention from the University of Barcelona. She works at Instituto Fazendo Historia, a nonprofit organization in Sao Paulo, on projects related to early childhood interventions in alternative care, foster care services, and children's literature. The degree and a summer course about children's participation at the University of Groningen deepened her knowledge about child protection, foster care, and children's rights. Naddeo is currently taking a graduate course in psychoanalysis and works in private practice with children, young people, and adoptive families.

Mimi Petersen, PhD, is an Associate Professor in the Department of Social Work at the University College Copenhagen, Denmark. Her research and teaching interests focus on children's rights and the interplay between participation, citizenship, and empowerment. She has obtained in-depth practice and research experience, knowledge, and skills from practicing social work with children and young people in different countries. She is an experienced researcher, teacher, supervisor, and project manager. Petersen is a member of the board of the Nordic Association Against Child Abuse and Neglect and the research network entitled Child Rights Institute at Lund University in Sweden. She is the founder of the Nordic Network for Children's Right to Participation in Social and Educational Work—Practice, Research, and Development. Petersen has published several journal articles and books on children and young people's participation in social work and research in Nordic countries.

Daniela Reimer is a Professor at the Zurich University of Applied Sciences (ZHAW) in Switzerland. She earned her PhD degree at the University of Siegen, Germany. From 2006 to 2018, she conducted extensive research on the biographies of young people in foster care. Reimer's research focuses on young people's biographical experiences. Her research is qualitative, and she is profoundly interested in social pedagogical perspectives and narratives. She has researched the transition into foster care from children's point of view, foster family cultures and family images, the supervision of foster families, the interplay of normality and identity in young people in foster care, and breakdowns in foster care. She is currently conducting a longitudinal qualitative study with young adults who were in foster care. Reimer is working on translating research into practice and policy, developing new advanced vocational training opportunities for social workers and educators.

María José Rodrigo is Professor and Director of the master's degree program in Family Intervention and Mediation at the University of La Laguna, Spain. She was the President of the European Association of Developmental Psychology from 2008 to 2011. Since 2010, she has been a Fellow of the Association for Psychological Science (APS) for sustained and outstanding distinguished contributions to the field. She serves as an expert commissioned by the Spanish Ministry of Health, Social Policy, and Equality to promote good practices among professionals in using evidence-based and preventive approaches to family work. Her research interests lie in evidence-based parenting programs to promote positive parenting for marginalized families and prevent child maltreatment. She designed, implemented, and evaluated group parenting programs and published numerous articles. She also researches the neurological and personality bases of maternal insensitivity to infant signals in mothers who neglect their children. She published several articles in international outlets on the neural networks activated in adolescents in risky decision-making in social contexts. ORCID: https://orcid.org/0000-0001-5504-886X

Talia Meital Schwartz-Tayri, MSW, PhD, is a faculty member in the Spitzer Department of Social Work at Ben-Gurion University of the Negev and a former postdoctoral research affiliate in the school of Social Welfare at the University of California, Berkley. Meital Schwartz-Tayri is a researcher in social services and social work practice. Her work focuses on the characteristics and outcomes of personal welfare services in Israel and the United States, including the engagement of social workers and social work students in policy advocacy. In her most recent studies, Meital Schwartz-Tayri utilizes linked child-family services big data and novel machine learning methods to enhance our understanding of the impact of social welfare services consumption on children and families and expand theory in social service research. ORCID: https://orcid.org/0000-0002-8073-2775

Harry Shier was born in Ireland and worked in England for many years in children's play, then in children's rights and participation. In the 1990s, he developed the "Article 31 Children's Consultancy Scheme," which enables children to act as consultants to the management of cultural institutions, an experience crystallized in his 2001 paper "Pathways to Participation," which introduced a tool for analyzing children's participation now widely used throughout the world. In 2001, he moved to Nicaragua in Central America to work with local community education organization CESESMA, supporting child workers on coffee plantations in claiming and defending their rights. In 2016, he was awarded a PhD degree at Queen's University Belfast for his study on Nicaraguan children's perceptions of human rights in school. He now lives in Ireland, where he is semi-retired, though still working on a range of children's rights and participation initiatives.

Professor Marit Skivenes, who holds a PhD degree in political science from the Department of Political Science at the University of Bergen in Norway, is Professor and Director of the Centre for Research on Discretion and Paternalism at the University of Bergen. Skivenes is the Principal Investigator of several international research projects on child protection systems and has received a Consolidator Grant from the European Research Council. She has published numerous scientific works on child protection decision-making, children's rights, migrant children, child welfare systems, and broader welfare issues. She is an editor of *The Oxford Handbook of Child Protection Systems* (2023). Skivenes has recently been appointed to lead the Norwegian government's expert committee on child protection (2021–2023).

Roar Sundby is an Associate Professor in the Department of Social Work at the Norwegian University of Science and Technology (NTNU). From 2016 to 2019, he participated in a joint project with the children in the Change Factory. He published two books on social work while contributing to multiple books and articles with his expertise in child protection. Sundby is a board member of the International Consortium for Social Development (ICSD) and served as the president of the European branch from 2005 to 2015.

Mijntje ten Brummelaar obtained her PhD degree at the University of Groningen, the Netherlands. Her dissertation focused on the participation of young people in decision-making procedures in secure residential care. Hereafter she worked as a project leader with the Alexander Foundation, specializing in youth participation and participatory research practices. She currently works at Cornerstones Youth Care, a professional foster care provider, and at the University of Groningen as a researcher and teacher. The focus of her research is on participatory research and care practices.

Nigel Patrick Thomas is Professor Emeritus of Childhood and Youth at the University of Central Lancashire and founder of the Centre for Children and Young People's Participation. He was previously a social work practitioner, manager, advisor, and social work educator. His research interests are principally in child welfare, children's rights, children and young people's participation, and childhood and intergenerational relations theories. He is currently part of a study of ethical practice and the meaning of child safety in different institutional contexts, funded by the Australian Research Council. His publications include *Children, Family and the State: Decision-Making and Child Participation* (Macmillan, 2000; Policy Press, 2002); *An Introduction to Early Childhood Studies* (with Trisha Maynard, Sage 2004, 2009); *Social Work With Young People in Care: Looking After Children in Theory and Practice* (Palgrave, 2005); *Children, Politics and Communication: Participation at the Margins* (Policy Press, 2009); *A Handbook of Children and Young People's Participation: Perspectives From Theory and Practice* (with Barry Percy-Smith, Routledge, 2010); and *Participation, Citizenship and Intergenerational Relations in Children and Young People's Lives* (with Joanne Westwood, Cath Larkins, Dan Moxon, and Yasmin Perry, Palgrave Macmillan, 2014).

Kevin R. O. van Mierlo, who lived in out-of-home care in the Netherlands, is a master's student in Political Science at the University of Waterloo, Canada. His academic background lies in Religious Studies (the University of Tilburg, the Netherlands). Van Mierlo completed a research assistantship within the Audre project at the University of Groningen during his undergraduate years. He co-edited the book *Working With LGBTQIA+ Youth in the Child Welfare System: Perspectives from Youth and Professionals*, published by Groningen University Press.

Monica Vidiz holds a master's degree in Sociology of Childhood and Children's Rights from the Institute of Education at University College London (UCL) and majored in Psychology at the Pontificia Universidade Católica in Sao Paulo, Brazil. She has nine years of work experience with children and young people in alternative care at the Instituto Fazendo Historia in Sao Paulo. She participated in publishing several books, coordinated the Befriending Program, and took part in advocacy issues. Her current interests include children's participation in care, intersectional inequalities, and a sense of belonging.

Debora Vigevani majored in Psychology at Pontificia Universidade Católica, Sao Paulo, Brazil. She has worked with children and young people in alternative care at Instituto Fazendo Historia (Sao Paulo) for 12 years, coordinating Fazendo Minha História since 2014. Her current interests include supporting families in the adoption process, ensuring greater participation of children and adolescents, and maintaining their identities after adoption.

1
Introduction

Katrin Križ and Mimi Petersen

This volume shows how children and young people, child protection practitioners, scholars, and nongovernmental organizations promote children's participation in their practice and research. It presents multiple pathways to children and young people's participation in various national contexts. Its starting point is Article 12 of the 1989 United Nations Convention on the Rights of the Child (UNCRC), the legal platform establishing children's right to participation at the international level. Article 12 emphasizes that UN member states must ensure that children express their views and that these views count according to children's age and maturity in administrative and judicial proceedings (United Nations, 2020; United Nations Department of Economic and Social Affairs, n.d.). General Comment 12 about Article 12 further explains the scope of participation:

> The views expressed by children may add relevant perspectives and experience and should be considered in decision-making, policymaking and preparation of laws and/or measures as well as their evaluation.
>
> . . . These processes are usually called participation. The exercise of the child's or children's right to be heard is a crucial element of such processes. The concept of participation emphasizes that including children should not only be a momentary act, but the starting point for an intense exchange between children and adults on the development of policies, programmes and measures in all relevant contexts of children's lives. (United Nations Committee on the Rights of the Child, 2009, p. 5)

Aims

This book has two aims. Its primary aim is to highlight different pathways to children's and young people's participation in child protection by providing

Katrin Križ and Mimi Petersen, *Introduction* In: *Children and Young People's Participation in Child Protection*.
Edited by: Katrin Križ and Mimi Petersen, Oxford University Press. © Oxford University Press 2023.
DOI: 10.1093/oso/9780197622322.003.0001

recent international examples of participatory research and practices that constitute or promote participation by children and young people. We hope that these examples can inspire children and young people, children's rights activists, child protection and international development practitioners, students, scholars, and public policymakers in child protection, so they initiate, design, and implement participatory practices that protect children and young people from maltreatment. We interchangeably use the terms "children's participation" and "children and young people's participation." The term "child protection systems" includes laws, policies, and practices by individuals and public and nonprofit organizations that aim to protect children from maltreatment, primarily in the family. The participatory practices include child protection practice and system innovations initiated and implemented by children and young people. They also encompass participatory practice programs, methods, and tools that professionals utilize in the public and nonprofit child protection sectors.

The secondary aim of this volume is to analyze a variety of participatory practices and research approaches. The book chapters examine these questions: What are the pathways to children's and young people's participation that children, youth, and adults forge? What are their advantages and benefits? What are the difficulties in creating opportunities for children's participation, and what are strategies to overcome them? Are there unique challenges to developing and implementing participation in practice and research depending on children and young people's experiences, identities, and social positions? What are the outcomes of children and young people's participation?

Concepts and Questions

This book is grounded in the assumption that children can and should have agency in decisions that affect their lives. We define children's participation as children's ability to develop and express opinions taken seriously by other children and young people and adults working with children in social change and decision-making processes about their lives (Hart, 1992; Shier, 2001; Archard & Skivenes, 2009). Decisions that children can drive and participate in occur in public child protection, research, and the development of activities and services that protect children from maltreatment.

Participation refers to children's and young people's opportunity to make meaningful choices, develop a sense of agency, possess the resources to exercise agency, and achieve their life choices (Shier, 2001; Kabeer, 2005). Our understanding of participation has been influenced by the definitions developed by the UNCRC and the operationalization of participation by scholars in the field, including Roger Hart (1992), Harry Shier (2001), Nigel Thomas (2002), David Archard and Marit Skivenes (2009), and Gerison Lansdown (2010). What these definitions have in common is an emphasis on creating opportunities and resources for children's agency and power in decision-making and social change initiatives. We believe that adults must protect children and young people from maltreatment and support their participation in decision-making and social change by creating conditions that make their participation possible.

Following the central tenet of a child equality perspective (Križ et al., in preparation), we understand children and young people as moral equals to adults: they have the same right as adults to exercise power in decisions over their lives. These ideas about genuine participation have informed this book: (1) Children and young people receive information to reflect and develop their views. (2) Adults support children and youth in developing a sense of agency. They listen to them and take their opinions seriously when making decisions about their lives. (3) Children and young people collaborate with adults to initiate decisions. They develop actions that lead to social change based on their experiences, views, and interests.

The theoretical paradigms that inspired this volume are the child-centric perspective developed by Skivenes and Strandbu (2006) and intersectionality proposed by Kimberlé Crenshaw (1989, 1991) and Patricia Hill Collins (1993). A child-centric view recognizes children's position at the structural level through rights to participation in law and policies (Skivenes & Strandbu, 2006). It acknowledges children's position at the individual level, first through recognition by adults, including parents, professionals, and other adults who recognize children as having interests and needs in the present rather than the future, and second through respect for children's views of the world, which differ from those of adults (Skivenes & Strandbu, 2006).

The second conceptual pillar that undergirds this volume is Collins's (1993) idea of intersectionality. Collins proposed that race, class, and gender are intersecting categories of oppression and resistance that structure our relationships and biographies. Based on this paradigm, we started this book assuming that children and young people's experiences with participation in child protection will vary depending on their social positions. We presumed that children's experience with participation would differ by age, social class, race, ethnicity, gender, ability, sexuality, migrant background, nationality, and so on. Following this idea, we have included a heterogeneous sample of case studies that reflect differences in children's social positions. We will describe in the section on "chapter selection" below how we selected the book chapters.

Significance

This book was motivated by the fact that there is no single edited volume on children and young people's participation in child protection from an international perspective in English. There is a lack of this type of book despite a recent surge in scholarship on children and young people's involvement in child protection over the past 5 years. (See, for example, Arbeiter & Toros, 2017; Balsells et al., 2017; Berrick et al., 2015, 2018; Bessell, 2011, 2015; Burford & Gallagher, 2015; Duncan, 2020; Duramy & Gal, 2020; Gerdts-Andresen & Hansen, 2021; Knag et al., 2018; Križ, 2020; Križ & Roundtree-Swain, 2017; Križ & Skivenes, 2017; Race & O'Keefe, 2017; Rafeedie et al., 2019; Schoch et al., 2020; Skivenes, 2015; ten Brummelaar et al., 2016; Petersen & Kornerup, 2021; Pösö & Enroos, 2017; Vis & Fossum, 2015; Wolff et al., 2016.)

Prior book-length scholarship focuses on child-centric professional social work practice or children and young people's experiences in one country (Duncan, 2020; Race & O'Keefe, 2017), two countries with different approaches to child protection (Križ, 2020), or the Nordic countries (Petersen & Kornerup, 2021). It analyzes children and young people's participation in various fields in high-income countries (Gal & Duramy, 2015) and low-income countries (Duramy & Gal, 2020). Children's participation in society overall (in child protection, education, politics, etc.) has also been documented by the country reports about the status of children to the United Nations Committee on the Rights of the Child (United Nations Human Rights Office of the High Commissioner, 2019).[1] However, the country reports and committee observations are country specific and voluminous and do not facilitate a view on children's participation in child protection primarily aimed at children and youth and practitioners and scholars of child protection. This volume extends this extant literature by highlighting children and young people's voices and agency in different countries. It brings together scholars and practitioners who showcase innovative participatory practices in children and young people's collective change initiatives and their individual participation in child protection practice and research. Adults and young people have written the book chapters, which emphasize children and young people's actions, experiences, and voices.

Chapter Selection

The empirical evidence for the book consists of recent research on children's participation in child protection by over 20 scholars and practitioners in the field of child protection that spans four continents: Asia, Europe, North America, and South America. We employed purposeful sampling and convenience sampling when choosing the case studies included here. We took two steps when selecting the cases. First, we chose case studies from presentations given at the 2018 European Scientific Association on Residential and Family Care for Children and Adolescents (EUSARF) meetings. We used these selection criteria: we chose presentations that focused on children and young people's voices and actions to change public child protection systems. Given our theoretical interest in intersectionality, we aimed for diversity in the social positions of children and young people because we wanted to highlight possible differences in experiences. We also chose presentations about current participatory practices initiated by practitioners in public child protection agencies and nongovernmental organizations. We primarily selected studies of child protection systems that had not been widely discussed in scholarly journals in English. We then contacted the authors of the presentations that fit these criteria and invited them to participate in this book project. Most of the authors we asked were enthusiastic. (Four did not respond to our invitation or declined it.)

Second, we invited scholars with a long track record of studying children's participation in child protection to contribute a foreword and afterword that synthesized their empirical and theoretical contributions in the field. The contributions of two of them— Marit Skivenes and Nigel Patrick Thomas— can be found in this volume. The third, Harry Shier, graciously offered to extend his foreword into an entire chapter.

Organization of the Book

The book begins with Marit Skivenes's foreword, which introduces the significance of the book's topic based on her longstanding scholarly research in the field of child protection. Skivenes describes why children's participation in child protection is important and the reasons adults often do not allow children to participate. The main body of the book consists of three parts. The first part is entitled "Children and Young People as Change Agents." Its three chapters highlight children and young people's actions for social change to protect children from violence. We begin by presenting children and young people's collective initiatives and efforts in public child protection in Europe before showcasing how children and young people in the Middle East and Latin America have initiated systemic changes to protect children from violence. Chapters 2 and 3 describe how children and youth who were in out-of-home care collaborate with adults to change public child protection systems in Norway and Denmark. In Chapter 2, Roar Sundby describes how children and young people with lived experience in the child protection system in Norway participate in training future child protection caseworkers in relational skills and collaborative case practice. In Chapter 3, Mimi Petersen shows how children and young people in Denmark participate in researching and developing public child protective and community services in Denmark. In Chapter 4, Talia Meital Schwartz-Tayri and Hadas Lotan discuss how care leavers in Israel help design and develop public child protective services and policies. In Chapter 5, Harry Shier describes children's collective initiatives to reduce violence against children in Nicaragua.

The book's second part is called "Participatory Practice Approaches by Child Protection Professionals." It focuses on what participatory practices by practitioners, or so-called street-level bureaucrats (Lipsky, 1980), could or should look like. The practitioners work for nonprofit organizations or public child protection agencies in Brazil, Germany, Spain, the Netherlands, and the United States (California). Most of the chapters examine children and young people's experiences with participation in public child protection systems. Each substantive chapter lists discussion questions at the end.

The first part of the book starts with the experiences of LGBTQIA+ youth in out-of-home care in the Netherlands: in Chapter 6, Rodrigo González Álvarez, Miintje ten Brummelaar, Kevin R. O. van Mierlo, Gerald P. Mallon, and Monica López López discuss the participatory practice approaches by public child protection workers as viewed by LGBTQIA+ youth. The chapter provides insight into strengthening child welfare services and practices for LGBTQIA+ youth in a way that allows for their voices to have weight. In Chapter 7, Daniela Reimer describes how young people in foster care benefit from participation and how social workers need to reorient their professional identities and (pre)conceptions of children and young people. In Chapter 8, Megan Canfield, Emma Frushell, Jenna Gaudette, and Katrin Križ illustrate how child protection caseworkers provide (and block) participatory opportunities for children in the Californian child protection system depending on the children's age.

In Chapter 9, Nuria Fuentes-Peláez, Ainoa Mateos, M. Àngels Balsells, and María José Rodrigo show how researchers can use an arts-based research (ABR) approach with children to ensure children's participation in child protection program evaluation. In Chapter 10, Monica Vidiz, Lara Naddeo, and Debora Vigevani showcase a nonprofit organization in Brazil that aims to ensure that children in foster and residential care know and own their past, present, and future stories, which facilitates their participation in decisions about their lives.

In Part III of the book, we offer concluding remarks. Chapter 11 describes the main takeaways from the book about the variety of pathways to participation. We will discuss the different participatory approaches presented in the chapters, the contexts in which children and young people's participation occur, and the outcomes of participation. In an afterword, Nigel Patrick Thomas summarizes the book's findings and calls for interpersonal relationships based on recognition and organizational structures and cultures based on esteem, love, and respect.

Notes

1. Except for the United States, which has not ratified the 1989 United Nations Convention on the Rights of the Child (UNCRC), state parties to the UNCRC and nongovernmental organizations working on children's rights periodically prepare reports to the committee. The committee discusses the reports and presents the state with concluding observations to monitor states' progress toward implementing the UNCRC. The committee reports thus represent a soft policy mechanism to influence states to enforce the rights embedded in the UNCRC, including children's rights to participation.

References

Arbeiter, E., & Toros, K. (2017). Participatory discourse: Engagement in the context of child protection assessment practices from the perspectives of child protection workers, parents and children. *Children & Youth Services Review, 74*, 17–27.

Archard, D., & Skivenes, M. (2009). Hearing the child. *Child & Family Social Work, 14*, 391–399.

Balsells, M. Á., Fuentes-Peláez, N., & Pastor, C. (2017). Listening to the voices of children in decision-making: A challenge for the child protection system in Spain. *Children & Youth Services Review, 79*, 418–425.

Berrick, J., Dickens, J., Pösö, T., & Skivenes, M. (2015). Children's involvement in care order decision-making: A cross-country analysis. *Child Abuse & Neglect, 49*, 128–141.

Berrick, J. D., Dickens, J., Pösö, T., & Skivenes, M. (2018). International perspectives on child-responsive courts. *International Journal of Children's Rights, 26*, 251–277.

Bessell, S. (2011). Participation in decision-making in out-of-home care in Australia: What do young people say? *Children & Youth Services Review, 33*(4), 496–501. https://doi.org/10.1016/j.childyouth.2010.05.006

Bessell, S. (2015). Inclusive and respectful relationships as the basis for child inclusive policies. The experience of children in out-of-home care in Australia. In T. Gal & F. Durami (Eds.), *International perspectives and empirical findings on child participation: From social exclusion to child-inclusive policies* (pp. 183–205). Oxford University Press.

Burford, G., & Gallagher, S. (2015). Teen experiences of exclusion, inclusion and participation in child protection and youth justice in Vermont. In T. Gal & B. F. Duramy (Eds.), *International perspectives and empirical findings on child participation. From social exclusion to child-Inclusive policies* (pp. 227–255). Oxford University Press.

Collins, P. H. (1993). Toward a new vision: Race, class, and gender as categories of analysis and connection. *Race, Sex & Class, 1*(1), 25–45.

Crenshaw, K. (1989). Demarginalizing the intersectionality of race and sex: A Black feminist critique of antidiscrimination doctrine, feminist theory and antiracist politics. *University of Chicago Legal Forum, 1*, 139–168.

Crenshaw, K. (1991). Mapping the margins: Intersectionality, identity politics, and violence against women of color. *Stanford Law Review, 43*, 1241–1299.

Duncan, M. (2020). *Participation in child protection: Theorizing children's perspectives.* Palgrave Macmillan.

Duramy, B. F., & Gal, T. (2020). Understanding and implementing child participation. Lessons from the Global South. *Children & Youth Services Review, 119*, n.p. https://doi.org/10.1016/j.childyouth.2020.105645

Gal, T., & Duramy, B. F. (Eds.). (2015). *International perspectives and empirical findings on child participation. From social exclusion to child-inclusive policies.* Oxford University Press.

Gerdts-Andresen, T., & Hansen, H. A. (2021). How the child's views are weighted in care order proceedings. *Children & Youth Services Review, 129*, n.p. https://doi.org/10.1016/j.childyouth.2021.106179

Hart, R. (1992). *Children's participation: From tokenism to citizenship.* UNICEF International Child Development Center. http://www.unicef-irc.org/publications/pdf/childrens_participation.pdf.

Kabeer, N. G. (2005). A critical analysis of the third Millennium Development Goal. *Gender & Development, 13*(1), 13–24.

Knag, F. M., Taylor, J., & Iversen, A. (2018). Precarious participation: Exploring ethnic minority youth's narratives about out-of-home placement in Norway. *Children & Youth Services Review, 88*, 341–347.

Križ, K. (2020). *Protecting children, creating citizens: Participatory child protection practice in Norway and the United States.* Policy Press.

Križ, K., Krutzinna, J., Pösö, T., & Skivenes, M. (in preparation). *The Child Equality Standards: An analytical tool to evaluate children's equality in public decision-making.*

Križ, K., & Roundtree-Swain, D. (2017). "We are merchandise on a conveyer belt": How young adults in the public child protection system perceive their participation in decisions about their care. *Children & Youth Services Review, 78*, 32–40.

Križ, K., & Skivenes, M. (2017). Child welfare workers' perceptions of children's participation: A comparative study of England, Norway, and the United States (California). *Child and Family Social Work, 22*(S2), 11–22.

Lipsky, M. (1980). *Street-level bureaucracy: Dilemmas of the Individual in public service.* Russell Sage.

Lansdown, G. (2010). The realization of children's participation rights: Critical reflections. In B. Percy-Smith & N. Thomas (Eds.), *A handbook of children and young people's participation: Perspectives from theory and practice* (pp. 11–23). Routledge.

Petersen, M., & Kornerup, I. (2021). *Børn som deltagere i professionel praksis (Children as participants in professional practice).* Hans Reitzels Forlag.

Pösö, T., & Enroos, R. (2017). The representation of children's views in Finnish court decisions regarding care order. *International Journal of Children's Rights, 25*(3–4), 736–753.

Race, T., & O'Keefe, R. (2017). *Child-centred practice. A handbook for social work.* Macmillan.

Rafeedie, J., Hudson, S. M., Deavenport-Saman, A., Rao, S., Rogers, K., & Roberts, S. (2019). Decision-making in foster care: A child-centered approach to reducing toxic stress. *Children & Youth Services Review, 96*, 10–16.

Schoch, A., Aeby, G., Müller, B., Cottier, M., Seglias, L., Biesel, K., Sauthier, G., & Schnurr, S. (2020). Participation of children and parents in the Swiss child protection system in the past and present: An interdisciplinary perspective. *Social Sciences, 9*(8), 1–19.

Shier, H. (2001). Pathways to participation: Openings, opportunities and obligations. *Children & Society, 15*(2), 107–117.

Skivenes, M., & Strandbu, A. (2006). A child perspective and children's participation. *Children, Youth & Environments, 16*(2), 10–27.

Skivenes, M. (2015). The space for children's participation (in Norwegian). *Tidsskrift for Velferdsforskning, 1*, 48–60.

Ten Brummelaar, M. D., Knorth, E. J., Post, W. J., Harder, A. T., & Kalverboer, M. E. (2016). Space between the borders? Perceptions of professionals on the participation in decision-making of young people in coercive care. *Qualitative Social Work, 17*(5), 692–711.

Thomas, N. (2002). *Children, family and the state. Decision-making and child participation.* Policy Press.

United Nations. (2020). *Convention on the Rights of the Child.* https://www.ohchr.org/en/professionalinterest/pages/crc.aspx

United Nations Committee on the Rights of the Child. (2009). *General comment no. 12. The right of the child to be heard.* https://www2.ohchr.org/english/bodies/crc/docs/AdvanceVersions/CRC-C-GC-12.pdf

United Nations Department of Economic and Social Affairs. (n.d.). *Definition of youth.* https://www.un.org

United Nations Human Rights Office of the High Commissioner. (2019). *The Committee on the Rights of the Child.* https://www.ohchr.org/en/hrbodies/crc/pages/crcindex.aspx

Vis, S. A., & Fossum, S. (2015). Organizational factors and child participation in decision-making: Differences between two child welfare organizations. *Child & Family Social Work, 20,* 277–287.

Wolff, R., Flick, U., Ackermann, T., Biesel, K., Brandhorst, F., Heinitz, S., Heinitz, S., Patschke, M., & Robin, P. (2016). *Children in child protection.* Nationales Zentrum Frühe Hilfe.

PART I
CHILDREN AND YOUNG PEOPLE AS CHANGE AGENTS

PART I

2
The Change Factory's Participation in Social Work Education in Norway

Roar Sundby

Introduction

Children's right to express themselves and participate in decision-making has been well established in the United Nations Convention on the Rights of the Child (UNCRC), Article 13 (United Nations, 1989), and the Norwegian Child Welfare Act (Barnevernloven, 1992, § 6-3). However, the professionals in the public child welfare services (CWS) in Norway have often made decisions without including children's voices and sufficiently documenting their opinions in legal documents (Eidhammer, 2014; Oppedal, 1999; Paulsen, 2015, 2016; Križ & Skivenes, 2015; Skauge, 2010; Ulvik, 2015; Skivenes & Strandbu, 2006; Vis & Fossum, 2015; Willumsen & Skivenes, 2005). The CWS has recently faced a high level of conflict: there have been protests and demonstrations stating that the CWS kidnaps children (Barnevernet Steals Children, n.d.). These protests are particularly prevalent among ethnic and racial minority groups and families of migrant background. Children of migrant background are overrepresented in the Norwegian child welfare system[1] (Skivenes, 2015). Their participation in child protection processes is tenuous, as research by Knag Fylkesnes et al. (2018) has shown. By October 2017, the European Court of Human Rights (ECHR) had investigated 27 cases from the CWS. Most of these cases involve the violation of Article 8—the right to respect of private and family life (see, for instance, ECHR, 2019). The CWS could have avoided some of these conflicts with a more cooperative child welfare practice that promotes the active participation of children and families.

In some municipalities, the CWS has begun to promote the development of cooperative practices based on new terminology and relationship with children. In the last few years, the Change Factory (*Forandringsfabrikken*), an

Roar Sundby, *The Change Factory's Participation in Social Work Education in Norway* In: *Children and Young People's Participation in Child Protection*. Edited by: Katrin Križ and Mimi Petersen, Oxford University Press.
© Oxford University Press 2023. DOI: 10.1093/oso/9780197622322.003.0002

organization of children with experience in the CWS, has been instrumental in advocating for children's rights to be heard in child welfare processes. (The children and young people in the Change Factory call themselves the "PROs," or professionals in child welfare.)

The terms "co-production" and "cooperation," which I will use in this chapter, indicate an equitable and positive relationship between child welfare workers and children. They refer to child welfare workers including children in decision-making processes about their lives. The term "co-production" denotes a kind of interaction between children and child welfare workers beyond participation; it is an equal relationship or partnership between children and professionals in public services. "Co-production" refers to the uppermost possible level of cooperation between children and adults and signifies genuine participation. It corresponds to the actual involvement of children as described by Shier (2001). In "cooperation" between children and adults, children take the initiative in the decision-making process (see Bell, 2002; Shier, 2001). The cooperation between children and adults is a condition for children's right to express themselves. The overall aim of providing children who encounter the CWS with the necessary help, care, and protection at the right time and guaranteeing that children experience safety, love, and understanding by professionals as established by the Child Welfare Act (Barnevernloven, 1992) depends significantly on the quality of the relationship between children and child welfare workers. There is evidence that children's participation in child welfare proceedings increases the success of out-of-home care arrangements and feelings of well-being for children (Vis et al., 2010a). In treatment services, an alliance between children and service providers is significantly related to both youth's and parents' reports of symptom improvement (Hawley & Weisz, 2005). And, as Crowe (2007) states: "the embracing of youth as partners is an essential component of... positive youth development" (p. 140).

The most recent national guidelines for child welfare education programs in Norway (RETHOS, 2019), developed by the Norwegian Directorate for Children, Youth, and Family Affairs, included children's knowledge as one of the three platforms of knowledge alongside practical knowledge (knowledge from the practice field) and, of course, traditional academic evidence-based scientific knowledge. The guidelines encourage children with lived experiences with different aspects of the child welfare system, including child welfare investigations and experience in foster care and residential care homes,[2] to participate in the training of future child welfare professionals.

(In Norway, the child welfare and social work higher education system is responsible for training the professionals in this area of social work practice.) Social work education programs can develop relational and cooperative skills based on safety, trust, and reciprocity in the interactions between social work students, teachers, PROs, and practitioners in social work education. The PROs participate in the education and training of future child welfare workers. They use their knowledge about how they are listened to in the CWS to advise students about how they can include children in the child welfare process. The main idea behind the guidelines is that the education system should include collaborative skills in the training of future child welfare workers by including children who have experienced different types of services in the CWS (RETHOS, 2019).

This chapter aims to demonstrate how education can improve the cooperation with children through the inclusion of children's lived experiences in the curriculum and training of relational competencies. Positive relational skills have resulted in a more sustainable outcome with better solutions for children involved with the child welfare system (Hawley & Weisz, 2005; Vis et al., 2010b). This chapter examines how this cooperation changes the contents of how we educate future child welfare workers today. It shows how the collaboration between children with lived experiences in the CWS and higher education in social work improves the quality of social services.

I will first describe the "My Life Education" project and its ideological basis before discussing the impact of the Change Factory. I will discuss the practical methods associated with universities including children's knowledge in social work education. I will describe the experiences of how this knowledge is changing how educators in social work education conceptualize the child welfare education curriculum. Finally, I will present the results from evaluations and interviews with the PROs, students, and teaching staff involved in the project.

The Change Factory

Developed in 2008, the Change Factory is a foundation that aims to organize children with lived experiences in the CWS and engage them to become a part of the social services through systematically collecting their knowledge and experiences. The children, known as the PROs, work in collaboration with the CWS and other public authorities. They come from a variety of backgrounds in terms of gender and ethnicity and have had a variety of experiences with the CWS. They present their knowledge and perspectives to decision makers at all levels of government: child welfare workers in the CWS, educators, and national-level politicians, including the Norwegian prime minister. The PROs have shared their experience and knowledge with CWS workers for more than a decade and have made an essential contribution to changing and improving the CWS, mental health care services, schools, and the juvenile justice system. The guiding philosophy of the Change Factory is "Listen to (young) people!" As they state in their own words: "The Change Factory's philosophy ... is built on a simple idea: Listening to what (young) people in welfare systems think about what is of help, and what should change for the help to feel appropriate and actually help" (Forandringsfabrikken, n.d., About us, n.p.). The Change Factory's methodology is "based on the idea that the people who know the most about problematic systems are those within them, and no one can better identify solutions for development" (Forandringsfabrikken, n.d., About us; INTRAC for Civil Society, 2017). The use of participatory "change-methodology, which is based upon Participatory Learning and Action (PLA) to encourage young people ... to honestly talk about and evaluate their situation" (Forandringsfabrikken, n.d., About us, n.p.), is central to their mission (INTRAC for Civil Society, 2017). The Change Factory has since 2008 met with and collected experiences from more than 5,500 children in schools and 1,500 children involved with the child welfare system (Forandringsfabrikken, n.d., Om forandringsfabrikken kunnskapssenter).

In 2018, the Norwegian government recognized the Change Factory as a so-called National Knowledge Center, thus valuing the knowledge from children and youth as equally important as knowledge from other research centers. It is the only Knowledge Center that exclusively gathers direct knowledge from children and young people. The creation of this Knowledge Center is a significant step toward recognizing the value of children's lived experiences as essential knowledge for public care systems. The Change Factory has published these books with collected experiences from children in different areas, including child welfare, violence, abuse, and substance abuse: *Children's Child Welfare: Safe, Useful and Cooperative for Children* (Forandringsfabrikken, 2018); *Mental Health Care From Us Who Know It* (Forandringsfabrikken, 2019a); *If I Were Your Child: About the Use of Coercion in Residential Care Homes* (Forandringsfabrikken, 2019b); and *Just and Safe: About Reporting, Investigation and Legal Process From*

Children Who Have Experienced Violence or Assault (Forandringsfabrikken, 2019c). Knowledge from children presented in these publications differs from the research on children. Children's statements are not analyzed or interpreted; they are published and delivered without any "corrections" by adults.

The My Life Education Project

My Life Education is a so-called innovation project[3] based on a cooperation between the child welfare education programs at the University of South-Eastern Norway (USN), the Norwegian University of Science and Technology (NTNU), and the Change Factory. The Norwegian Directorate for Children, Youth, and Family Affairs financed this project. Its purpose is to include lived experiences from children in the child welfare education and training process, improve the cooperational competencies for students in child welfare education through practical training of skills, and develop pedagogical tools to enhance children's participation in social work education. More than 1,000 students were exposed to various trainings from children with lived experience with the child welfare system.

This project was necessary for three reasons: First, children involved with the CWS expressed clearly that the CWS did not sufficiently consider their voice, interests, and viewpoints. The PROs presented several striking examples and advice for improvement. Second, several research projects indicate that the CWS and child welfare workers spent little face-to-face time with children. In addition, contrary to the legal requirements, professionals did not sufficiently document children's viewpoints and interests in the CWS case files (Skauge, 2010). Lastly, the curriculum of child welfare workers appears not to improve (and even discourage) university students' competencies in collaborative practices with children, although communication training, such as role-plays, and communication theory are a part of social work education and training. In fact, after the training activities, social work students' communication with children seems to have been even more challenging for students. The threshold for communicating seemed to increase (not decrease), and students' impression prevailed that talking with children is complicated and difficult (Gamst, 2011; Grytbakk et al., 2019). Recent research on the decisions by the CWS shows that children are not sufficiently listened to (Magnussen & Skivenes, 2015). It appears that the two findings—students' challenges in communicating with children and children's experiences with not being heard—are connected.[4]

Framework and Terminology

The project transforms the PROs' experiences into suggestions about how the CWS should perceive and treat children. The project includes recommendations for changes in working methods and values. Examples of the PROs' advice include:

> Always talk to the child first to be sure to get the child's opinion on the situation (this can be quite different from their teachers' or parents' viewpoint).
> Always ask the child if the information can be shared and with whom.
> Include the child's viewpoint in the decision-making concerning the child. (Forandringsfabrikken, n.d., About us, n.p.)

The Change Factory is strongly value based and has expressed several values that should form the basis of all types of professional practice with children. The core values in child welfare work supported by the PROs are:

- Openness: all information relevant to the child's situation should be available to the child if cooperation is authentic.
- Humility means that child welfare workers should listen to and respect children's understanding and opinions.
- Co-decisions are understood as decisions discussed between the involved parties where the different positions have been heard.
- Love is a core value of child welfare practice. After an intense discussion about how it should be understood in the legislation, it is now included in the Norwegian Child Welfare Act. This value has initiated a debate in the academic system about how love should be understood in a professional setting (Neumann, 2016; Thrana, 2016).

The advice by the PROs and the Change Factory's values emphasizes the perception and recognition of children as equals. This view of children can best be expressed in these words by the Change Factory: "Children and youth have important knowledge about their own life, they have the same value as all people, they need love, they need to be trusted and taken seriously" (Forandringsfabrikken, n.d., About us, n.p.). Attempting to change the dynamics of the relationship between children and child welfare workers by placing greater emphasis on recognizing children as equal, valuable human beings requires a new set of terminology in the CWS. The tradition of labeling children as *service users* or *clients* with diagnoses or other behavioral characteristics lingers in social work and other helping professions. However, children may perceive this language as rhetoric that only further alienates them from social workers. As the PROs stress, "Use my name and listen to my history" (Forandringsfabrikken, 2017). It has been a salient aspect of the PROs' work to catalog the terms that conceptualize children as clients, service users, and so on. The "child welfare caseworker" became "the contact person," "the foster family" became "my family," and so on. (Forandringsfabrikken, 2017). These changes should be reflected by higher education and training in social work.

Co-production
When child welfare workers perceive children as equal to adults and carriers of knowledge with the same value and importance as other parties, it allows for a new relationship and communication between child welfare workers and children. Frank discussions, mutual understanding, and open dialogue replace orders, messages, behavioral descriptions, and diagnoses. (Moore [2011] discusses the importance of critical dialogue in the construction of children's citizenship.) Children and adults make decisions because of open arguments where different parties, including the children, can express their opinion.

Challenging the Education System in Child Welfare

Social work education involves training students in skills for a professional practice that will influence the quality of the work in child welfare. Recent changes in the guidelines for child welfare education now define three platforms of knowledge: *evidence-based knowledge* included in the science-based curriculum of social work education; *practice knowledge* as in the skills and experiences from child welfare workers sharing their methods and experiences; and *knowledge from the children* who are involved with the services (RETHOS, 2019).

The impact of children's lived experiences varies considerably between different educational institutions. Only the individuals who receive the service can ultimately be the ones who evaluate it. Children's participation in child welfare education is crucial to changing the understanding in social work education and the social services about what constitutes excellent social work. Including cooperation with children in social work requires a revised paradigm in the education system. It involves a type of education that teaches people's values, dialogue, and empathic and relational skills and activities alongside evidence-based knowledge. Evidence-based expertise, based on scientific knowledge, has traditionally dominated the academic world. The relational competencies of experienced social workers are not easy to pinpoint and transfer to the education system. In relational and cooperative practices, skills and values appear more crucial than methods, manuals, or programs. However, academic education has excluded emotional and even relational aspects of professional practice. Therefore, when the PROs reintroduce values, social relations, and communication as central components of the child welfare system, they positively alter the content of social welfare services and academia toward a more inclusive paradigm of education and public services.

Ways of Including the PROs in Social Work Education

The PROs have participated in the education of child welfare workers, particularly in communication training, in various ways. They act as lecturers or co-lecturers with an adult specialist or scientist, as consultants and commentators on student projects, as conversation partners in one-to-one communication training, and as participants in evaluating students' communicative skills. Educators incorporated conversations between students and the PROs into exams by testing students' ability to listen, share, be responsive, and exhibit appropriate body language. (Exams consist of oral and written parts.) The students' and PROs' reflections on the quality of the meetings may also be part of exams. The students document their conversation(s) with the PROs with a short video and a written reflection as a basis for the oral exam.

The young people participating in child welfare education have been between 15 and 20 years old, and they have had recent involvement with the CWS. The projects consistently follow the steps that are necessary to ensure their safety; for example, one of the principles followed in the training sessions are that the PROs are always placed with individuals they know and can support them in the meetings with the students. These individuals are representatives from their organization or professors whom the PROs know and trust. The Change Factory prepares the PROs for the conferences and debriefs them if they find their interactions with the students uncomfortable or challenging.

Another protection for the PROs who participate guarantees that their stories, suggestions, and perspectives are never "interpreted" or modified in a session. The statements by the PROs are respected as they express them. The stories that they choose to share often include difficult and personal aspects of their lives and interactions with the care system; therefore, it is of utmost importance that the students and teaching staff treat the PROs' experiences with respect in and beyond the classroom.

The first time the PROs participated in the teaching at the two universities, the responses from the students were overwhelmingly positive. For example, they stated that "to work together with these children is really the meaning of studying child welfare" (this is a quote from students' evaluation). The reactions of the teaching staff were more mixed. They felt they had a new responsibility to alter their past syllabi to align with the terminology and experiences introduced by the PROs. One teacher wrote, "From now on, I'll have to change all my lectures." Some sounded wearier. Teachers pointed to concerns about the privacy and confidentiality of the PROs and their families. There was general concern among the teaching staff that the discussions of the difficult life histories that the PROs shared may retraumatize them and pose an additional burden in their lives. Some teachers found these questions so complex that they withdrew their participation in the pedagogical activities with the PROs. My evaluation[5] of the project showed that the input and experiences from the PROs have led to a new understanding of how to train skills in child welfare education.

Students' Relational Understanding

The participation of the PROs in child welfare education in the My Life Education project allowed for a renewed focus on relational and communication skills in social work education. The changes in relational skills training for a more cooperative child welfare practice can be summarized as follows: A more equal and open two-way communication replaces the traditional subject-object or therapist-client relationship. There has been less focus on manuals and structured interviews. The focus has shifted from children's behavior toward their lived histories as narrated and experienced by them. Educators and students have become increasingly aware of the sensitivity it takes to handle the power relations between students and the PROs. Despite this, the information shared in the types of educational settings created by the My Life Education project seems to be both more open and genuine than the information gathered in top-down relationships in education.

Students' Communication Skills

One of the main reasons for not allowing children to participate in child welfare cases has been communication difficulties between children and child welfare workers (Vis et al., 2010a). This issue requires attention to developing skills in working with children through participatory processes (Vis et al., 2010a). Several evaluations of traditional communication training in child welfare education reveal that the activity becomes dysfunctional because students felt that the assessment interview with children was difficult. The students lost self-confidence and felt that they could not manage the meeting (Vis, 2004). The use of role-play as a technique in training, in which students interacted with different cases and took on various social worker roles, became challenging because it felt artificial and did not give students the feeling of "real" communication. As a former social work student stated: "You leave three years of education and are afraid of talking with children." This kind of sentiment does not serve as a positive reference for the education system. It is not helpful for public services if future child welfare workers exit their education feeling trepidation about talking with children.

Based on the communication difficulties experienced by social work students, there has been an attempt in social work education to shift from role-play to communication between real people: between students or between students and young people in the child welfare system. The focus in training has become participation in "open conversations." An approach emphasizing open dialogue and getting to know the other (Haarakangas et al., 2007) inspired these conversations. A trauma-informed care perspective, which focuses on trust and safety more than investigating specific events or situations, influenced this approach as well (Bath & Seita, 2018). The ease and intuitiveness inherent in these conversations give students a feeling of connectedness that should be a primary condition for all kinds of genuine cooperation.

Awareness of Students' Personal Histories

Understanding social relations in child welfare work practice includes an insight into social workers' attitudes and presentation of self. Awareness of one's history is a prerequisite to being open and attentive to a child's history. Some students have traumatic or difficult relationships and backgrounds, contributing to why they chose this profession. However, past trauma or involvement in the child welfare system may also constitute an obstacle or create unhealthy patterns in the students' meetings with the children because their trauma can affect their work. This dynamic necessitates that the students become aware of their personal history as an essential element of communication training. The My Life Education project worked with methodologies such as Life Story and the River of Life (see Ryan & Walker, 2016, for more information) with small groups of six to seven students, where students could share their histories. The outcome of these training sessions seems to be a more vital self-awareness of students' limits in relationships and of their comfort zone in interacting with others. The students in the project reported a community feeling based on a more profound knowledge of fellow students, an improved level of cooperation among students, the development of a stronger mutual connection and interpersonal relationships between students, and, most importantly, the importance of listening to others' life stories without prejudice. By acknowledging one's limits in training, social work students can be better social workers in practice.

The PROs' Messages to the Students

The PROs find themselves in a unique and autonomous position where they can educate social work students about the realities of the child welfare system. They inform the students about their lived experiences and interactions with the system: the positive aspects, but also, more importantly, the unproductive, harmful, or traumatizing facets of the system. They may offer suggestions about improving the child welfare system and other public systems designed to help people. Their advice may be included in students' textbooks. The core messages from the PROs include consistent, honest, and productive communication while respecting the child's voice and opinion to guarantee the protection of children and promote cooperation and co-production in decision-making.

Here are some quotes that evidence the kind of knowledge the PROs express in the participation process. The first quote is about why children involved with the CWS have found participation helpful:

> In the first meeting with the child welfare services, I met with two persons who wanted to know how I was doing and what the situation at home was. They took what I said seriously, therefore I was able to tell them what had happened. It certainly took some time before I was able to trust them. But when my experiences were seen as real, I dared to tell them what was hurting the most. It made me feel worthy of receiving help. (Forandringsfabrikken, 2017, p. 82)

In contrast, there were things that the CWS did that the children did not find helpful:

> It felt as if my contact person did not understand that there were reasons behind when I did silly things. It felt as they just saw that I did this and that, without trying to find the cause. They put tags on me instead of investigating if there were bigger things behind them. Then I lost a lot of trust in my contact persons and became frustrated. In addition, they figured out different ways of helping me that in my opinion was [the] wrong kind of help. (Forandringsfabrikken, 2017, p. 107)

The PROs considered cooperation necessary, as this quote illustrates:

> Today I know that decisions are not taken over my head. All kinds of plans, goals and decisions about me and my life are discussed with me firsthand. It makes me feel like a captain in my own life. When I have that captain's hat, I am more eager to direct my life in a positive direction. Then the child welfare services and I have the same goals, and we can cooperate much better. (Forandringsfabrikken 2017, p. 73)

Evaluations by Students, the PROs, and Teaching Staff

The researchers evaluated the My Life Education project by analyzing 200 written exams of first-year and second-year students in the child welfare programs of 2016 and 2017, containing reflections of their conversations with the PROs. The students participating in the dialogues with the PROs were, in their descriptions, focused on what these encounters teach them. One first-year student wrote: "We also had this conversation with the PROs that was really interesting. To experience the real practice so early in the study made us a lot stronger and gave a better perspective on the education and the work to come." A second-year student commented: "The conversation with the PROs; a scary but really useful experience. A pain that makes you stronger." Another second-year student said: "In the conversations, many feelings appeared; there was laughter and joy, irritation, sorrow, and wonder." This is what this student took away from the training: "We have discovered how important the atmosphere is experienced. The atmosphere should express friendliness and calm. It's about the context of the dialogue in addition to our body language." Another second-year student wrote: "It is important to be mentally present to have the possibility to go deeper. Grasp the opportunity to approach personal themes!" And another second-year student thanked the PROs this way: "We ... are very grateful that the PROs are willing to share their experiences and give us useful suggestions on our way."

Some of the students' quotes reflect the students' preparation for good co-operation, including the following: share from your own life, use daily language, be attentive so you can listen, refrain from judging, and so on. One of the PROs reported: "They [the students] proceed in a way so that I just talk, talk, talk.... [T]hey are so clever. To talk about your life makes it easier to live your life."

The students' reflections are applicable beyond the classroom in that the dialogue with the PROs is meaningful for future professional practice and builds vital skills. The thoughts of the PROs are equally fascinating and revealed their positive experiences with the students. None of the PROs we interviewed expressed any negative feelings about their participation in the project. Some of them indicated that telling their story had a healing effect. Many of them felt that it was satisfying that their stories could influence the life of another child in the system. Most of the PROs had told their history before in different settings and were ready for their own and other people's reactions.

The project staff gathered the PROs' immediate reactions to the encounters with the students through focus group interviews (see Gibbs, 1997) just after their sessions with the students. One PRO explained:

> I never liked having to go to therapy, but I like to talk to students because they can also tell us something about themselves. They seem so fresh, and they react freshly, so it makes us feel good. Because I have a good feeling in my stomach that kids in the future are lucky to meet such beautiful people as we have met here. It feels good to talk about your own life when you know that you are not judged.

The PROs observed that the traditional education system does not improve the students' communicative and relational skills. One of them said, "I remember some time ago I was in a first-year class, and the students were so engaged, and when we came back in the third year, they were really scared to talk with children."

This is an inherent challenge of the education system: to improve students' relational skills through experience from interaction with people in real settings. It is essential to note in the context of the PROs' evaluations that the PROs who participated in the project may have had dramatic background histories of abuse and neglect. They may have experienced meetings with schools, mental health care institutions, child welfare services, or other social services that they may have felt did not work in their best interests. It could be daunting and make deep impressions on them to meet young people with totally different life experiences.

The third group involved in this cooperation was the academic staff members. Staff members from nine child welfare programs were interviewed in 2021 as part of the project (Skauge et al., 2021). The responses among the staff varied from solid resistance to full cooperation with the PROs. Those who supported the collaboration with the PROs cited Article 12 of the UNCRC and found that the PROs' lived experiences were a valuable contribution to professional training (Skauge et al., 2021). One teacher who questioned the PROs' involvement stated:

> If we use the Change Factory . . ., we must be sure that the participants have approval from their biological parents, then we are dependent on the approval from the youth themselves and we are dependent on the eventual approval from the foster family and approval from the CWS if they talk about

their child welfare services, so it is a lot of persons involved. (Skauge et al., 2021, pp. 205–223)

The idea of professional distance has characterized the history of professionalization in social work. Professionals should not get involved in social relations with their clients. Therefore, the My Life Education project and students' interaction with the PROs challenge several well-established truths in the academic tradition. The teaching staff's reactions to children's participation can be interpreted in this light.

Discussion

The innovation project My Life Education aims to integrate knowledge from children with lived experiences in the CWS into the education and training of social work students at the university level in Norway. By enhancing the collaborative and relational skills of future child welfare workers, this kind of training aims to improve the CWS's ability to include children in the process of decision-making. One of the first reactions to this project by the teaching staff was that the PROs are vulnerable and may suffer or be retraumatized by being exposed and presenting their story to the students. The most common argument against the PROs sharing their histories with students in an educational setting is their potential vulnerability. The teachers who opposed the involvement of the PROs argued that the PROs could not give authoritative consent to their participation because they are too young. The teachers surmised that the PROs might regret sharing their stories or perspective at a later point in time.

On the other hand, the PROs reported increased self-confidence and personal importance related to their valuable contributions to the education of child welfare workers. An additional objection is legal concerns about the right to privacy and confidentiality that most social services are obligated to respect. Educators believe that universities should respect confidentiality in sensitive cases. On the other hand, it is vital to protect universities as places of freedom of expression for young people. However, the reactions of the teaching staff were generally positive. They emphasized that the introduction of lived experiences from children and parents who are interacting or have interacted with the child welfare system is improving higher social work education and the competencies of future child welfare workers and contributes to the improvement of the CWS and children's lives.

The next step will be to develop pedagogical designs relevant for involving children's knowledge in child welfare education. These designs ought to work for the number of students taught. So far, the number has varied from several hundred students to one-to-one encounters between students and PROs. Another dimension is the involvement of the academic staff in the presentations. Educators are debating whether they should respect the PROs' experiences as independent narratives about their lives or comment on or moderate their contributions to relate the stories to other parts of the curriculum.

Political and Ethical Reflections

In social work education in Norway, the teaching staff has usually agreed about the criteria for evidence-based knowledge and how they ought to present it to students in the classroom. The participation of children with lived experiences in the CWS in the education of child welfare workers has triggered both political and ethical reflections. Here are some critical questions: How do educators select the young people who participate in social work education? Should there be an age limit for children who participate? Are there children in particularly vulnerable situations who should not participate? Can children give consent to participating in social work education and training? Can it be harmful to the PROs to participate? Will the children regret it at a later point in time as others may identify and stigmatize them as clients in the CWS? How should the PROs' privacy be protected and balanced against the child's right to expression? These are questions we have encountered throughout the My Life Education project. We are currently still in an early phase of developing suitable forms of inclusion of children's knowledge in social work education.

Adults have repressed the fundamental human right of many social groups to express themselves who are considered vulnerable: children, primary and secondary school students, clients of the social services, people with disabilities, and people with lived experiences in mental health institutions. Professionals may speak on behalf or in place of these vulnerable groups, claiming that they do not know what is in their best interest.

The PROs' experience with their participation in social work education and training at the university level in Norway has been that they gained self-respect when standing up and telling their experience with the CWS. The PROs thought that talking in front of a group of listeners is valuable for later life and that sharing their stories might be helpful to others in the same situation. There is no evidence of difficult experiences or regrets from the numerous PROs who have participated in the education and training programs during the project period. The evaluation of the project by the young people participating in child welfare education is overwhelmingly positive, given that they are well prepared and cared for before and after their meetings with the students.

Conclusion

Research has shown that child welfare workers rarely and infrequently talk with children in their child welfare investigations due to a lack of established routines, low self-confidence, and lack of relational competencies in conversations with children (Vis et al., 2010a). The right for children and young people to express themselves in a safe environment can liberate praxis and give them a voice in the public sphere. The education system must play a crucial role in improving this situation. It is a profoundly ethical approach in child welfare for professionals to meet children with mutual respect and recognize them as equal partners in open dialogues (Honneth, 1995). The participation of young people with challenging or unique life experiences in the CWS in the education and training of future child welfare workers has changed the terminology and understanding of how child welfare workers should practice. Based on the work of the My Life Education project, I conclude by saying that it should be impossible to work in child welfare without talking to and including children's opinions in decisions, even from a very young age. The relationship between child welfare workers and children is and must continue moving toward a more equal, human-to-human relationship. The inclusion of values and emotions in creating these relationships makes them safer and more trustworthy for children.

Improving social work students' ability to use open dialogue and cooperation with children are two crucial aspects of improving child welfare routines. Students in the child welfare field must become familiar with talking to and listening to children's opinions during their studies and fieldwork. The development and cultivation of cooperational, relational, and communication skills with children is an aspect of children's involvement in the child welfare process that needs further research and development.

Reflection Questions

(1) What is the difference between learning about children's problems and learning from children with challenges?
(2) How should children participating in social work education and training be protected and cared for in their encounters with social work students?
(3) Is there a conflict between children's and families' right to privacy and to participate and be heard?
(4) How can children who contribute their personal stories to the advancement of social work education empower future children both individually and as a group?

Notes

1. Children who were born in Afghanistan, Eritrea, Iraq, Russia, Burma, Iran, and Somalia belonged to the top seven groups of children born outside Norway who were in the child welfare system in 2009 (Kalve & Dyrhaug, 2009). Children who were born in Norway and whose parents were born in Russia, Iran, Iraq, Afghanistan, Morocco, Eritrea, and Vietnam were in the top seven groups in the system (Kalve & Dyrhaug, 2009).
2. The Norwegian CWS works with approximately 55,000 children each year. This number accounts for nearly 5% of the child population. Of these 55,000 children, 15,000 are in out-of-home care (Statistics Norway, 2019).
3. Innovation projects are projects funded by the Research Council of Norway or other government departments following a public call.
4. David (2002) has provided a very useful discussion of the methodological problems encountered in this kind of action research and innovation project as the one between the Change Factory as an interest group and the universities.
5. I have obtained the empirical material for the description of the results presented here through different sources and methods: formal and informal interviews, conversations, written reflections and citations from meetings and teachings, and direct participation in the innovation project.

References

Barnevernet Steals Children [A Facebook Community]. (n.d.). *Norway, give us back the children you stole.* Retrieved July 7, 2021, from https://www.facebook.com/BarnevernetStealsChildren

Barnevernloven. (1992). *The Child Welfare Act of July 17, 1992* (new version only available in Norwegian). https://lovdata.no/dokument/NL/lov/1992-07-17-100

Bath, H., & Seita, J. (2018). *The three pillars of transforming care: Trauma and resilience in the other 23 hours.* University of Winnipeg.

Bell, M. (2002). Promoting children's rights through the use of relationship. *Child and Family Social Work, 7*(1), 1–11.

Crowe, K. M. (2007). Using youth expertise at all levels: The essential resource for effective child welfare practice. *New Directions for Youth Development, 113,* 139–149. https://doi.org/10.1002/yd.206

David, M. (2002). Problems of participation: The limits of action research. *International Journal of Social Research Methodology, 5*(1), 11–17. https://doi.org/10.1080/13645570110098037

Eidhammer, S. (2014). *Youth and participation in the child welfare service* [Master's thesis, NTNU].

European Court of Human Rights (ECHR). (2019). *Case of Strand Lobben and others v. Norway* (Application no. 37283/13). https://hudoc.echr.coe.int/eng#{%22itemid%22:[%22001-195909%22]}

Forandringsfabrikken [The Change Factory]. (n.d.). *About us (English).* Retrieved February 23, 2023 https://forandringsfabrikken.no/en/metoden/

Forandringsfabrikken [The Change Factory]. (n.d.). *Om forandringsfabbriken kunnskapssenter* [About the Change Factory's knowledge center]. Retrieved February 23, 2023, from https://forandringsfabrikken.no/en/kunnskapssenter/

Forandringsfabrikken [The Change Factory]. (2017). *Barnevernet fra oss som kjenner det* [Child welfare from us who have experienced it]. Universitetsforlaget.

Forandringsfabrikken [The Change Factory]. (2018). *Barnas barnevern: Trygt, nyttig og samarbeidende for barn* [Children's child welfare: Safe, useful and cooperative for children]. Universitetsforlaget.

Forandringsfabrikken [The Change Factory]. (2019a). *Psykisk helsevern fra oss som kjenner det* [Mental health care from us who know it]. Universitetsforlaget.

Forandringsfabrikken [The Change Factory]. (2019b). *Hvis jeg var ditt barn. Om tvang i barnevernsinstitusjon* [If I were your child. About coercion in a residential care home]. Universitetsforlaget.

Forandringsfabrikken [The Change Factory]. (2019c). *Rett og sikkert: Om anmeldelse, avhør i barnehuse og rettsak fra unge som har opplevd vold eller overgrep* [Just and safe: About reporting, investigation and hearing from children who have experienced violence or assault]. Universitetsforlaget.

Gamst, K. T. (2011). *Profesjonelle barnesamtaler: å ta barn på alvor* [Professional conversations with children: Taking children seriously]. Universitetsforlaget.

Gibbs, A. (1997). *Focus groups. Social Research Update, 19.* Sociology at Surrey. http://Surrey.ac.uk

Grytbakk, A., Skauge, B., & Sundby, R. (2019). From client to partner. Children changing the child welfare services and the education of child welfare workers. In M. Aferbauer,

G. Berc, A. Heimgartner, L. Rither, & R. Sundby (Eds.), *Social development: Ways of understanding society and practising social work* (pp. 167–182). LIT Verlag.

Haarakangas, K., Seikkula, J., Alakare, B., & Aaltonen, J. (2007). Open dialogue: An approach to psychotherapeutic treatment of psychosis in northern Finland. In H. A. D. Gehart (Ed.), *Collaborative therapy: Relationships and conversations that make a difference* (pp. 221–233). Routledge.

Hawley, K. M., & Weisz, J. R. (2005). Youth versus parent working alliance in usual clinical care: Distinctive associations with retention, satisfaction, and treatment outcome. *Journal of Clinical Child and Adolescent Psychology, 34*(1), 117–128.

Honneth, A. (1995). *The struggle for recognition: The moral grammar of social conflicts.* Polity Press.

INTRAC for Civil Society. (2017). *Participatory Learning and Action (PLA).* https://www.intrac.org/wpcms/wp-content/uploads/2017/01/Participatory-learning-and-action.pdf

Kalve, T., & Dyrhaug, T. (2009). *Barn og unge med innvandrerbakgrunn i barnevernet 2009* [Children and youth with immigrant origin in the child welfare system 2009]. SSB report 39/2011. Statistics Norway.

Knag Fylkesnes, M., Taylor, J., & Iversen, A. (2018). Precarious participation: Exploring ethnic minority youth's narratives about out-of-home placement in Norway. *Children and Youth Services Review, 88*, 341–347.

Križ, K., & Skivenes, M. (2015). Child welfare workers' perceptions of children's participation: A comparative study of England, Norway and the USA. *Child & Family Social Work, 11*(S2), 11–22.

Magnussen, A., & Skivenes, M. (2015). The child's opinion and position in care order proceedings: An analysis of judiciary discretion in the county boards decision-making. *International Journal of Children's Rights, 23*, 705–723. https://doi.org/10.1163/15718182-02304001

Moore, S. (2011). Constructing critical citizenship with young people: Alternative pedagogies. *International Journal of Child, Youth and Family Studies, 3/4*, 494–509. https://dx.doi.org/10.18357/ijcyfs23/420117764

Neumann, C. B. (2016). Children's quest for love and professional child protection work: The case of Norway. *International Journal of Social Pedagogy, 5*(1), 104–123. https://doi.org/10.14324/111.444.ijsp.2017.08

Oppedal, M. (1999). *Rettsikerhet ved akutte vedtak etter barnevernloven* [The rule of law in acute decisions under the Child Welfare Act]. Universitetsforlaget.

Paulsen, V. (2015). *Children and youths' participation in the child welfare service.* Presentation. NTNU Trondheim, Norway. Retrieved February 23, 2023 https://www.researchgate.net/publication/284726636_Children_and_youthsparticipation_in_the_child_welfare_service

Paulsen, V. (2016). Ungdommers erfaringer med medvirkning I barneveret [Youths' experiences with participation in child welfare]. *Fontene Forskning, 1*, 4–15.

RETHOS. (2019). *Forskrift om nasjonal retningslinje for barnevernspedagogutdanning* [Legal regulation of the National Guidelines for Child Welfare Education in Norway]. https://lovdata.no/dokument/SF/forskrift/2019-03-15-398

Ryan, T., & Walker, R. (2016). *Life story work.* Coram (Adoption and Fostering Academy) BAAF.

Shier, H. (2001). Pathways to participation: Openings, opportunities and obligations. *Children and Society, 15*, 107–117. https://doi.org/10.1002/CHI.617

Skauge, B. (2010). *Er det noen som vil høre på meg?* (Isn't there anyone who wants to listen to me?) NTNU Institute of Social Work. https://ntnuopen.ntnu.no/ntnu-xmlui/bitstream/handle/11250/267722/402461_FULLTEXT01.pdf?sequence=1&isAllowed=y

Skauge, B., Roar, S., & Sørlie, H. E. (2021). Kærlighed og professionalisme i det faglige arbejde med børn [Love and professionalism in professional work with children]. In M. Petersen & I. Kornerup (Eds.), *Børn som deltagere i professionel praksis: Åbninger, muligheder og rettigheder* [Children as participants in professional practice: Openings, possibilities and rights] (pp. 205–223). Hans Reitzels Forlag.

Skivenes, M. (2015). How the Norwegian child welfare system approaches migrant children. In M. Skivenes, R. Barn, K. Križ, & T. Pösö (Eds.), *Child welfare systems and migrant children: A cross country study of policies and practices* (pp. 39–61). Oxford University Press.

Skivenes, M., & Strandbu, A. (2006). A child perspective and children's participation. *Children, Youth and Environments, 16*(2), 10–27.

Statistics Norway. (2019). *Child welfare 2018.* https://www.ssb.no/en/sosiale-forhold-og-kriminalitet/statistikker/barneverng/aar/2019-07-03

Thrana, H. M. (2016). Kjærlighetens inntreden i barnevernet – en utfordring for den profesjonelle relasjon? [Introduction of love into child welfare – a challenge for the professional relationship?] *Tidsskriftet Norges Barnevern, 2*, 96–109.

Ulvik, O. S. (2015). Talking with children: Professional conversations in a participation perspective. *Qualitative Social Work, 14*(2), 193–208.

United Nations. (1989). *Convention on the rights of the child.* https://www.ohchr.org/Documents/ProfessionalInterest/crc.pdf

Vis, S. A. (2004). *Samtaler med barn i barnevernet* [Conversations with children in child welfare]. Skriftserie. Barnevernets utviklingssenter i Nord Norge, Tromsø.

Vis, S. A., & Fossum, S. (2015). Organizational factors and child participation in decision-making: Differences between two child welfare organizations. *Child & Family Social Work, 20*, 277–287.

Vis, S. A., Holtan, A., & Thomas, N. (2010a). Obstacles for child participation in care and protection cases—Why Norwegian social workers find it difficult. *Child Abuse Review, 21*(1), 7–23. https://doi.org/10.1002/car.1155

Vis, S. A., Strandbu, A., Holtan, A., & Thomas, N. (2010b). Participation and health—A research review of child participation in planning and decision-making. *Child & Family Social Work, 16*(3), 325–335. https://doi.org/10.1111/j.1365-2206.2010.00743.x

Willumsen, E., & Skivenes, M. (2005). Collaboration between service users and professionals: Legitimate decisions in child protection - A Norwegian model. *Child & Family Social Work, 10*, 197–206.

3
Child-Directed Child Welfare Research and Development in Denmark

Mimi Petersen

Introduction

This chapter discusses children and young people's participation in two child welfare research and development projects in Denmark. Both projects analyzed how participation could generate a process of empowerment for a group of marginalized children and young people in a local community.[1] One study was a 3-year research project called "Signs of Safety/Safety Plans" that I conducted in Roskilde[2] from 2011 to 2014. (I will refer to this as "the Roskilde Project" here.) The second project involved adolescents as researchers and agents of change in another local community. This project, called "Project Bella," ran from 2016 to 2019. The purpose of this chapter is to emphasize the importance of children's participation and explore openings, opportunities for change, professional obligations, and considerations based on what I have learned as a researcher and social work educator. The chapter demonstrates that child-directed social work practice and research can positively affect children and young people; however, researchers and practitioners need to consider intersectionality and children's resiliency and strengths. They need to approach children's participation by considering the intersectionality of their social positions, including their age, gender, ethnicity, migrant background, socioeconomic background, and so on. This chapter also raises questions about how researchers and professionals can recognize children and young people as competent actors and transcend the dichotomy between children as vulnerable or resourceful.

These are the questions that the chapter addresses: What do social work practice and research with children look like in practice? What were the outcomes of participation for children in a child-directed project? What are the takeaways for social work practice and research from the two projects?

Mimi Petersen, *Child-Directed Child Welfare Research and Development in Denmark* In: *Children and Young People's Participation in Child Protection.* Edited by: Katrin Križ and Mimi Petersen, Oxford University Press.
© Oxford University Press 2023. DOI: 10.1093/oso/9780197622322.003.0003

These questions are essential because of the shortage of research on projects directed by children in child protection in Denmark and elsewhere.

The theoretical platform of my research consists of several conceptualizations of children's participation: Hart's ladder of youth participation (Hart, 1992), Shier's (2001) idea of pathways to participation, the concept of intersectionality as developed by Crenshaw (1989, 1991), the theory of recognition by Honneth (2003, 2006), and the idea of empowerment as devised by Kabeer (2005) and Shier (2010). Based on these concepts, I approached my research with these assumptions: Genuine participation is about being recognized. It is a process where individuals can understand, deal with their situation, try to act, and find solutions. Children and young people have different opportunities and limitations regarding their participation as active agents in their lives depending on their gender, ethnicity, socioeconomic background, living conditions, and so on.

I will start by briefly describing the legislative context for children's participation in social work in Denmark. I will then discuss young people's involvement in the Roskilde Project and Project Bella. I will focus my discussion of the Roskilde Project on describing the approach we developed in Roskilde that we used in Project Bella afterward. From 2011 to 2014, the government chose the municipality of Roskilde to use safety plans as an alternative to out-of-home placements in child welfare. The city developed an agreement with University College Copenhagen (Københavns Professions Højskole, or KP) to assess whether the safety plans influenced children and young people's well-being and examined the results, challenges, and opportunities. In this chapter, I will highlight the lessons I learned about children's participation from these projects.

Child Welfare in Denmark

The number of children younger than 18 was 1,152,995 in Denmark in 2021 (Statistics Denmark, 2021a). The total population was 5,840,045 (Statistics Denmark, 2021b). The number of children and adolescents in out-of-home care is approximately 13,000. The proportion of children in out-of-home care greatly varies by municipality and ranges from 0.23% to 0.53% of the child population (Ulum, 2018).

Since the ratification of the United Nations Convention on the Rights of the Child (UNCRC), the government has amended the children's rights legislation to a certain extent (Nielsen, 2004). The Law on Social Services gradually strengthened the legal position of the child: the amendment of the Child and Youth Code in the Social Assistance Act from 1993 included a requirement for conversations between social work professionals and children 12 years or older. In 1997, the Social Services Act stated that "the [social] support must be based on the child's resources, and the child's or young person's views must always be included and weighed according to their age and maturity."[3] Despite this change, the law maintained the 12-year threshold for the participation of children until 2003. Since then, the law has stated that all children should be involved in matters about their lives regardless of age, for example, when social service agencies place a child in care. In 2011, amendments to the Social Services Act entered into force because of children's rights reform. These legislative changes further improved the legal position of the child.

The government introduced more changes to the Social Services Act with a law on abuse and violence in 2013. These changes required that children must be involved in child welfare processes through conversations regardless of age. The municipal authorities must speak with children if they suspect abuse. The law states that in the case of an investigation into child maltreatment,[4] the municipalities must ensure that child welfare professionals talk with the child. Child welfare workers must give children the option to exclude their parents from attending the professionals' meeting with the child.

Chapter 11 of the Social Services Act ensures that children and young people who need support services can achieve the same opportunities for personal development, health, and independent adult life as their peers. The act emphasizes that the support services must be based on the child or young person's resources. Social service agencies must weigh children's views according to their age and maturity. (This corresponds to Article 12 of the UNCRC.) From 2020 to 2021, politicians, social work professionals, and nongovernmental organizations undertook immense efforts to create a law for children in Denmark. Some of the main points of the law (called Children First) are as follows: the country's legal code needs to include more rights for children, the child's wishes must be at the center of decision-making about a child's life, the child should have the right to reject contact with their biological parents, all children have a right to stability and knowledge about their rights, and children's voices need to be heard in the case of children exposed to a crime (Social- og Ældreministeriet, 2021).

The Roskilde Project

The Roskilde Project aimed to investigate children and young people's participation in decisions about their safety and well-being. The focus of the Roskilde Project was the municipality's work with safety plans as service measures and alternative placements for children and families in vulnerable positions. The purpose of the safety plans was to ensure children's safety and well-being in the family. The project examined how helpful safety plans were as an alternative to out-of-home placements. One part of this evaluation investigated children's participation in decision-making about their safety. The project addressed these questions: (1) How are the children involved in the safety planning process? Are they informants, collaborators, or co-deciders? (2) How would the children like to be involved? (3) How do they view their role? (4) What are the children's suggestions for how children should participate in social work with vulnerable children? (5) In their view, how do safety plans help foster children's well-being?

We employed various research methods, including observations, interviews, participation in meetings, workshops, discussions with children, and case materials developed with the young people and social work students. When we began the Roskilde Project and Project Bella, KP did not yet have an ethics committee. It was up to KP researchers to conduct research in an ethical way. My colleagues and I have done so to the best of our knowledge by discussing the ethical considerations of the projects with other researchers and project participants in public seminars, workshops, and meetings. In Denmark, the government has only developed ethics regulations for scientific research in the past 10 years. Some Danish research universities have recently begun to establish internal ethics committees (C. S. Petersen, n.d.).[5] Article 2 of the 2011 Danish Act on Universities established that universities must safeguard ethics in science (C. S. Petersen, n.d.). The Ministry of Education published *The Danish Code of Conduct for Research Integrity* in 2014 (Uddannelses- og forskningsministeriet, 2014). We adhered to this code to the best of our knowledge.

In total, 95 children and youth aged 3 to 17 years participated in the two projects—86 in the Roskilde Project and nine in Project Bella. The children and young people who participated were mainly from low-income families and some of them with minority backgrounds. (The term "minority background" here refers to social groups that differ from the majority population in Denmark in terms of ethnic background, religion, living conditions, or sexuality.) The participants in Project Bella were from the Middle East and Africa.[6]

We involved three groups of children and young people in the Roskilde Project: we recruited 19 children from the principal investigator's (PI's) students' family networks and social networks, four children aged 3 to 13 with a safety plan, and 63 children from three fifth-grade classes of a local public school. We obtained informed, voluntary consent from both the children and parents of the 19 children. We also received informed and voluntary consent from the children who had a safety plan and their parents. In the case of the 3-year-old child, we obtained permission from her parents. We elicited the 3-year-old's perspective with the help of drawing and playing during the interview, which took place in her home. If we had additional questions, we asked the parents, who were present.

We sought and obtained consent from the children and parents for the discussions and meetings with the help of the school superintendent. All children whom the superintendent approached said that they wanted to participate.[7] In our letter to the parents, we clearly explained the purpose of the research and its benefits and risks and emphasized that participation was entirely voluntary. The superintendent and the teachers met with the children and described the study, confidentiality, and voluntary involvement on several occasions. Dr. Petersen organized a joint meeting with all of the children. In this meeting, she again explained the purpose, risks, and benefits of the study and emphasized that their participation was entirely voluntary.

Over half of the participants had encountered social service agencies regarding their safety and well-being (Table 3.1). The number may be relatively high because the school served a highly disadvantaged community. The children and youth, students from the social work program at KP, social workers from the child welfare department of the municipality, teachers, and community social workers were involved in gathering, analyzing, and presenting the data. Tables 3.1 and 3.2 illustrate the participants and their roles in the two projects.

The children, youth, and undergraduate students were co-researchers in the Roskilde Project and active researchers in Project Bella. We developed several approaches to collecting children's perspectives because we found that the semi-structured interviews with children, which we began with, were not optimal for involving children in the study. The children did not show interest, answered very briefly, or were utterly silent. (I have learned from my experience talking with many children over the years that it is not

Table 3.1. The Roskilde Project: Participants, Roles, Activities, and Duration

Participants	Roles and Activities	Duration
Eight social workers from the municipality	Acted as dialogue partners about project organization and implementation Participated in two focus group interviews	2011–2014
Two researchers from KP	Implemented project PI: Mimi Petersen	2011–2015
Manager at the municipality	Project owner	2011–2015
38 case journals by the municipalities	The PI read the case journals	2011–2014
Children and youth aged 8–15 years (about 10 participants per meeting) Parents, family members, and professionals from child welfare services and school	Participated in 15 safety plan meetings observed by the PI	2011–2014
28 undergraduate social work students	Conducted pilot interviews with the children and young people Developed first draft of case vignette	2011–2012
19 children aged 8–16 years	Participated in study Collaborated with students in developing first draft of case vignette	2011–2012
Two master's degree students	Undertook administrative tasks	2012–2015
20 undergraduate social work students in their final semester Five first-year undergraduate students	Conducted interviews with the children, parents, and professionals and participated in other project activities, including organizing seminars, family day, etc., and wrote bachelor theses Participated in dialogue meetings with 63 children in 2014	2011–2014
63 children from fifth grade	Met with social work students to discuss case vignette Participated in interviews Co-developed case vignette	2014

(continued)

Table 3.1. Continued

Participants	Roles and Activities	Duration
Four children with a safety plan	Participated in interviews and discussions about the case vignette and developed a new approach	2012–2013/2014
	Participated in the family day in 2014 (two children)	
Senior lecturer from KP	Supervised and examined the students on bachelor theses and participated in the family day workshop in 2014	2011–2014
Senior lecturer from KP	Co-authored report with PI Presented results at conferences	2013–2015
Six parents	Participated in interviews with PI	2012–2014
Manager from the municipal child welfare services	Participated in interviews with PI	2012–2013
Five teachers	Participated in research meetings	2014
	Supported study participants	
School superintendent	Disseminated information about the project to children and parents	2014
	Provided administrative support and helped seek and obtain children's and parents' informed consent	

optimal to start a conversation with children in difficult life situations by asking them directly about their lives.) My experience has taught me that it is better to use metaphors and case vignettes to begin a dialogue with children. We used observations, dialogue meetings, and workshops with children and developed case material together with the children and students.

The case vignette served as a helpful entrance into children's views on children's rights, children's participation, and dilemmas in social work with vulnerable children and adolescents. The researchers presented the children with a case vignette about Sille, a 12-year-old girl, and her younger brother, Storm, 7 years old. They live with their parents in a home characterized by parental alcohol abuse and constant arguments and yelling matches between the parents. We gradually modified the case vignette in collaboration with

Table 3.2. Project Bella: Participants, Roles, Activities, and Duration

Participants	Roles and Activities	Duration
Nine young people	Participated in the project together with social workers, teachers, and a researcher from KP	2016–2018
One teacher and two social workers	Helped locate participants and implement project Supported the young people's project Participated in conference, trip to Ærø, workshops, and seminars Social workers: served as moderators for youth's activities	2016–2018
Child welfare services manager	Co-wrote the project application Provided project financing and financing of trip to Iceland and conference attendance Provided diplomas for each young participant	2016–2018
PI (Mimi Petersen)	Located young study participants Implemented project Supported young people Contacted parents and requested consent Conducted 14 interviews with young people	2016–2018
Community social worker	Organized different activities, such as workshop and courses for the youth Participated in conference	2016–2018
Two lecturers from KP	Started project and wrote first draft of project application Collected the data One lecturer: co-authored project application, supported young people, and co-authored final project report	2016–2018
90 students from KP	Went on field visits organized by the youth participants	2018–2021

three groups of children and in conversation with the social work students. The vignette includes a description and several questions. (The final version of the vignette can be found in the appendix to this chapter.) We based our discussion with the children on the case vignette and the questions. We did not compensate the children monetarily, but we got fruit and juice for the rooms where children would take breaks.

We involved undergraduate students from the social work program at KP because we utilized the project's findings for a social work training program. It has been challenging for social work students to communicate with and involve children, and the students learned to support children and youth and build relationships in the projects. In total, 53 undergraduate social work students were involved in different roles. Thirty-three of them were engaged for a short time during the first stage of the projects when we developed the case. They participated in the discussions with the schoolchildren. Twenty social work students were more actively involved in the discussion meetings with children, youth, and parents. These students contributed to the study and undertook graduation projects based on different subjects related to vulnerable children and youth. Two master's degree students in social work collaborated with the project leader and undertook practical and administrative tasks.

The first phase of the Roskilde Project, which focused on the parents' and child welfare workers' perspectives, showed that children's participation was not sufficient even though the social services legislation in Denmark focuses on strengthening the rights of children and young people. The parents did not want the children to be involved. They emphasized the professionals' lack of knowledge about the children on their caseload. The purpose of children's participation was unclear to the parents and their children. The parents' reluctance was challenging for the children and the social workers.

In total, we asked nine parents who had 12 children ages 3 to 14 years who had a safety plan to participate in the study. We did not receive consent from five parents to interview their children. According to these parents, the children were already in contact with too many adults, and they thought that more contact would be an additional burden. We obtained consent from four parents to interview their children (four children in total). Six parents consented to the interview. Nine parents agreed to being observed in their meetings with the professionals.

The project embraced methodological flexibility and creativity to include the children's perspectives. Several ideas evolved based on discussions with the study participants: we organized family days, had discussions with schools and students, and developed case materials for conversations with children on children's rights and participation in child welfare processes for disadvantaged children and adolescents (see Table 3.1). We invited nine parents and 12 children to present the results of the first phase of the research about the safety plans in a 1-day workshop that we called a "family day." The entire family could attend the workshop and enjoy breakfast together with us, and then we had a discussion. I started the family day by presenting the project and describing the results. Afterward, we conducted interviews and ran focus group discussions. Three parents and three children participated in the family day. Five participants from KP (a colleague of mine, three undergraduate social work students, and I) participated.

From Child-Centered to Child-Directed Social Work

In this section, I will discuss children's thoughts on how they wanted to be involved and how their perspectives resulted in a new approach to children's participation. I would like to emphasize that none of the children in the project felt they were involved as active subjects when the child welfare authorities made decisions about their well-being. The professionals mostly used them as informants. My observations, participation in meetings, and document analyses corroborated the children's sentiment, which served as the impetus for children's wish to develop a new approach. All three groups of children who participated in the study expressed a clear desire for co-determination and self-determination. The children suggested that they play a more decisive role by choosing from different solutions in the decision-making process. The common feeling among the study participants' various (and diverging) views was that trust, feeling safe, and clarity (information and explanations) are essential prerequisites for vulnerable children to obtain an informed and/or participatory level of participation. One of the most significant findings was that children want to be equal actors in the decisions about the issues the family faces. They want to be involved in the decisions about their lives and contribute their ideas to solutions.

The adults who participated in the Roskilde Project approached their work with vulnerable children, young people, and their families with a perspective that places the child in the center. Figure 3.1 illustrates this perspective (see M. Petersen & Johansen, 2015). This perspective subjects the child to the power and decisions of adults. In the final phase of the Roskilde Project, we developed a model in cooperation with the children that focuses on the problem and decisions about solutions. Figure 3.2 depicts this approach. In this approach, the child is an equal actor and decision maker in a solution-focused social work practice (M. Petersen & Johansen, 2015). The children are involved from the very beginning of the child welfare process to define what the problems are and develop recommendations for solutions as equal actors together with the adults. The children stated that they do not want to be co-deciders because they absolutely must get what they want. They

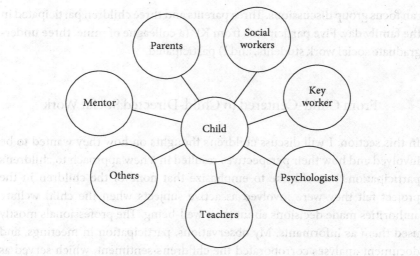

Figure 3.1. Child-centered social work.
From M. Petersen and Johansen (2015).

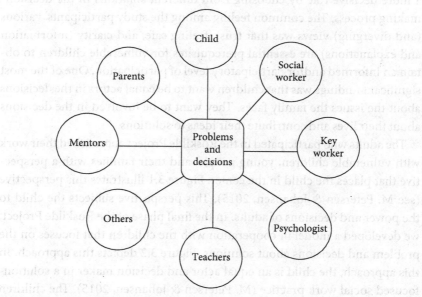

Figure 3.2. Child-directed social work.
From M. Petersen and Johansen (2015).

want to be seen and heard and want their views taken seriously when the authorities make life-changing decisions, such as placing them into out-of-home care, limiting their contact with parents, changing schools, and so on. The children were fully aware that these decisions are ultimately made by the authorities. They said that they were okay with this but thought that the social services agencies must explain why things turned out the way they did.

The children and young people who participated in the Roskilde Project were "co-researchers" with the adults and developed a problem-solving approach to child welfare work. The three groups of children explored, discussed, and defined the issues in the case vignette. When they talked about their experiences with being involved in decisions, it became clear that their experiences resembled the child-centered approach, not the problem-solving approach that views the child as a co-decider. In the child-centered approach, the adults discuss the child and their problems and develop solutions. The problem-solving approach served as the source of inspiration for Project Bella.

Project Bella

We conducted Project Bella in Bellahøj, an area in Copenhagen known as the home to Denmark's first high-rise building. The project focused on young people's participation and democratic formation to counter their marginalization and promote their motivation to pursue their education. The young participants in the project came from low-income, disadvantaged families. All of them were children of immigrants. Table 3.2 describes the participants and their roles and activities.

We began the project because we felt inspired by the approach we had developed with the children and young people in the Roskilde Project. We ran Project Bella concurrently with another project called "Together on Bellahøj." That project aimed at increasing a sense of belonging among vulnerable Bellahøj families by drawing on the area's diversity as a source of strength for community building (M. Petersen & Johansen, 2017). Project Bella highlighted ways to counter the risks to and marginalization of young people who lived in a public housing environment by strengthening their resilience and empowering them through creating participatory processes. The project aimed to enable young people to develop skills and abilities to research, document, and analyze themes relevant to them, such as well-being and safety in the local community, to act as change agents on behalf of themselves and others in their community. The nine young people (seven young men and two young women) learned to collaborate to plan and run meetings and conduct research and documentary work in their local community to contribute to positive local change. They undertook this work after school, and the project paid them as if it were a part-time, after-school job. The young people needed to study their community and develop into active and democratic citizens through genuine participation. We were ambitious and aimed to reach the sixth (and next to highest) rung of the youth participation ladder in Hart's (1992) participation model: joint decision-making between youth and adults initiated by adults. The young participants were between 14 and 17 years old when we began the project. Some of the youth knew each other before the project started. The teacher of the young people had chosen and asked them and their parents whether they wanted to participate and obtained informed consent.

The first meetings between all the individuals involved in the project (see Table 3.2) took place at KP in January and March 2016. The young people had the opportunity to develop the project description in these meetings. They decided what they should work on, how to accomplish their tasks, and what they wanted to achieve in the project period. In this initial phase, the group focused on unity, cooperation, and the atmosphere and culture of the meetings. The young people worked intensively to improve their meeting-related skills as moderators, create meeting agendas, and so on. They focused on deciding what they would like to do in the project. What would they change, and how? How would they disseminate their knowledge? What would their role in the project be? It was imperative to the young people that the project would receive funding. In fall 2016, the project received a quarter of a million Danish crowns (equivalent to US$40,000) from the A. P. Møller Fund. The foundation is among the largest private foundations in Denmark. It funds very costly projects and smaller, innovative projects (A. P. Møller Fonden, n.d.).

In fall 2016, all the young people went on a weekend trip to Ærø, one of Denmark's smallest island towns. The young people had collaborated with the adults to organize the trip. The trip was a milestone in the project: when they looked back at this trip, the young people found that the journey had strengthened their willingness to work together and increased their feeling of belonging to a community. On the trip, the youth collaborated on developing ideas about what they would like to research and how they would like to change Bellahøj. They worked on how to cooperate in a group, take joint responsibility for meetings, discuss their roles and tasks in planning meetings, divide their tasks, plan which data to collect and how, and present their findings to their parents and other interested parties.

They discussed what the project should be called in every language they spoke, which involved many discussions and led to several suggestions. The adults had given a very long name to the project ("Adolescents as Researchers and Agents of Change in a Local Community"). The youth were not fond of this long, academic name that they found strange, so they changed it to a simple, tangible name (Project Bella), thus taking ownership of the project. They decided that the project's focus should be on creating safety for everyone in their local community. They chose this focus because of the history of crime and drug use in their community.

The young people decided to give guided tours of their housing project. They acquired knowledge about Bellahøj and its inhabitants to prepare for the guided tours they gave for several professional groups. They attended engineering and environmental management meetings at Copenhagen City Hall and learned about the political decision-making processes. This cast more light on the construction of Bellahøj and along Degnemosen, the urban park surrounding Bellahøj, and gave them the confidence to talk about their community in the guided tours. In fall 2016, they visited the four resident boards[8] at Bellahøj and presented the project. These visits laid the foundation for further cooperation with the resident boards and gave the young people insight into resident democracy. They showed images based on their research on the positive and negative aspects of Bellahøj. They presented what it is like to grow up and be young in Bellahøj and how they could help create positive changes for young and older people in the community. Some of their recommendations included "conversation benches," where residents could sit and talk with each other, and more lighting in certain areas that were unsafe at night. In their research, which included interviews with residents, the young people had found out that older residents living in Bellahøj, especially those from a nonmigrant background, were afraid of young people like them who lived there. They realized that both groups harbored prejudices toward each other. The young people thought this was the case because the two groups of residents did not know each other. The conversation benches, which could be placed in different locations in the community, could be spaces for dialogue with others and reduce the lack of knowledge about and fear of "strangers" (M. Petersen & Johansen, 2017).

The young people also went on a trip to Reykjavik, Iceland, to attend the annual meetings of the International Federation of Social Workers (IFSW) in 2017. This trip was not part of the original project proposal but became possible because of the support from the local public authorities, including the child welfare department, the department that is responsible for supporting children and young people under the age of 18 who experience social and mental health issues (Københavns Kommune, n. d.). When we communicated with the Danish Social Workers Association, a trade union for social workers in Denmark, we found support for the young people submitting a presentation abstract in cooperation with the researchers and project staff. Five of the young people and four of the professionals involved in the project then had the opportunity to give a presentation and workshop at the IFSW meetings in Iceland in May 2017. At the conference opening meeting, the young people met with the president of Iceland, as Figure 3.3 shows.

The presentation and the workshop following it were well-attended—more than 75 social workers and researchers from all over the world participated in the workshop and engaged the young people in discussions about the project. Many of the attendees wanted to learn more. Figure 3.4 shows the youths as they are giving the presentation.

In the summer and fall of 2017, the youth gave several guided tours. In August 2017, a documentary premiered with the title *Skyscrapers at Bellahøj*

Figure 3.3. Project participants meeting with the president of Iceland in Reykjavik in 2017.
Image credit: JohnSteen Johansen.

Figure 3.4. Project participants giving a presentation at the International Federation of Social Workers meeting in Reykjavik in 2017.
Image credit: JohnSteen Johansen.

by Søren Houen Scmidt (2017), available at this weblink https://vimeo.com/229709930.

The film, which the Statens Kunstfond and Landsbyggefonden supported, was produced by Magma Media and produced in collaboration with the housing departments and organizations at Bellahøj in 2016–2017. The documentary featured some youth participants, who described what it was like growing up and living in Bellahøj. In October 2017, the youth presented their work at a conference about children's right to participation that KP and Metropol College organized.

The youth also worked with social work teaching staff in the undergraduate social work education program. The social work program at KP contains an international module entitled *Comparative Perspectives on Social Work With Young People*. The course aims to familiarize students with international and

Danish perspectives on policies, theories, methods, and social practices with children and young people. College students from several European countries attend the course, which is 10 weeks long. The course includes several field visits, one of which is a trip to Bellahøj. The young people in Project Bella are responsible for this field visit and guide the students through the area. They tell them about their lives as young people living in a socially disadvantaged residential area and the changes they are trying to enact. The young people get paid as guest teachers (about US$50 to $60 per hour). This collaboration, which started in 2018, has become a permanent part of the international module in the Social Work Program at KP. From 2018 until 2020, 90 students had taken this course. This cooperation aims to include the knowledge of "experts by experience" in social work education so that the program contains three forms of knowledge: (1) knowledge from young people, (2) knowledge from social work practitioners, and (3) knowledge from research.

The Young People Before and After Project Bella

The young people who participated in Project Bella did not attend school regularly. Most of the young people started attending school regularly because they participated in the project. It was sometimes difficult to create trust between the young people and the adults in the project—it took continuous work to create and recreate youths' faith in the adults and build and rebuild cooperation between them. The adults had to learn to trust the young people's abilities, skills, and knowledge; share power; not be afraid of failure; and begin a respectful, equal dialogue with the youth. They managed to gain the youths' trust and maintain productive cooperation.

Some of the young participants designed a brochure to present Project Bella on the tours they offer. In May 2019, the young people and other residents and professionals (teachers and social workers) took the mayor on a tour to improve the well-being of the residents and increase safety in the area. Discussions are now underway between the mayor's office and the young people, all of whom are now over 18. How will professionals continue to work with young people in the community? How can the young people develop the project further with the youth as role models who recruit younger residents for a new project? This project would establish a youth council in the community that would draw on the positive experiences from both projects.

Discussion of Outcomes and Lessons Learned

According to Article 12 of the UNCRC, "States parties shall ensure that a child able to formulate his or her own views is free to express those views in all matters relating to the child; the child's views shall be given appropriate weight in accordance with its age and maturity" (United Nations, 1989, n. p.). As Article 12 establishes, children are entitled to participate in decisions that affect their lives. Social work research and development has a direct impact on the lives of children and young people. Therefore, they must be involved in research and development processes in this field. Working with children and young people in various research and development social work processes requires professional knowledge in several areas. The considerations in each area are the basis for the participatory methods we must develop. In the following, I will discuss some of the lessons I learned about children and young people's participation in research and development processes with the help of the Roskilde Project and Project Bella. I will address these questions: What were the outcomes of involving children and youth as co-researchers in child protection (or welfare) practice, research, and development? How did the children and young people's participation contribute to empowering them and improving their well-being? What were the challenges?

Recognition of Children and Young People as Competent Actors

Recognition is a precondition for positive interactions between young people and adults. Honneth's (2003) concept of social recognition refers to the need for human beings to contribute to and be recognized by social communities. Recognition is the prerequisite for people experiencing themselves as socially successful, which is the overarching goal of social life. It is salient for people's identity and development to be listened to and given the opportunity to influence their everyday lives (Honneth 2003, 2006; Kornerup & Petersen, 2014; Petersen & Kornerup, 2015). Honneth's concept of recognition can be combined with the idea of participation and Antonovsky's (2000) understanding of the experience of coherence in life when it comes to the willingness of young people to be agents in their lives. This combination was evident in Project Bella.

Antonvosky (2000) describes recognition as a sense of coherence. Individuals need to experience comprehensibility, manageability, and meaningfulness to achieve coherence in life. To achieve a sense of coherence, they need to participate as active agents in their lives. According to Boyden and Ennew (in Powell & Smith, 2009, p. 124), "Participation is defined as taking part and the 'sense of knowing that one's actions are taken note of and may be acted upon.'" Boyden and Ennew conceptualize participation as aiding individuals in collaborating and experiencing that their actions matter because others consider them. This is central to a relationship being characterized as a mutually respectful partnership (Boyden & Ennew in Powell & Smith, 2009). Individuals' participation in the decisions that affect their lives and impact their society is the foundation of a democratic society. Increased opportunities for participation will reduce the risk of future schisms between young people and the community in which they live and contribute to them developing resilience. A lack of participatory opportunities can lead to children's negative self-understanding and lack of motivation and the risk that young people carry a negative social heritage into adulthood (Jenkins, 2006; Yuval-Davis, 2010).

Young people must be actively involved in the decision-making processes around them to experience meaning and coherence, according to Antonvosky. At the same time, they must understand what is at play and how and why marginalization processes affect them to cope with and transcend these processes. In this way, young people's resilience is linked to the concept of recognition and participation. Children and young people's aims, knowledge, and understanding of their society ensure that they experience coherence in the decisions they make. Social work practice must ensure that they achieve participation and understand the decision-making process and motivation for social change. Social work professionals can mobilize their abilities to transcend marginalization processes and create change by encouraging children's experiences of comprehensibility, manageability, and meaningfulness. Comprehensibility means that individuals are reality oriented and understand their situations. Manageability implies that individuals can manage to act and try to do something. Meaningfulness is about finding it meaningful to try and solve problems and understand the crisis you are experiencing and see it in context. These three characteristics help individuals develop a sense of coherence, which allows them to manage difficult life circumstances (Antonvosky, 2000). The development of educational and social interventions, as in Project Bella, involves and motivates young people to undertake significant changes. The children and adolescents' participation in the two projects showed that one of the prerequisites for success is the consistency of people and trusting relationships. It also showed that the success of the projects could be measured in many ways.

The children in the Roskilde Project exhibited a great deal of commitment and interest in participation. As they understood it, they had been "chosen" to help some students from a social work education program and researchers to solve some problems (develop the case vignette) and help the students become better at building relationships and communicating with children. The following quotes from children in the Roskilde Project illustrate how they thought about their participation in the project. One participant told us: "We think it was very odd in a way . . . something new . . . not really, anything we tried before, but it was a lot of fun, I think. So strange, in a good way." ' Another participant said: "It is different from what we tried when we talked to adults in the municipality and people like that." A 12-year-old boy who participated in the Roskilde Project said: "Just call me anytime you need help." The child-directed participation in the social work approach that focused on problems and solutions in the Roskilde Project was a profound inspiration for the professionals and researchers in the field. It was the model that inspired our approach to Project Bella.

The young people in Project Bella were proud to participate in the project. The project created a better understanding and dialogue between young people and professionals (teachers, social workers, community workers, etc.). It gave them insight into the roles and responsibilities of professionals (teachers and social workers). This knowledge, in turn, created understanding and changed the views of young people and other residents in the area. Young people gained great motivation for change from the project. The following quotes from participants in Project Bella illuminate the importance that recognition and successful experiences can have when we involve children and adolescents in research and development processes. The young participants said, "We have become brave. We stood up in front of many people and did something we never knew we could do. We had a great experience. We traveled to another country to get the chance to talk about our project. . . . It was cool to come as young people and teach the adults something. We were very proud.... We were happy to be heard." One of the social workers stated: "This project has had a huge impact.... It has been extremely important that you [the researchers] have not seen the young people as cases but as equal co-researchers."

It requires a different approach and a profound understanding of empowerment to share and, in some cases, completely relinquish power to young people. This lesson brings me to my next point: empowerment should not be understood as someone with power going out into the world and empowering others (the powerless). The two projects demonstrated the need for a different understanding and approach to empowerment in educational and social work settings with children and adolescents, starting, in our case, with a child-directed approach. The starting point must be that we, the child welfare practitioners, cannot empower anyone, but we can help create empowerment processes.

According to Kabeer (2005) and Shier (2010), the following criteria must be present for individuals to experience empowerment: (1) Capability: individuals must be able to do things; possess knowledge, competence, skills, and information; and think and act as individuals and in cooperation with others and quickly learn from others and their own experiences. (2) Conditions and opportunities: individuals must be in an environment that provokes and recognizes their abilities, competencies, and skills, such as in an organization or a group together with other children and adolescents. (3) Attitude: individuals must recognize their skills and knowledge and feel that they can act and that their actions have influence. They must know their rights, be able to defend them, and be prepared to engage with others in groups to achieve goals they have set. They must possess high self-esteem and be prepared to face challenges. Young people and professionals must know this approach in decision-making processes and activities. Shier (2019) uses the concept of "protagonismo infantil," which means that the child or young person should be the main actor in their life. Through the participatory processes that the child participates in together with adults, the child can achieve respect, equal value, and development. Learning processes are required in which children and adults gain awareness of their rights, increase their self-esteem and consciousness as competent members of a society to achieve their life goals, express their opinions, and organize their lives. The question remains whether adults (researchers, practitioners, etc.) are ready to consider sharing their decision-making power with children and young people.

The manager of the department of child welfare at Bellahøj said this about the approach of Project Bella: "It will certainly affect our way of doing social work in a completely different way. Professionalization? With this project, we can see that the professionals should have a role as facilitators." This quote illustrates that this approach requires a change in professionals' mindset—to a perspective where the professional considers children and young people as competent actors and the professionals as facilitators. Children's participation means more than interviewing children. Involving children in vulnerable positions in research and development requires a paradigm shift on many levels: First, professionally, concerning professional competencies. Second, organizationally, we must reimagine children's participation and the participation of practitioners. Third, at the political level, children's influence must be clarified and strengthened. For the children, it is evident: they want actual participation.

The young participants said they achieved a great deal of competence and more self-esteem through their participation in the project. They believe in their resourcefulness more and are engaged in organized cooperation with adults and other youth to create positive changes in their community. Some of them are even considering going into social work education (M. Petersen & Johansen, 2017). Project Bella tried to maintain this conceptualization of young people as the main actors. This perspective was not completely easy for the adults participating in the project. It was sometimes challenging for them to let go and let the youth manage the processes related to the project. (This was also the case in the Roskilde Project.)

Children and adolescents have different opportunities and limitations in terms of participation. In this regard, the lessons I drew concern the need for practitioners and policymakers to transcend the dichotomy of children as either vulnerable or resourceful and resilient. The literature points to a recurring discussion about professionals perceiving children and adolescents as vulnerable (exposed to social pressures and disadvantages) or resourceful. Children should be seen as competent or as individuals who are entitled to protection (Brembeck et al., 2004). The UNCRC contains the same duality by highlighting children's right to protection (vulnerability) and being heard (resourcefulness). However, this dichotomy is oversimplified because children can be both vulnerable *and* resourceful: symptoms of stress can coexist with coping strategies (Raghaillgah & Gilligan, 2010).

Social work has focused a great deal on children's vulnerabilities and not very much on posttraumatic growth. Many children who live through challenging experiences can develop in a very positive direction. Research has shown that children can get through traumatic life experiences and come out more robust on the other side and better cope with challenges (Garbarino et al., 1992; Jadidoleslami, 1998, 1999; M. Petersen, 2011; Raundalen & Dyregrov, 1993). Children can use their life experiences to create positive psychosocial development through building a kind of "resistant capital," as Yosso (2005) calls it. Many children and adolescents in the Roskilde Project and Project Bella have experienced harsh living conditions and many strains in their lives. Despite (or because of) them, they were enormously competent in engaging with the project, making it their own, producing results, and initiating change in their community.

Another lesson I learned from the projects was the need to approach children's participation in social work research and development from the view of intersectionality. How can we understand the intersections that arise in this work? How many social categories, such as gender, ethnicity, religion, culture, age, class, and so on, intersect? As practitioners and researchers, we must address how we should consider multiple social inequalities and identities in children's participation. We must consider the intersections between overlapping forms of social distinction, such as gender, race, ethnicity, age, sexuality, national origin, social class, and disability. As Crenshaw (1991) argued in her famous essay on intersectionality, we need "to account for multiple grounds of identity when considering how the social world is constructed" (p. 1245). The advantages or disadvantages that characterize particular social characteristics may be compounded as they intersect. This point is important to consider for the participation of children and young people. The term intersectionality comes from the English word intersection, which refers to crossing or overlapping. U.S. English uses the word for road junctions. Different dimensions or categories meet each other at the crossroads, creating intersectionality (Christensen & Jensen, 2011). The concept of intersectionality is used to describe and analyze the interplay between different power inequalities. The idea is that researchers (and practitioners) keep their eyes on various forms of oppression and look at how they play out together and help create one another. Scholars who apply intersectionality seek an explanation of how and why power and inequality are woven into perceptions of class, ethnicity, nationality, gender, generation, and so on, and create boundaries between them and us (de los Reyes & Mulinari, 2005).

Social work professionals must identify and address the subjective understanding and experiences of the children and young people they work with when they decide about their participation. These experiences can vary widely depending on children's age, gender, socioeconomic and migrant background, housing situation, ability, the conditions in which they grew up, and so on. The crossroads of various social categories can be crucial to children's experiences and their understanding of themselves and the world and its opportunities. This point was driven home in Project Bella, when some of the young women participating in the project could not join the other young participants on the trip to Iceland because they did not have a Danish passport. Their nationality became a barrier to participation. At other times, the intersection of children's gender, ethnicity, and socioeconomic background constituted a participation barrier regarding how other people viewed them. The boys reported experiencing stereotyping and criminalization because of their gender, skin color, and Middle Eastern heritage. These marginalization processes resulted from an undifferentiated image that some White, native-born majority residents of Bellahøj projected onto the children. They created an "us versus them" boundary.

Researchers and practitioners must take an intersectionality perspective because it helps focus their attention on several factors that may influence a specific child or young person's opportunities and limitations with participation. This approach would be more holistic and would result in more ways of incorporating children and young people in social work research and development relevant to their lives. Researchers and practitioners need to keep in mind that adult responsibility does not mean that adults should protect the child from exercising their rights (Åkerström Kördel & Brunnberg, 2017), including their right to participation.

Reflection Questions

(1) What would a problem-solving approach that treats children and young people as collaborators and co-deciders look like in your community, practice, and/or research? How would your environment need to change to create one?
(2) How can social work students and workers incorporate the idea of intersectionality in their work with children and young people in terms of participation?

Appendix Case Vignette: Sille

Sille is 12 years old and in sixth grade. She lives with her father, mother, and younger brother, Storm, who is 7 years old. Sille's parents have their own company and have therefore always worked a lot. Sometimes they have come home in the middle of the night. When they get home, they argue and yell at each other very loudly. The next day, Sille has to get up in the morning and make Storm breakfast and follow him to school, because their mom and dad are still in bed. Sometimes Sille is so busy in the morning that she even forgets to eat breakfast before she goes to school. It is often Sille who must do the shopping, because her father and mother do not always have time for that. If Sille and Storm go straight home after school, Sille must play with Storm, because they cannot disturb mom and dad, who sometimes still sleep when they get home from school. Sille and Storm therefore rarely get homework done because their mother and father are not there to help them. *How do you think Sille feels when she is at home? What would you do if you were in Sille's place? What do you think Sille dreams of?*

One day at school, Sille has Danish and math, which are her favorite subjects. Although Sille has the subjects she likes best, she cannot concentrate. While Sille sits and thinks, her teacher suddenly stands in front of her and asks if she's listening. Sille nods and says she's obviously listening. Suddenly the bell rings out for break and Sille gets up from her seat. On the way out of the classroom, the class teacher pulls Sille aside and asks if they can talk.

What do you think the class teacher wants to talk to Sille about? What do you think Sille will tell her teacher? How do you think Sille feels about the class teacher pulling her aside? What do you think the teacher should do?

Out in the schoolyard, Sille finds her best friend, Maria. Maria and Sille have been in the same class ever since the second year. They are often together at school and during school breaks, and sometimes they are together after school. Sille likes it best when they are at Maria's home, but they're not there often anymore because Sille must follow Storm home after school. Sille does not like Storm being home alone. Sille sometimes wonders if she should tell Maria about the things that are going on at home.

Why do you think Sille does not like Storm to be home alone? Why do you think Sille doubts if she should tell Maria about the things that are going on at home? What do you think Maria will say if Sille talks about the things that are going on at her house? Do you think there are others that Sille would rather talk to (than Maria)? Do you think it would be easier for Sille if she had someone to talk to about her situation?

Sille's parents have always drunk a lot of red wine. This is something you do when you're out, Sille's mother says. Sille can sometimes smell that her parents smell like beer or red wine, even if they haven't been out. They smell in the morning and when they come home from the office in the afternoon. When Sille's father and mother are home, they argue a lot. When they yell at each other, they say a lot of nasty things. Sometimes her mother says she wants a divorce. When they argue loudly, Sille tries to ignore them. One night Sille's teacher calls, and her father picks up the phone. Sille thinks about what her father is talking to the teacher about, but she can only hear her father getting angry and annoyed. He tells the class teacher not to interfere and then he slams down the phone. Sille asks her father what he talked to the teacher about. Sille's father does not answer her but leaves without saying goodbye and slams the door on her. After a few days, Sille's parents receive a letter from the municipality, in which they are called to a meeting with a social worker. Sille is told by her father that she's going to the meeting with him.

Why do you think the father gets mad at the teacher? Do you think Sille wants to go to the meeting? Why? What do you think Sille is going to do at the municipality?

When they go to the meeting at the municipality, they are greeted by a woman named Bente. Bente is a social worker and she's the one they are going to talk to. Bente says that she wants to hear how things are going at home. She also says she'd like to talk to Sille alone. She asks Sille if she wants to talk to Bente alone or if she would like her parents to be part of the conversation.

What do you think Sille wants most, talking to Bente alone or with her parents? Why? What do you think Bente wants to talk to Sille about? What do you think Sille wishes to talk to Bente about? What would you do if you were Bente? What would you ask Sille? What do you think Bente can help Sille and her family with? How would you help Sille if you were Bente?

A while after Sille and her parents have been to the municipality, her grandmother and grandfather start to visit Sille and her family often. It is something that the municipality has asked them to do. Sille likes when her grandmother and grandfather visit because they have a good time; they bake buns and watch movies. If Sille and Storm have homework to do, the grandfather helps them. Sille knows that the municipality helps her father and mother not to be out so late at night anymore, and that they no longer smell of beer and red wine. Sille and Storm think it has become a lot easier to be at home and they both feel really good.

Why do you think Sille is happy that the grandmother and grandfather have started coming to her home? What do you think of the way the municipality has chosen to help Sille's family? What further help do you think Sille's family should get?

Final Questions:
What do you think of the story?
How do you think you can spot children who are having a hard time at home?

Notes

1. More detailed information about the projects can be found in M. Petersen & Johansen (2015), M. Petersen (2016), and M. Petersen & Johansen (2017).
2. Roskilde is a Danish city in eastern Zealand to the southeast of Roskilde Fjord with 52,000 inhabitants. It is one of Denmark's oldest cities.
3. All translations in the text are mine.
4. In Denmark, the municipal child welfare authorities investigate when they suspect that a child or young person needs support services. The municipality initiates an investigation (a so-called Section 50 investigation) if it receives a report indicating that a child or young person is in need or there is a risk to the child or young person's development. As part of the investigation, child welfare workers must talk with children (Socialnettet, 2021).
5. There are significant discrepancies regarding research ethics regulations across Europe. The European Union established ethics regulations for research only recently. It published the first European Code of Conduct for Research Integrity in 2011 and revised it in 2017 (Desmond & Dierickx, 2021).

6. According to placement statistics from the National Board of Appeal and Population Statistics from Statistics Denmark, immigrant children with backgrounds from the Global South are placed outside the home significantly more often in the age group of 10 to 17 years than are other children of the same age group. Among younger children, immigrant children are placed outside the home disproportionately less frequently. Immigrant boys from countries of the Global South aged 14 to 17 are especially likely to be placed outside of the home. Children and young people of Danish origin are most often placed in foster families. Children and youth of Global South origin are placed in residential and foster care to the same extent. By the end of 2013, Danish-origin children and youth accounted for 90% of all children placed in care.
7. To our great surprise, several other classes also approached the superintendent and asked why they had not been invited. We had chosen these three fifth-grade classes on the superintendent's recommendation.
8. Public housing is governed very democratically in Denmark. The resident board comprises residents who organize themselves to make decisions about their local community (Domea, n.d.).

References

Åkerström Kördel, J., & Brunnberg, E. (2017). *Participation—A right, phenomenon and everyday practice in health and welfare work*. Student Literature.

A. P. Møller Fonden (n.d.). *Om fonden* [About the fund]. Retrieved on July 28, 2021, from https://www.apmollerfonde.dk/om-fonden/

Antonvosky, A. (2000). *Healing mystery*. Hans Reitzels Forlag.

Brembeck, H., Johansson, B., & Kampmann, J. (2004). *Beyond the competent child: Exploiting contemporary childhoods in the Nordic welfare societies*. Roskilde University Press.

Christensen, A.-D., & Jensen, S. Q. (2011). Intersectionality as sociological concept. *Danish Sociology, 22*(4), 71–88.

Crenshaw, K. (1989). Demarginalizing the intersectionality of race and sex: A Black feminist critique of antidiscrimination doctrine, feminist theory and antiracist politics. *University of Chicago Legal Forum, 1*, 139–168.

Crenshaw, K. (1991). Mapping the margins: Intersectionality, identity politics, and violence against women of color. *Stanford Law Review, 43*, 1241–1299.

De los Reyes, P., & Mulinari, D. (2005). *Intersectionality: Critical reflections over (on) the landscape of equality*. Liber.

Desmond, H., & Dierickx, K. (2021). Research integrity codes of conduct in Europe: Understanding the divergencies. *Bioethics, 35*(5), 414–428. https://doi.org/10.1111/bioe.12851

Domea. (n.d.). *Beboerdemokrati*. Retrieved on July 27, 2021, from https://www.domea.dk/beboere/beboerdemokrati/

Garbarino, J., Dubrow, N., & Kostelny, K. (1992). *Children in danger: Coping with the consequences of community violence*. Jossey-Bass.

Hart, R. A. (1992). *Children's participation: From tokenism to citizenship.* UNICEF International Child Development Centre. https://ideas.repec.org/p/ucf/inness/inness92-6.html

Honneth, A. (2003). *Behovet for anerkendelse.* Hans Reitzels forlag.

Honneth, A. (2006). *The struggle for recognition.* Hans Reitzels forlag.

Jadidoleslami, M. (1998). *Barn av krig, Om irakisk-kurdiska barns livssituation under decennier av krig och forfoljelse* [Children of war. On the life situations of Irqui-Kurdish children during the years of war and persecution]. C-uppsats, Stockholms universitet, Socialhogskolan.

Jadidoleslami, M. (1999). *Jag vill leta efter deras foraldrar—En studie om irakisk-kurdiska foraldralosa barn* [I want to look for their parents. A study of Iraqui-Kurdish orphans]. D-uppsats, Lunds universitet, Socialhogskolan.

Jenkins, R. (2006). *Social identity.* Academica.

Kabeer, N. (2005). Gender equality and women's empowerment: A critical analysis of the third Millennium Development Goal. *Gender and Development, 13*(1), 13–24.

Københavns Kommune [Community of Copenhagen]. (n.d.). *Borgercenter—børn og unge* [Citizens center for children and young people]. Retrieved on July 27, 2021, from https://www.kk.dk/bbu.

Kornerup, I., & Petersen, M. (2014). Børns rettigheder og medborgerskabs- dannelse. In: I Kornerup, I. og Næsby, & T. (Eds.), *Pædagogens grundfaglighed. Grundbog til pædagoguddannelsen* (s.145–166). Frederikshavn: Dafolo Forlag.

Nielsen, E. H. (2004). *Kursen i dansk børnepolitik* [Course in Danish child policy]. Socialrådgiveren, nr. 5. Retrieved on April 12, 2021, from http://socialrdg.dk/Default.aspx?ID=2062

Petersen, C. S. (n.d.) *Responsible conduct of research.* Retrieved on July 27, 2021, from https://forskerportalen.dk/en/safeguarding-rcr-at-universities/

Petersen, M. (2011). *Mobilitet, barrierer & muligheder: Et studie af unge flygtninges tilhorsforhold og positioner* [Mobility, barriers and opportunities: A study of young refugees' affiliations and positions] (Dissertation, Institut for Sociologi, Socialt Arbejde og Organisation, Aalborg Universitet).

Petersen, M. (2016). *Children's participation in decision-making in social work.* Working paper 2: Researching children's perspectives when norms and values are in conflict. Conference proceedings edited by Bodil Rasmusson and Kerstin Svensson.

Petersen, M., & Johansen, J. S. (2015). *Safety at the center: Safety plans in social work with children and families in vulnerable positions.* Department of Social Work Scripture Series 15.

Petersen, M., & Johansen, J. S. (2017). *Vi er lige begyndt: afsluttende rapport om roject Bella* [We have just begun: Final report on project Bella]. Professionshøjskolen Metropol. Retrieved on July 28, 2021, from https://viden.sl.dk/

Petersen, M., & Kornerup, I. (2015). Children's participation in each day's decisions and change processes. In I. Kornerup & T. Næsby (Eds.), *The basic professionalism of the pedagogic* (pp. 211–232). Dafolo.

Powell, M. A., &Smith, A. B. (2009). *Children's participation rights in research.* Sage.

Raghaillgah, M. N., & Gilligan, R. (2010). Active survival in the lives of unaccompanied minors: Coping strategies, resilience, and the relevance of religion. *Child and Family Social Work, 15,* 226–237.

Raundalen, M., & Dyregrov, A. (1993). *Barn och familjer i krig* [Children and families at war]. Radda Barnen.

Scmidt Houen, S. (2017). *Skyscrapers at Bellahøj*. https://vimeo.com/229709930.
Shier, H. (2001). Pathways to participation: Openings, opportunities, and obligations. *Children & Society*, 15(2), 107–117.
Shier, H. (2010). Pathways to participation revisited: Learning from Nicaragua's child coffee workers. In B. Percy-Smith & N. Thomas (Eds.), *A handbook of children's and young people's participation: Perspectives from theory and practice* (pp. 215–229). Routledge.
Shier, H. (2019). Student voice and children's rights, participation, empowerment and "protagonismo." In M. Peters (Ed.), *Encyclopedia of teacher education* (pp. 27–31). Springer Nature. https://rd.springer.com/content/pdf/10.1007/978-981-13-1179-6_27-1.pdf
Social- og Ældreministeriet [Ministry of Social Affairs and the Elderly]. (2021). *Børnene først: Et trygt hjem og flere rettigheder il udsatte børn* [Children first: Safe home and more rights for vulnerable children]. https://im.dk/media/19474/boernene_foerst_t.pdf
Socialnettet. (2021). *§ 50 undersøgelsen—den børnefaglige undersøgelse* [Article 50 investigation—the child welfare investigation]. Retrieved on July 25, 2021, from https://socialnettet.dk/paragraf-50-undersoegelse
Statistics Denmark. (2021a). *Children*. Retrieved on July 25, 2021, fromhttps://www.dst.dk/en/Statistik/emner/befolkning-og-valg/husstande-familier-boern/boern
Statistics Denmark. (2021b). *Population of Denmark*. Retrieved on July 25, 2021, fromhttps://www.dst.dk/en/Statistik/emner/befolkning-og-valg/befolkning-og-befolkningsfremskrivning/folketal
Uddannelses- og forskningsministeriet [Ministry of Education and Research]. (2014). *Den danske kodeks for integritet i forskning* [The Danish code of conduct for research integrity]. Retrieved on July 27, 2021, from https://ufm.dk/publikationer/2015/filer/file
Ullum, A. (2018). *Andel af anbragte børn svinger fra 0,23 til 3,53 procent. Se tal for alle kommuner her* [The proportion of children in care ranges from 0.23 to 3.53 percent. See the figures for all municipalities here]. NB Økonomi. https://nb-okonomi.eu/2018/12/06/andel-af-anbragte-boern-svinger-fra-034-til-352-procent-se-tal-for-alle-kommuner-her)
United Nations. (1989). *Convention on the Rights of the Child*. https://www.ohchr.org/en/professionalinterest/pages/crc.aspx
Yosso, T. J. (2005) Whose culture has capital? A critical race theory discussion of community cultural wealth. *Race Ethnicity and Education*, 8(1), 69–91.
Yuval-Davis, N. (2010). Theorizing identity: Beyond the "us" and "them" dichotomy. *Patterns of Prejudice*, 44(3), 261–280.

4
Care Leavers' Participation in Designing Child Welfare Services and Policy in Israel

Talia Meital Schwartz-Tayri and Hadas Lotan

Introduction

Research in the field of young people's participation in decision-making has focused predominantly on the engagement of children and youth in decision processes related to their lives as individuals (Ben-Arieh & Attar-Schwartz, 2013; Gunn, 2005; van Bijleveld et al., 2014). Adults—parents and professionals—often dominate these processes. This chapter explores youth engagement in child welfare policy advocacy as an emerging domain of youth engagement in policymaking. Our study seeks to expand the knowledge of the engagement of disadvantaged youth in policy design. More specifically, we aim to examine the experiences of care leavers who served as advisory board members in policy-related decision-making processes in Israel. We analyze the impact of their experiences on their political resources, self-efficacy, and opportunities to engage in policy advocacy. When we started our study, we assumed that their participation in the advisory board would introduce them to both challenging and empowering experiences.

First, we will review the main features of the Israeli child protection system and discuss the policy discourse about youth participation in public child welfare services. Second, we will describe the framework of advisory groups involving youths' transition from care and discuss the implementation and model of youth engagement in service and national policy design as established by the Israeli Council for the Child in Care in 2015. Third, we will present the methods and findings of the study. Finally, we will discuss our main conclusions and reflect on significant issues that emerged from our results.

Talia Meital Schwartz-Tayri and Hadas Lotan, *Care Leavers' Participation in Designing Child Welfare Services and Policy in Israel* In: *Children and Young People's Participation in Child Protection*. Edited by: Katrin Križ and Mimi Petersen, Oxford University Press. © Oxford University Press 2023. DOI: 10.1093/oso/9780197622322.003.0004

Child and Youth Welfare Services in Israel

Israel is a multicultural country composed of about 9 million citizens and permanent residents. There are 6.5 million Jews, 1.5 million Muslims, 170,000 Christians, and 140,000 Druze. There are about 3 million children younger than 18; of these, 71.5% are Jewish, 22.5% Muslim, 1.6% Druze, and 1.5% Christian, and 2.9% had no specified religion (Israeli Central Bureau of Statistics, 2019).

In Israel, local welfare services are mandated by the government and are universal social care services. While the Israeli welfare state has developed a comprehensive universal system of family and child welfare services, a large proportion of families with children continue to face numerous social problems.[1] In 2015, 34.7% of children lived in families with incomes below the poverty threshold. Among the 443,548 children who were known to social services, 365,981 were identified by child welfare (or protection) services as children at risk due to poverty, physical abuse, emotional abuse, sexual abuse, neglect, psychiatric hospitalization, involvement in criminal activities, suicide attempts, and addictions (Israel National Council for the Child, 2016).

In Israel, child protection practice is carried out by social workers in the social care departments of the local authorities. The child welfare system includes a range of preventive services in the community and out-of-home placements (Israeli Ministry of Social Services and Social Affairs [IMSSSA], 2014a). Community therapeutic services, educational and social daycare centers for infants at risk, foster care agencies, residential care facilities, and group homes are among the services provided by the system. In 2016, 10,779 children known to the child welfare services lived in out-of-home placements: 26.7% were in family foster care, and the majority were in different types of care facilities, mostly group homes (Sabah, 2017). Many care leavers are unable to return to their birth families when they age out of care (at the age of 18) due to past abuse and neglect. In response to this issue and other challenges care leavers face in their transition to independence (Sulimani-Aidan, 2014), the Israeli Council for the Child in Care founded the first nationwide independent living program in Israel in 2005.

The Israeli Council for the Child in Care is a national nonprofit organization supporting children and youth from all demographic groups in residential group homes and foster families. For the past 30 years, the council has been operating social, therapeutic, and educational programs for children in care. Its "Bridge to Independence" program serves over 1,000 youths who left care settings at age 18 without family support (Schwartz-Tayri & Spiro, 2017). The program provides them with accommodation; social, emotional, and instrumental supports during their military or civic-national service; educational and vocational counseling; life skills development; and other kinds of support during their transition to adulthood (Schwartz-Tayri & Spiro, 2023).

Young People's Participation

Public participation in policymaking occurs when citizens have a voice in policy choices, such as community meetings, citizen advisory committees, and administrative law (Bishop & Davis, 2002). These types of participation extend democracy, enhance active citizenship (Bryson et al., 2013), and potentially reduce social exclusion (Gunn, 2002). Children and youth have had the most limited access to decision-making arenas (Arnott, 2008; Tisdall & Davis, 2004) and thus lack political power (Kosher & Ben-Arie, 2009). This leaves children to depend on adults to be their voice in decision-making processes, such as policy design (Bowers-Andrews, 1998). The United Nations Convention on the Rights of the Child (UNCRC; 1989) led to a major shift in welfare states' construction of children as mere "dependents" (Arnott, 2008; Makrinioti,, 1994). Still, in only a few countries, such as Norway and Scotland, children and youth have been active participants in designing policies that affect their lives as a collective (Leeson, 2007; Rampal, 2008; Tisdall et al., 2008).

Israel's ratification of the 1989 UNCRC in 1991 (Article 12) required government authorities to constitute a child's right to participate in the decision-making processes about their lives in legislation and practice. In 1997, the government established a committee, chaired by district court judge Saviona Rotlevi, to examine Israeli law regarding the subjects of children's rights, legal status, and welfare, according to the guidelines of the UNCRC (Gottfried & Ben-Arieh, 2019). The Rotlevi commission's role was to translate these rights into legislation (Israeli Ministry of Justice, 2003). The 2008 child welfare reform led by the Israeli Ministry of Social Services and Social Affairs introduced significant changes into specific practices of the local committees involved in child protection and decision-making. The reform set up new procedures to regulate local committees' duty to weigh children's voices in their decisions about children at a personal level (Alfandari, 2017).

In Israel, children's right to participate in policy choices is constituted by law only in school decision-making. All types of schools (from elementary to high school) are required to encourage establishing a student council, which the students elect. Usually, the school council is actively involved in the school's social education. It provides constant feedback to the school principal's office in face-to-face meetings (Israeli Ministry of Justice, 2000). The government has only made a few efforts to engage children in policymaking outside educational contexts, for example, in the Rotlevi commission deliberations (Israeli Ministry of Justice, 2003) and in special programs operated by local authorities (Nir & Perry-Hazan, 2016), such as local children's parliaments and "Friendly City for Children" (The Knesset, 2016). As part of these programs, some city councils operate various activities that aim to facilitate children's participation in defining and addressing the needs and challenges of children and youth in their city and establish think tanks to suggest proper local solutions. In one of the cities, children were members of the city development strategy committee. In another, children co-planned the content, structure, duration, and marketing strategy of the summer school break activities with members of the city council. However, these programs are not mandatory and are not implemented nationally.

Care Leavers' Advisory Boards

Youth advisory boards are one type of citizen participation of young people (Wandersman & Florin, 2000). Inspired by England and Canada, advisory boards of youth aged out of care were established in the United States in the late 1980s, following the Independent Living Initiative of 1986. This law mandated the first U.S. transitional programs from care to independent living services. These programs included educational and employment support and personal development workshops and conferences. The first U.S. care youth advocacy boards originated from these workshops and conferences (Havlicek & Samuels, 2018). They served as the primary method that states use to include foster youth in decision-making about child welfare policy and practice (Collins, 2004). Some advisory boards were implemented exclusively through public child welfare agencies and others through public-nonprofit partnerships (Forenza & Happonen, 2016). Their activities included group meetings, newsletters, and weekend retreats in which participants learned "about their rights and built skills for leadership and advocacy" (Havlicek & Samuels, 2018, p. 248). Researchers have found that while all boards engaged in policy advocacy, they varied in their design of decision-making processes (Havlicek et al., 2018) and their use of parliamentary procedure and evaluation strategies (Havlicek et al., 2016).

In 2015, the Council for the Child in Care established the first care leavers' advisory board in Israel as a part of Bridge to Independence," the independent living program operated by the council. As a part of their participation in the program, youths were invited to join the board. The staff members who supervised the apartments of Bridge to Independence encouraged current participants and program alums to join the board in individual face-to-face meetings, apartment meetings, and group meetings of alums. The young people who agreed to join the board were all invited to meet the council's CEO to plan the aims and core activities of the board. Among 25 youths who attended the first meeting, 14 participants decided to become official board members. Between 2015 and 2019, three youths left the board, and three joined it. There have been no eligibility criteria to join the board. Therefore, the board is introduced to each new care leaver, who joins Bridge to Independence as part of the first intake session with the staff member.

The board aimed to create a social support network that would facilitate the engagement of care leavers in national child welfare and transitional program services and policies. This aim was based on the idea that young people are relevant partners in decision procedures pertinent to their own lives and service and policy design (Hart, 1992). The original board included 14 young people who aged out of group homes and foster care and had no family to accommodate or support them. Their ages ranged from 19 to 23 years. Four of them lived in the program's apartments in Jerusalem, six in small cities in the north of Israel, and two in the cities in the center of Israel. The others were Bridge to Independence alums who lived independently in the center of Israel. All members wished to voice their knowledge shaped by their experiences growing up in care as a part of the council's advocacy activities.

The board's activities included participation in 2-hour, biweekly meetings and an annual weekend seminar. Two of the social workers at the Council for the Child in Care facilitated the meetings and the seminar, and the youths chose the main issues for discussion. The young people received 200 Israeli shekels (about 45 euros or 60 U.S. dollars) for each meeting to cover their effort and travel expenses. The board activities aimed to influence the services operated by the Council for the Child in Care and other child welfare agencies and influence national child welfare policy. In 2017, as a part of the implementation of the Israeli foster care law (Israeli Ministry of Justice, 2016, Section 7), the Israeli Ministry of Social Services and Social Affairs invited the board to be involved in the design of the first ombudsman agency for children in care. The ministry asked the board members to take an integral part in the deliberation about the constitution of the agency. The youths partnered with the minister of social affairs and the agency's first official to conceptualize the model of the agency. In addition, board members operated in the Israeli parliament (the Knesset). They joined deliberations of the Knesset committees that negotiated the Foster Care for Children Act and ratified the final procedures of the ombudsman agency. In some of the Knesset committees, board members lobbied for a new law mandating a comprehensive set of services for care leavers. Two board members initiated a meeting with the chair of one of the national agencies for civic-national service to promote special assistance for young adults aged out of care whom this agency served.

In addition to their advocacy activities on the national level, the board decided to work on the following objectives: (1) create social networks for youth who graduated from the independent living program, those who were artists and wished to collaborate in search of employment channels, or those who served in civic-national service; (2) increase the life skills for participants before leaving the program, mainly in financial management; (3) organize community events for the program participants, such as annual retreats and designer clothing giveaways. Three of the four board members led the planning and implementation of each objective. Their activities at the council level included attending routine meetings with the CEO of the Council for the Child in Care and leading management in discussing the design of services. As a result of their meetings, the board decided to create a new program in which graduates of the independent living program will receive ongoing mentorship as part of program participation and while transitioning into independent living.

Care Leavers' Engagement in the Political Arena

Youth aging out of care is a vulnerable population of young people. While in most modern welfare states children in care grow up in foster families, in Israel, most children in care grow up in residential care facilities (Gottfried & Ben-Arieh, 2019). Unlike family foster care, these facilities operate as closed or "total institutions" (Grupper & Freizler, 2018) and provide children with fewer opportunities to develop and exercise their daily living functions. These youth deal with "instant adulthood" (Stein, 2006) when transitioning out of state care with no family support. This situation forces them to cope with developmental issues and responsibilities (Arnett, 2007) that youth who were not in care can postpone as a part of their emerging adulthood (Courtney & Dworsky, 2006).

The process of political socialization takes place at home. The political socialization of children who grew up in care provides limited outcomes compared to children who did not grow up in care. Prior research demonstrated that political attitudes and behaviors are transmitted across generations in the family (Brady et al., 2015). Generally, individuals' social status is the strongest predictor of political engagement (Verba et al., 1995). More educated parents are more politically engaged themselves. They are more likely to provide politically stimulating home environments for their children through consuming information about politics, discussing political issues, and modeling civic engagement. However, regardless of their social status, parents can expose their children to alternative political simulation through involvement in the community. Parents involved in the civic sphere, such as their local churches, mosques, synagogues, or temples or on school parents' boards, expose their children to organizations that usually operate in a democratic environment and offer a variety of opportunities for civic and political engagement. These exposures prepare children for future political activities in school and other social organizations. Through these activities, children can acquire critical political resources, such as civic skills and political information; develop their political efficacy; and increase their political interest (Putnam, 1993; Verba et al., 1995). Youth who grow up in care settings, away from their birth families, typically lack the critical opportunities for the development of political skills, efficacy, and interest. Therefore, they are less likely to engage in political activism. In addition, due to the correlation between social status and political resources, their families would not provide them with proper political socialization even if they returned home for weekends and holidays.

Studies showed that youth's civic development improves when they are encouraged to take on leadership roles (Christens & Peterson, 2012; Zeldin, 2000). Youth participation in macro-level decision-making is associated with a decrease in youth mistrust, increased self-confidence, and a sense of belonging (Larson et al., 2005; Serido et al., 2011). Obstacles to youth participation were often associated with programs focusing on youth vulnerability (Finn, 2001; Richards-Schuster, 2012), fear of speaking out (Felix, 2003), and youth feeling that they are told what to do instead of asked to participate (Independent Sector, 2001). However, little is known about the unique experiences of care leavers advisory boards' members, the challenges they encounter, and what helps them overcome these challenges. One study documented that care youth advisory board members faced intensive pressure to deal with their mistrust, revisiting painful experiences, low self-esteem, and low self-efficacy (Havlicek & Samuels, 2018).

Methods

After obtaining the ethical approval of the Tel Aviv University Review Board, the second researcher, who was a graduate student at the time of the study, conducted face-to-face, in-depth semi-structured interviews with 12 of the 14 youths who served as advisory board members for at least a year before the interview. They included 10 women and two men. Their ages ranged from 19 to 24 years. Three youths served in civic-national service, four in the army,[2] and four in professional or academic programs. All of them worked odd jobs during their service or studies. One participant, who completed her civic-national service, was working in a part-time sales job. Two came from Muslim-Arab families; five came from Jewish families who emigrated from North African countries, such as Morocco, Algiers, Tunisia, and Asian countries (Yemen). Three participants were from Jewish families who emigrated from Ethiopia, and two from Jewish families who emigrated from the former Soviet Union countries. Ten participants aged out of residential care settings and two from family foster care. Of these, one graduated from ultra-orthodox residential care and another from a group home. All of them participated in the Bridge to Independence program. At the interview, some of them lived in the program's apartments or utilized the program's services, such as counseling and employment services.

The board facilitators presented the study to the board members in one of their routine meetings. They asked for their permission to provide the second researcher with a list of potential participants. The second researcher contacted the list of potential participants via emails and phone calls to further explain the study and request the youths' consent to join the study. Among 14 board members, 12 agreed to participate in the study and voluntarily consented to participate. Each interview lasted between 60 and 90 minutes and was conducted in a location chosen by the participant.

The interviews were conducted between April and July 2018. Interview guidelines included open-ended questions and were adapted to the interviewees' personal stories (Lune & Berg, 2017). We invited participants to tell us about their experiences in the board's meetings, in the board's meetings with managers of the Council for the Child in Care, and with national-level policymakers. We asked participants to retrospectively evaluate the impact of joining the board on their personal lives.

The interviews were recorded and transcribed. To identify patterns and themes within the data, we employed theoretical thematic analysis (Braun & Clarke, 2006) and an incident-by-incident coding process that involved two readers (the interviewer and the researcher). In this process, we read every portion of the interview transcript and coded it for important themes (Charmaz, 2006). Each reader interpreted each interview and extracted a list of themes. We then reanalyzed the incident codes to identify the main themes in the interviews.

Findings

The study participants reported having a positive experience with their membership on the board. They expressed satisfaction from their meetings with the Council for the Child in Care managers and policymakers. One of the participants summarized his experience in the following words: "It made me feel that what I have to say has meaning in the eyes of others and that others believe in me and my competencies."[3] Retrospectively, most participants experienced their membership on the board as empowering and stated that it helped them discover their strengths and capabilities. One youth expressed what it meant to her to have her voice heard by policymakers for the first time: "It is the first time that I have received a stage. It made me feel good about myself, finally." Some participants expressed their appreciation for the board facilitators, social workers from the council. They noted that they were not judged for their opinions during the meetings even if they expressed criticism of some services provided to them.

The Board as a Support and Self-Help Group

The participants portrayed the atmosphere in the board meetings as supportive and accepting. They provided thick descriptions of the warm and intimate relationships that evolved between members who did not know each other before. They agreed that their relationship with the social workers from the council had become gradually closer and helped them authentically speak their minds. In the board meetings, members spoke openly about their experiences in care, the struggles of transitioning to independence, and the need to deal with powerful systems. One of the participants said, "Once someone talked about all that she's been through, and how nobody listened to her, everyone supported her. All of us know that we will care for each other from now on...." The interviewees indicated that the strong sense of belonging and solidarity increased their motivation to explore opportunities to help other youth who share similar experiences: "We all came from care, we have a lot in common, we became very close after the seminar, and we feel that together we can initiate things. It is amazing that together we can change things for others." Unlike most, one interviewee stated that sharing her story in the group and with policymakers was a very stressful experience: "Testifying in the Knesset [the Israeli parliament] . . . everybody is talking, it is something that is super hard for me. Within our group, it was also so difficult. It exposes you. It's too much. It breaks me."

From Mistrust to Cooperation With Politicians

The participants described their mistrust of managers in the child welfare services, government officials, and parliament members. They criticized them for not doing their job. They thought they did not serve the people; did not protect children, Holocaust survivors, and single parents in need; and instead mainly fought to maintain their position. Two participants noted that they learned how to manipulate politicians to effect policy change in the meetings in parliament and with government officials: "Many times, we had to raise our voice, and, sorry to say, but we had to manipulate them and make them cry when hearing our stories. I know it sounds disgusting, and it might sound like I'm selling myself, but it worked, and finally, you see things changing after that. We learned that, and it is our way to affect the process."

According to the interviewees, the invitation to join the board, preparing for meetings with government officials, and the outcomes of testifying in parliament committees contributed to the change in how they perceived politics and working with politicians. One participant explained how this change occurred:

> I felt that the managers and ministers, they just came to power to help their own specific community and completely neglected welfare policy. I hated that policy "forgets" about me, as a young person with no family to support her. . . . [E]very part of my body suffers from this situation . . . so I felt mistrust towards the ministers in the government. . . . [B]ut after this year, and after the policy actually changed now because of the help of the Knesset member, that gives me hope.

Gaining Communication Skills and Self-Confidence

The interviewees described self-expression and public speaking as the two communication skills they practiced the most while on the board. They expressed that their self-confidence significantly increased due to their public appearances. They explained that they practiced new skills by watching their peers and acquiring skills when they prepared to testify in parliament committees, prepared to lobby for policy change, and met with the CEO of the Council for the Child in Care, the managers of the transitional housing programs, and government officials. One of the participants put it like this:

> I learned how to speak in a way that may help me not only in the Knesset but also in other areas in my life, and it is not just how to debate; it is how you stay focused on the idea that you have to be prepared in advance. This is one of the main skills I have practiced repeatedly on the board.

The participants provided various examples about their involvement in the policymaking process, such as deliberating in the Knesset committees to pass legislation. Their knowledge when preparing to testify and debating demonstrated the skills they accumulated in their lobbying efforts. They reported that working with each other increased their belief that young, disadvantaged individuals can change policy. Working as a group with the endorsement of the Council for the Child in Care was vital to gaining political power. For example, one participant stated that "working with the board made me feel that I am a part of something bigger and that I'm taking part in activism that is a collective effort of a group ... together, to something that has power, and we can think of [policy] solutions that I could never think of alone."

One of the interviewees exemplified how her political self-efficacy increased due to the membership on the board:

> I was talking to the manager of the civic-national service agency, and he provided me with this "politician's answers," saying that he could not do this and that. And I said nicely, "no, I'm sorry, but we cannot accept this," and so, as a board, we could continue to negotiate with him. This is undoubtedly something that being a part of this board gave me—I know that they had my back when I was talking with him.

Challenges With Participation

The participants mentioned a few obstacles to participation on the board and perseverance in activism. The majority noted at least three challenges that they struggled with during their participation in the board's activities. They emphasized that traveling to the meetings was time-consuming and that they struggled with the decision to come or whether to use that time for working or studying. The financial compensation they received for each meeting and travel expenses was crucial for their membership. Four mentioned that they had to travel more than 2 hours to each session and use three buses each way.

The participants agreed that being socially active is challenging for youth who transition from care to independent living. One of the interviewees said that they face many changes and painful situations in moving to independent living and therefore have little time left for activism. Another participant explained why it was even harder for youth who were aging out of care to become part of an activist group: "Not everyone who aged of out care has the time to do it. It is not only the financial hardship. It's also because our schedule is much more hectic than that of others our age. It was a hard choice. It is even harder for us."

Another challenge that most interviewees emphasized was their lack of experience in expressing their opinions. Many noted that they had low expectations of things changing and did not think it was "worth it" to express what they had to say and that they did not believe in themselves and their skills. One of the participants remarked: "I did not believe in myself and the system, and when you are not confident in yourself, you are not sure of your opinion, and so you wouldn't share it. You wouldn't create the stage to express yourself. I have huge insecurity, but I learn to put it all aside."

A few participants believed that their lack of self-confidence and skills was due to their experiences in their family and care settings. One youth explained that during her participation in the council transitional housing program, the staff member who oversaw the department made all the decisions. There was very little left for the youths to decide. Some participants mentioned that in residential care, the care providers usually made all decisions and they always heard "no" when they wanted to change decisions. However, one interviewee explained that her lack of competency was related to her family: "I'm so insecure, it is like I said, I come from a family that does not know how to move things, get things, and it has become part of me. It is hard for me to demand things. But now, if I want something, I change it, I do it."

A Life-Changing Experience

One of the study participants said this about her board membership: "It helped me stop feeling like a victim.... I understood that my voice matters and that big changes might begin from simple people." The youths described their overall experience of participating in the board's activities as life changing. The interviewees described a change in the way they perceived themselves. The majority mentioned a transition from feeling like a victim to becoming someone who can influence others' lives. They said it was the first time they had received a stage to express their opinions and share their knowledge as former child welfare service users. The youths felt empowered working alongside the Council for the Child in Care staff and managers, who had previously provided them with services. They thought that these empowering experiences, together with the strong sense of belonging and acceptance they received on the board, caused a change in their personality. Some emphasized that the successes they had achieved as a group had changed the way they felt about themselves:

> Suddenly you start to feel normal because everyone on the board knows how it is, and now you don't feel that you are strange. You suddenly get to

know the Council's CEO, and you get to understand the system and how it operates. Beyond that, you start to have confidence, and I believe that we will continue to work together because . . . I know it sounds kitschy, but we're a family now.

One participant explained how her participation in the board's activities changed the way she perceived herself and drastically increased her self-esteem:

When you join the board, you know that you'll eventually share your story, all that you've been through, especially during your childhood in care. You learn to accept what happened and make the best of what you've experienced. I didn't tell anyone my story after aging out of residential care because if I had told someone at work or even on a date, people would have pushed me away. I learned to be ashamed of what I am, but now, after working in this group, I speak proudly of my experience and how I survived because I also want the children in the same situation to know that they can make it. I'll give you an example: once I figured out that a client in the store [where the participant was working as a retail assistant] also grew up in care. She [the client] was 50 years old, and she came and hugged and kissed me like she'd survived care with me.

Discussion

In this chapter, we explored the experience of youths who aged out of care who participated in child welfare services and policy design as part of their membership in an advisory group established by the Israeli Council for the Child in Care. The youth thought that their engagement on the board and their efforts to lobby for better child welfare policies were empowering. They felt that they were not alone in handling their hardships as care leavers and that they could finally raise their voices as youth who grew up in care and had to face difficulties on their own. Most of the study participants were very insecure and had low self-esteem when they joined the board. However, in time, they experienced increased self-confidence, self-esteem, and better communication, organization, and negotiation skills. These served as crucial assets for effective political advocacy. Many of them indicated that working together in the political arenas reshaped their beliefs about the policymaking process, despite having ambivalent attitudes toward politicians. Their actions increased their sense of political efficacy because they witnessed their impact on politicians and policy. As a result of these experiences, they moved from feeling like victims to feeling like they had control over their lives.

The increase in youths' perceived power and competencies was facilitated by peers, members of the boards, and social workers who facilitated the meetings. The young people had the opportunity to exercise political skills in a safe environment. The warm and accepting relationships with their peers and social workers helped board members to overcome the traditional barriers faced by disadvantaged individuals in political spheres (Verba et al., 1995) and the specific challenges of youth in care when serving as advocates (Havlicek & Samuels, 2018).

These findings support the notion that care leavers' advocacy boards may empower and cultivate leadership skills among members (Crowe, 2007). They corroborate the idea that peer groups of graduates of the child welfare system help build peer networks and social capital among care leavers (Snow & Mann-Feder, 2013). Their relationships with their peers provide youth with social acceptance (Brown & Larson, 2009; Schneider, 2000) that later helps them navigate political arenas and transition from supervised to independent living.

In line with previous research related to youth mistrust as a challenge for civic engagement (e.g., Havlicek & Samuels, 2018; Serido et al., 2011), the participants in our study had to overcome their criticism and feelings of mistrust to negotiate with politicians and government officials. Drawing upon Lareau's work (2002), we argue that this mistrust is a long-term consequence of youth and their families' interactions with representatives of educational and welfare systems, such as child protective services workers. These kinds of interactions are described in our findings and extensively by Lareau (2002) as disempowering experiences. The causes for this long-standing mistrust provide a possible explanation for interviewees' claims that to work with welfare managers and other policymakers, they had to manipulate them. Some of them recoiled from the need to use manipulation to adapt to the social class culture of the politicians.

The findings of our study challenge the civic voluntary model's basic assumptions about the political capital of disadvantaged youth (Verba et al., 1995). We argued that disadvantaged youths' knowledge is excluded from the policy process due to their limited political stimuli in the family and care facilities because vital social processes, such as the policy process, are designed with and draw upon upper- and middle-class knowledge (Bourdieu & Passeron, 1977). This mechanism may suggest that the knowledge and competencies of youth in care are not helpful and therefore cannot be synchronized with the standard policy design processes. However, our findings showed that political socialization is continuous and allows for the development of political skills and efficacy in young adulthood. Youth membership on the board helped centralize the marginalized implicit knowledge of young people who were born into immigrant communities, grew up in disadvantaged families, and were in care. In line with Yosso's application of critical race theory (2005), our findings showed that the experiences accumulated by youth in care could be viewed as resistant capital, which translated into the vital knowledge they required in designing child welfare policy.

Despite the similarities between the care leavers advisory board models that emerged in the United States and Israel, they differ in their primary purposes and micro-politics. The U.S. model initially aimed to provide youth leaving care with a platform for personal development through sharing experiences and learning about their rights. The U.S. approach was initiated as part of federal law (Forenza & Happonen, 2016). The advocacy role of the U.S. groups emerged because of youths' personal development and empowerment processes. In many cases, the board's decision-making processes were adult led instead of youth led (Havlicek & Samuels, 2018).

In Israel, on the other hand, the original purpose of the board was to prepare youth to serve as advocacy groups, and therefore, the board's youth members set the agenda. The empowerment and personal development experienced by the youth were an outcome of their efforts to become advocates. In both the United States and Israel, the supportive relationship with the board's facilitators and peers enabled the youths to share their stories and impact policymaking processes (Havlicek et al., 2018).

Conclusion

Membership in the Israeli Council for the Child in Care advisory board was a life-changing experience for the board's youth members. The board provided them with opportunities to self-reflect on their experiences as clients of the care system. It challenged the way they perceived themselves, their strengths, and their attitudes toward power relations. For youth who aged out of care, sharing their life stories and partnering with professionals to achieve policy change can help heal past wounds and empower them to become proactive advocates for their rights as individuals and as a collective (Weiss-Gal, 2009).

The participation of young people of diverse ages upholds their rights as citizens and fulfills the state's legal responsibility for child protection, ensures effective service delivery, and empowers children by enhancing their skills and involvement in democratic processes (Hart, 2008; Lansdown, 2010; Sinclair & Franklin, 2000). A close relationship with others who shared similar hardships and a strong sense of solidarity with other service users can increase care youth advisory board members' engagement with the political process. Our findings suggest that the process of political socialization of care leavers was reshaped by their strong, empowering engagement in multilevel shared decision-making. Board members gained the resources required for effective engagement in the policy process even though they belong to a disadvantaged social group. Advisory boards should be considered a component of personal development programs for children in out-of-home placements and independent living programs for care leavers. They can strengthen the political socialization of youths in care. Program facilitators should create a democratic environment in care settings and provide the youth with hands-on experience in macro-political arenas to effectively enhance their political resources, efficacy, and interest.

Reflection Questions

Youth engagement in public policymaking is considered a complex concept for implementation. The results of our study raise a few issues:

(1) What is the long-term impact on youth who exposed their personal stories as a part of their lobby for service and policy change?
(2) Which interests motivate policymakers to promote youth participation, and to what extent do youth voices count in their policy decisions?
(3) Are there best practices to cultivate care youth participation in policy design?

Notes

1. The Israeli statistics do not capture whether specific groups of children are overrepresented among children in poverty, in contact with the child welfare system, and in out-of-home care. One of the authors (Talia Meital Schwartz-Tayri) is currently working on a big data project that will allow analyses about the representation of ethnic groups of children in the child welfare system.
2. The army is mandatory for all young people at the age of 18. Young people who cannot join the army due to religious restrictions may serve in the civic-national service.
3. All the translations are by the authors.

References

Alfandari, R. (2017). Evaluation of a national reform in the Israeli child protection practice designed to improve children's participation in decision-making. *Child & Family Social Work, 22*, 54–62. https://doi.org/10.1111/cfs.12261

Arnett, J. J. (2007). Aging out of care towards realizing the possibilities of emerging adulthood. *New Directions for Youth Development, 113*, 151–161. https://doi.org/10.1002/yd.20302

Arnott, M. A. (2008). Public policy, governance and participation in the UK: A space for children. *International Journal of Children's Rights, 16*, 355–367. https://doi.org/10.1163/157181808X311196

Ben-Arieh, A., & Attar-Schwartz, S. (2013). An ecological approach to children's rights and participation: Interrelationships and correlates of rights in different ecological systems. *American Journal of Orthopsychiatry, 83*(1), 94–106.

Bishop, P., & Davis, G. (2002). Mapping public participation in policy choices. *Australian Journal of Public Administration, 61*(1), 14–29. https://doi.org/10.1111/1467-8500.00255

Bourdieu, P., & Passeron, J. (1977). *Reproduction in education, society and culture*. Sage.

Bowers-Andrews, A. (1998). An exploratory study of political attitudes and acts among child and family services workers. *Children & Youth Services Review, 20*(5), 435–461. https://doi.org/10.1016/S0190-7409(98)00016-4

Brady, H. E., Schlozman, K. L., & Verba, S. (2015). Political mobility and political reproduction from generation to generation. *Annals of the American Academy of Political & Social Science, 657*(1), 149–173. https://doi.org/10.1177/0002716214550587

Braun, V., & Clarke, V. (2006). Using thematic analysis in psychology. *Qualitative Research in Psychology, 3*, 77–101. http://dx.doi.org/10.1191/1478088706qp063oa

Brown, B., & Larson, L. (2009). Peer relationships in adolescence. In R. Lerner & L. Steinberg (Eds.). *Handbook of adolescent psychology* (3rd ed., pp. 74–103). Wiley.

Bryson, J. M., Quick, K. S., Slotterback, C. S., & Crosby, B. C. (2013). Designing public participation processes. *Public Administration Review, 73*(1), 23–34. https://doi.org/10.1111/j.1540-6210.2012.02678.x.

Charmaz, K. (2006). *Constructing grounded theory: A practical guide through qualitative analysis*. Sage.

Christens, B. D., & Peterson, N. A. (2012). The role of empowerment in youth development: A study of sociopolitical control as mediator of ecological systems' influence on developmental outcomes. *Journal of Youth & Adolescence, 41*(5), 623–635. https://doi.org/10.1007/s10964-011-9724-9

Collins, M. E. (2004). Enhancing services to youths leaving foster care: Analysis of recent legislation and its potential impact. *Children & Youth Services Review, 26*(11), 1051–1065. https://doi.org/10.1016/j.childyouth.2004.08.005

Courtney, M. E., & Dworsky, A. (2006). Early outcomes for young adults transitioning from out-of-home care in the USA. *Child & Family Social Work, 11*, 209–219. https://doi.org/10.1111/j.1365-2206.2006.00433.x

Crowe, K. M. (2007). Using youth expertise at all levels: The essential resource for effective child welfare practice. *New Directions for Youth Development, 113*, 139–149. https://doi.org/10.1002/yd.206

Felix, A. (2003). Making youth voice a community principle. *Youth Service Journal, 10*, 1–8.

Finn, J. (2001). Text and turbulence: Representing adolescence as pathology in the human services. *Childhood, 8*(2), 167–191. https://doi.org/10.1177/0907568201008002003

Forenza, B., & Happonen, R. G. (2016). A critical analysis of foster youth advisory boards in the United States. *Child & Youth Care Forum, 45*(1), 107–121. https://doi.org/10.1007/s10566-015-9321-2

Gottfried, R., & Ben-Arieh, A. (2019). The Israeli child protection system. In L. Merkel-Holguin, J. Fluke, & R. Krugman (Eds.), *National systems of child protection* (pp. 139–171). Springer. https://doi.org/10.1007/978-3-319-93348-1_8

Grupper, E. & Freizler, R. (2018). Residential education and care for children and young people in Israel. In T. Islam & L. Fulcher (Eds.), *Residential child and youth care in a developing world: Middle East and Asian perspectives* (pp. 67–81). CYC-net Press. https://www.fkn.org.il/webfiles/fck/files/Middle-East-and-Asia_Perspectives-ebook.pdf#page=68

Gunn, R. (2002). *Young people's participation in social services policy making* (Doctoral dissertation, University of Leicester).

Gunn, R. (2005). Young people's participation in social services policy making. *Research Policy & Planning, 23*(3), 127–137.

Hart, J. (2008). Children's participation and international development: Attending to the political. *International Journal of Children's Rights, 16*, 407–418. https://doi.org/10.1163/157181808X311231

Hart, R. (1992). Children's participation: From tokenism to citizenship. *Innocenti Essays*, no. 4. UNICEF.

Havlicek, J., Curry, A., & Villalpando, F. (2018). Youth participation in foster youth advisory boards: Perspectives of facilitators. *Children & Youth Services Review, 84*, 255–270. https://doi.org/10.1016/j.childyouth.2017.12.016

Havlicek, J., Lin, C. H., & Villalpando, F. (2016). Web survey of foster youth advisory boards in the United States. *Children & Youth Services Review, 60*, 109–118. https://doi.org/10.1016/j.childyouth.2015.11.023

Havlicek, J., & Samuels, G. M. (2018). The Illinois state foster youth advisory board as a counter space for well-being through identity work: Perspectives of current and former members. *Social Service Review, 92*(2), 241–289. https://doi.org/10.1086/697694

Independent Sector. (2001). *Giving and volunteering in the United States.*

Israel National Council for the Child. (2016). *The state of the child in Israel: 2016 statistical yearbook* [Hebrew].
Israeli Central Bureau of Statistics. (2019). *Central Bureau of Statistics - Population of Israel* Israeli Central Bureau of Statistics. (2019). *Statistical abstract of Israel 2018.* No. 69, Chapter 2—Population (Hebrew). https://www.cbs.gov.il/en/publications/Pages/2018/Population-Statistical-Abstract-of-Israel-2018-No-69.aspx.
Israeli Ministry of Justice. (2000). *Pupils' Rights Law.* Retrieved from pupilsrightslaw.pdf (jewishvirtuallibrary.org).
Israeli Ministry of Justice. (2003). *Minister of Justice's commission on fundamental issues concerning children and law and their implementation in legislation* (Chairperson: S. Rotlevi) [Hebrew].
Israeli Ministry of Justice. (2016). *Foster Care for Children Act.* Retrieved from https://www.gov.il/he/departments/ministry_of_justice/govil-landing-page
Israeli Ministry of Social Services and Social Affairs. (2014a). *The Commission to Examine the Ministry's Policy in Relations to Children's Removal to Out-of-Home Placement and Custody Arrangements.*
Israeli Ministry of Social Services and Social Affairs. (2014b). *Planning, Intervention, and Evaluation Committee: The implementation team's decisions.*
The Knesset. (2016). *Children and youth participation in decision and policy making.* Center for Research and Information.
Kosher, H., & Ben-Arie, A. (2009). Child participation in social policy design: The role of social work [Hebrew]. *Social Security, 81,* 107-134.
Lansdown, G. (2010). The realisation of children's participation rights—Critical reflections. In B. Percy-Smith & N. Thomas (Eds.), *A handbook of children and young people's participation: Perspectives from theory and practice* (pp. 11-23). Routledge.
Lareau, A. (2002). Invisible inequality: Social class and childrearing in black families and white families. *American Sociological Review, 67*(5), 747-776.
Larson, R., Walker, K., & Pearce, N. (2005). A comparison of youth-driven and adult-driven youth programs: Balancing inputs from youth and adults. *Journal of Community Psychology, 33*(1), 57-74. https://doi.org/10.1002/jcop.20035
Leeson, C. (2007). My life in care: Experiences of non-participation in decision-making processes. *Child & Family Social Work, 12*(3), 268-277. https://doi.org/10.1111/j.1365-2206.2007.00499.x
Lune, H., & Berg, B. L. (2017). *Qualitative research methods for the social science.* Pearson Education.
Makrinioti, D. (1994). Conceptualization of childhood in a welfare state: A critical reappraisal. In J. Qvotrup, M. Bardy, G. Sgrittaand, & H. Wintersberger (Eds.), *Childhood matters: Social theory, practice and politics* (pp. 267-284). Avebury.
Nir, T., & Perry-Hazan, L. (2016). The framed right to participate in municipal youth councils and its educational impact. *Children & Youth Services Review, 69,* 174-183. https://10.1016/j.childyouth.2016.07.012
Putnam, R. D. (1993). *Making democracy work. Civic traditions in modern Italy.* Princeton University Press.
Rampal, A. (2008). Scaffolded participation of children: Perspectives from India. *International Journal of Children's Rights, 16*(3), 313-325. https://doi.org/10.1163/157181808X311169

Richards-Schuster, K. (2012). Empowering the voice of youth: The role of youth advisory councils in grant making focused on youth. *New Directions for Evaluation, 136*, 87–100. https://doi.org/10.1002/ev.20036

Sabah, Y. (Ed.). (2017). *Annual review of social services 2016* [Hebrew]. Ministry of Labor, Welfare and Social Services. Retrieved November 14, 2019, from https://www.gov.il/he/Departments/publications/reports/molsa-social-services-review-2016

Schneider, B. H. (2000). *Friends and enemies: Peer relations in childhood. Texts in developmental psychology*. Oxford University Press.

Schwartz-Tayri, T. M., & Spiro, S. E. (2017). The other side of the bridge: A follow-up study of Israeli young adults who participated in a transitional housing program after aging out from care. *Residential Treatment for Children & Youth, 34*(3–4), 311–324. https://doi.org/10.1080/0886571X.2017.1334164

Schwartz-Tayri, T. M., & Spiro, S. E. (2023). The contribution of replicated follow-up studies to improving transitional housing programs for youths aging out of care in Israel. *Children and Youth Services Review, 106863*. https://doi.org/10.1016/j.childyouth.2023.106863.

Serido, J., Borden, L. M., & Perkins, D. F. (2011). Moving beyond youth voice. *Youth & Society, 43*(1), 44–63. https://doi.org/10.1177/0044118X09351280

Sinclair, R., & Franklin, A. (2000). *Young people's participation - Quality protects—Research briefing no. 3*. Department of Health. Retrieved November 14, 2019, from http://www.rip.org.uklpublicationsldocuments/QPBIQPB3.PDF

Snow, K., & Mann-Feder, V. (2013). Peer-centered practice: A theoretical framework for intervention with young people in and from care. *Child Welfare, 92*(4), 75–93. http://www.ncbi.nlm.nih.gov/pubmed/24851476

Stein, M. (2006). Research review: Young people leaving care. *Child & Family Social Work, 11*, 273–279. https://doi.org//10.1111/j.1365-2206.2006.00439.x.

Sulimani-Aidan, Y. (2014). Care leavers' challenges in transition to independent living. *Children & Youth Services Review, 46*, 38–46. https://doi.org/10.1016/j.childyouth.2014.07.022

Tisdall, E. K. M., & Davis, J. (2004). Making a difference? Bringing children's and young people's views into policymaking. *Children & Society, 18*(2), 131–142. https://doi.org/10.1002/CHI.816

Tisdall, E. K. M., Davis, J. M., & Gallagher, M. (2008). Reflecting on children and young people's participation in the UK. *International Journal of Children's Rights, 16*, 343–354. https://doi.org/10.1163/157181808X311187

Van Bijleveld, G. G., Dedding, C. W. M., & Bunders-Aelen, J. F. G. (2014). Seeing eye to eye or not? Young people's and child protection workers' perspectives on children's participation within the Dutch child protection and welfare services. *Children & Youth Services Review, 47*, 253–259.

Verba, S., Schlozman, K. L., & Brady, H. E. (1995). *Voice and equality: Civic voluntarism in American politics*. Harvard University Press.

Wandersman, A., & Florin, P. (2000). Citizen participation and community organizations. In J. Rappaport & E. Seidman (Eds.), *Handbook of community psychology* (pp. 247–272). Springer.

Weiss-Gal, I. (2009). Teaching critical perspectives: Analyses of professional practice in the film Ladybird, Ladybird. *Social Work Education, 28*(8), 873–886. https://doi.org/10.1080/02615470802702157

Yosso, T. J. (2005). Whose culture has capital? A critical race theory discussion of community cultural wealth. *Race, Ethnicity and Education, 8*(1), 69–91. https://doi.org/10.1080/1361332052000341006

Zeldin, S. (2000). Integrating research and practice to understand and strengthen communities for adolescent development: An introduction to the special issue and current issues. *Applied Developmental Science, 4*(1), 2–11. https://doi.org/10.1207/S1532480XADS04Suppl_1

5
Children Claiming the Right to Live Without Violence in Nicaragua

Harry Shier

Introduction

All children have the inalienable right to live without violence, and this chapter is about how children themselves can organize to claim and defend this right. Drawing on case studies from Nicaragua in Central America, the chapter aims to show how, when children are informed and empowered as rights holders and recognized as active citizens, transformations occur throughout communities, leading to a safer, less violent society. Before proceeding, however, it is necessary to enter a crucial caveat. Keeping children safe from violence and harm is essentially an adult responsibility. We adults must assume the role of duty bearers in relation to the child's right to live without violence and the obligations that go with it. Most of the work to be done in ensuring child protection is done by and with adults throughout the world, and it is often challenging work.

Having made this point, we can return to our focus in this chapter, namely the children's role. The chapter is structured in three parts. Following this introduction, the first part introduces and unpacks the concept of "a rights-based approach to keeping children safe," drawing on specific rights established in the United Nations Convention on the Rights of the Child (UNCRC; United Nations, 1989). The second part presents 10 examples of how children and adolescents have taken practical action to defend their right to live without violence, all drawn from my own experience supporting child workers on the coffee plantations of northern Nicaragua between 2001 and 2012. In the third part, I reflect on these experiences to share some of the lessons I learned along the way.

Harry Shier, *Children Claiming the Right to Live Without Violence in Nicaragua* In: *Children and Young People's Participation in Child Protection.* Edited by: Katrin Križ and Mimi Petersen, Oxford University Press.
© Oxford University Press 2023. DOI: 10.1093/oso/9780197622322.003.0005

A Rights-Based Approach to Keeping Children Safe

In general terms, the United Nations describes a human rights–based approach (HRBA) as a conceptual framework for the process of human development that is normatively based on international human rights standards and operationally directed to promoting and protecting human rights. It seeks to analyze inequalities at the heart of development problems and redress discriminatory practices and unjust distributions of power that impede development progress (UN Office of the High Commissioner for Human Rights, 2006, p. 15).

Let us rewrite this with a focus on keeping children safe:

> **A rights-based approach to keeping children safe** is a conceptual framework for keeping children safe from harm. It is based on the international human rights standards set out in the UNCRC. It is operationally directed to promoting and protecting every child's right to live without violence. It seeks to analyze inequalities that place some children at greater risk of violence and abuse and redress discriminatory practices and unjust distributions of power that perpetuate such risks.

A distinctive feature of the rights-based approach is that it recognizes all children as *rights holders* and identifies adults as *duty bearers* at different levels. The implementation of a rights-based approach, therefore, involves building the capacity of children, as rights holders, to claim their rights. It also involves building the capacity of duty bearers to fulfill their obligations (as well as calling those same duty bearers to account when they fail to do so and providing support and solidarity to children whose rights have been violated).

For children to claim their rights, and for duty bearers to respect and protect them, there must be a shared understanding of what those rights are, and here the first point of reference is the UNCRC, an international treaty binding on all the world's governments except for the United States. (The United States is the only United Nations member state that has not ratified the convention.) At the heart of a rights-based approach to keeping children safe lies Article 19 of the convention:

> **United Nations Convention on the Rights of the Child, Article 19.1**
>
> States Parties shall take all appropriate legislative, administrative, social, and educational measures to protect the child from all forms of physical

> or mental violence, injury or abuse, neglect or negligent treatment, maltreatment, or exploitation, including sexual abuse, while in the care of parent(s), legal guardian(s) or any other person who has the care of the child.

But rights do not stand alone, so we must also take account of:

Article 28.2: School discipline to be administered in a manner consistent with the child's human dignity;

Article 34: Protection from all forms of sexual exploitation and sexual abuse;

Article 35: Prevention of abduction, sale, or traffic in children;

Article 36: Protection against all other forms of exploitation prejudicial to the child's welfare;

Article 37: Protection from torture or other cruel, inhuman, or degrading treatment or punishment.

Together these constitute the child's fundamental "right to live without violence." "Violence" can be defined in many ways. For the purpose of this chapter, "the right to live without violence" can be understood as shorthand for the realization of the specific rights mentioned above.

A rights-based approach also needs to take on board the four underpinning principles of the convention:

- Enjoyment of all rights without discrimination of any kind (Article 2);
- The child's best interests to be a primary consideration in all decisions (Article 3);
- The right to life and development (Article 6);
- The child's right to speak out and be heard on all matters that affect them (Article 12; Committee on the Rights of the Child, 2003, pp. 3–4).

It further needs to be recognized that Article 12 is accompanied by Article 13 (the right to information and ideas), Article 14 (freedom of thought, conscience, and religion), and Article 15 (freedom of association and peaceful assembly). Together these are the core of what is commonly known as the child's "participation rights." When protection rights are coupled with participation rights, it is clear that children have the right to live without violence and the right to know, defend, demand, promote, and protect—in other words, to *claim*—that right.

I emphasized above that a rights-based approach involves building capacities both in children to claim their rights and in duty bearers to fulfill their obligations. Both aspects are essential to the rights-based approach, and the importance of up-skilling and motivating duty bearers cannot be overestimated. However, with our focus on "children's participation in child protection," I want to look more closely at how we can support the empowerment of children as rights holders to claim and defend their right to live without violence. Note that in this chapter, "empowerment" is not used in a hazy, ill-defined way but is a clearly defined concept with practical application; see Shier (2019a) for a complete account of this concept and further discussion of "empowerment" toward the end of this chapter.

In more traditional conceptions of child protection, adults in positions of power generally did not seek, did not hear, and therefore did not consider the child's views (Shemmings, 2000; Van Bijleveld et al., 2015). Indeed, it was seen as in a child's interests not to be heard, due to a common belief that

> too much responsibility and too much participation can be harmful to children. They need to be protected from participating in difficult decision-making or from feeling pressure to express their views on painful or controversial matters. (Lurie, 2003, n.p.)

This means a great deal of violence toward children, including sexual and physical abuse, went unnoticed and unreported. Children who did have the courage to speak out were ignored, disbelieved, or accused of fantasizing (Aronson Fontes & Plummer, 2010; Greeson et al., 2016). Increasingly these days, rights-based approaches require that children's views *are* sought, which means creating spaces where voices can be expressed and heard and adapting systems so that the views expressed can be taken into account in decision-making (Keeping Children Safe, 2011; Moore, 2017).

In child protection, this commonly happens at the micro level; that is, the individual child's views are sought to get the best possible outcome for that particular child in the prevailing circumstances (Wolff et al., 2016). But it can also happen at the macro level: the voices of a group of children can be brought together so that the sum of their individual experiences can become a driver for change at higher levels in the services or systems in question (Ruiz Casares et al., 2017; Willow, 2009). However, the focus, at least in wealthier countries where people rely on a range of social and legal services, is still on the child as a *service user*. The aim is to improve outcomes for the child through the provision of adequate and appropriate services (Shier, 2010a). In many places, however, children's experiences are very different.

Children Claiming the Right to Live Without Violence in Nicaragua

For 11 years (2001–2012), I worked with the children's rights organization CESESMA in the coffee-growing zone in Nicaragua in Central America, where extreme poverty and dependence on coffee production lead to a high incidence of child labor and associated social problems. Though the situation is improving, the Nicaraguan coffee industry still employs thousands of child workers who work long hours in difficult and dangerous conditions, receiving little or no payment for their efforts. Almost all drop out of school early, leading to a cycle of dependency, hunger, and destitution in these remote mountain communities (Shier, 2010b).

CESESMA was founded in 1994 by a group of local schoolteachers whose initial aim was to make the education offered in village schools more relevant to the lives of rural working children. During my time there, however, although CESESMA remained solidly Nicaraguan and firmly rooted in the local communities it served, its role and mission evolved as it embraced a child rights–based approach, focusing on supporting rural children and adolescents in promoting and defending their rights. Among the rights promoted and defended were the right to education, a healthy uncontaminated environment, dignity and respect at work, play and recreation, enjoying and sharing their own culture, and speaking out, organizing, and participating. For many children, however, the most important was the right to live without violence (CESESMA, 2012b).

As the organization evolved, my role in the team also evolved from an initial focus on training and capacity building to encompass a broad range of rights advocacy, facilitation, coordination, and research (which included accompanying and facilitating some of the processes described later in this chapter; Shier, 2007). For someone like me, who had previously worked in the United Kingdom, a major difference I encountered in Nicaragua was that the emphasis on the child as a "service user," which prevailed in the United Kingdom, would have meant little here since services for children were sparse and had to be fought for, rather than simply consumed (Shier, 2010a). To fully grasp CESESMA's way of working and find my place in it, I had to understand and embrace two related concepts that were new to me at the time: children as *active citizens* and *protagonismo infantil*.

"Citizenship" has been conceived and defined in many ways, but the active citizenship promoted by CESESMA was neither a legal status nor a geographical identity. It was instead a conscious decision on the part of young people themselves to assume responsibility in their community and take collective action to improve the conditions of life—of themselves and others—by promoting and defending their rights (Shier, 2010a, 2014). In Latin America, the need to stand up and defend one's rights in this way, rather than avail oneself of services provided by the state, has given rise to the theory and practice of *protagonismo infantil*. *Protagonismo* amplifies the idea of children as citizens, occurring when children themselves take a *leading* role in conceiving and carrying out actions to improve their lives (Shier, 2019b; Taft, 2017, 2019). Rooted in the history of movements of organized working children, *protagonismo* is not about individual children acting independently in defense of individual rights but rather collective action by organized, self-directed groups. *Protagonismo*, in turn, leads to empowerment of children and adolescents and, through them, to transformation in society. Almost all the literature on *protagonismo* is in Spanish, but Taft (2019) offers a detailed account in English, and Lavan (2012) explores *protagonismo* in an African context.

Here is a selection of projects and processes that I was privileged to support and accompany during my 11 years with CESESMA amid the Nicaraguan coffee plantations, where children and adolescents exercised their citizenship and exerted their *protagonismo* to defend the right to live without violence.

Youth Theater Against Violence in the Home

Youth theater groups supported by CESESMA devised, produced, and presented original plays that exposed issues of gender-based violence and economic exploitation that were seldom talked about in local communities. This proved effective in opening up discussion of these "taboo" issues and urging communities to address them. Young people's community theater was also a powerful medium in campaigns and protests, where groups devised and performed original plays to support campaigns against child abuse, corporal punishment, and exploitation of child labor (Shier, 2010b, 2012, 2014, pp. 17–19).

Festivals Against Violence Towards Children

Starting in 2006, Save the Children organized an annual National Festival Against Violence Towards Children. Organized groups traveled from all over the country to share their stories and creative approaches to tackling the issue through theater, song, banners, posters, and other media. The 2010 festival, held in La Dalia in the coffee-growing zone, gave the children's theater group Los Colibrís the opportunity to perform their play *Blows to the Soul* about the issue of domestic violence (see above) before an audience of over 2,000 children and adults in the town's baseball stadium (Shier, 2012, 2014, pp. 17–19).

Child Consultants Investigating the Problem of Violence on the Coffee Plantation

In 2007, a team of 12 working children aged 10 to 16 from the Santa Martha Coffee Plantation became expert consultants to research violence in their lives on the plantation. They interviewed 59 children and adolescents living and working on the plantation, then analyzed their data to produce a report with extensive recommendations for change. They then traveled to the capital city to present their findings at a national conference on the theme of violence against children. They were able to put their recommendations directly to the government minister responsible for children and families and challenge her to tell the conference what her department intended to do about the issue. It is unknown what direct effect this had on government policy, but the Children and Families Department introduced new programs to protect vulnerable children shortly afterward. The following year, the children retold their experience in words and pictures for publication (Shier, 2015, p. 210; Young Consultants of Santa Martha, 2009).

The Dragon of Violence

In 2008, children in Samulalí district created a Chinese-style carnival dragon that took to the streets in several marches and protests to awaken people to the reality of violence threatening women and children in rural communities and the need to face up to it without fear. When the National Festival Against Violence Towards Children came to La Dalia in 2010 (see above), the children decided that the Dragon of Violence should take to the streets again. However, the original dragon, whose head was made from cardboard boxes, was in bad shape and not up to another parade, so the children created a new dragon based on the original design, which led the festival parade (Shier, 2012, p. 7).

Young Women's Groups

Adolescent girls formed learning and action groups in their villages to spread the word about gender equality, women's rights, and sexual and reproductive health. These safe spaces for girls and young women effectively empowered girls and built assertiveness in the face of the "machismo" prevalent in local communities (Hernández Méndez & Quintanilla, 2016; Shier, 2010b). CESESMA also invited parents to parallel awareness-raising sessions. However, given the traditional attitudes to gender roles in these communities, it was inevitable that not all parents were happy about their daughters engaging in these activities. In these cases, members of the CESESMA team met individually with parents and usually won them over by convincing them of the long-term benefits to their daughters.

New Masculinities Program

Understanding that men too have to change their ways, CESESMA supported adolescent boys in forming action groups to spread the message that there are many ways to be a real man that do not involve violence toward women and girls (Shier, 2016, p. 81). These experiences were later consolidated in a facilitator's guide published by CESESMA (CESESMA, 2013). As an interesting aside, this guide recommends a shared viewing of the film *How to Train Your Dragon* as a way to help boys and young men explore how traditional gender roles, and parental expectations based on these, trap young men into stereotypical aggressive behavior and make life difficult for those who dare to step outside such prescribed roles (CESESMA, 2013, p. 20).

Transformative Research by Children and Adolescents

Based on the earlier model of children's consultancy (see example "Child Consultants Investigating the Problem of Violence on the Coffee Plantation" above), CESESMA developed a new approach called Transformative Research by Children and Adolescents (TRCA). It is beyond the scope of this chapter to describe the TRCA methodology, but it is explained in detail in Shier (2016, pp. 232–237). Using this methodology, children became researchers to investigate and report on issues that concerned them in their communities. A team from El Plomo investigated the concept of respect and how lack of respect leads to violence in families and communities. A team from Yasica Sur researched the violence that children and adolescents suffer in the home. Children in Samulalí examined the issue of parents who hit their children. And finally, a team from Yúcul decided to investigate the topic of alcohol and its relation to violence in the community. As well as producing research findings and recommendations, the four teams drew up action plans to publicize the results of their research and push for the implementation of their recommendations. They presented their reports first in their home villages and subsequently in municipal, and some cases national, forums. The four reports were compiled and published in book form by CESESMA, followed by an English translation, *Learn to Live Without Violence* (CESESMA, 2012b; Shier, 2015).

All four teams used their research to advocate for change, but the one that made the most impact was the team from Yúcul. They presented their findings to the government's newly formed Family Life and Security Commission, which decided to prioritize the alcohol problem for local action. Local government officials admitted they had been aware of the issue for years, but it was not until the children came forward with their research that they felt obliged to act. The local police also took action, confiscating illegal liquor and closing unlicensed cantinas. A popular national television channel then featured the young researchers on the evening news. Since then, the local authority has ensured that no new liquor licenses are granted in the Yúcul area (Shier, 2014, pp. 26–28).

Children Researching Children's Understanding of Sex and Sexuality

One of the most remarkable projects undertaken by child researchers was a survey to find out what their peers actually knew about sex and sexuality and what they felt they needed to know. This project occurred in the context of a wider project to develop a new learning initiative around sexual and reproductive rights in rural communities. It was important to decide how and when to involve children of different ages in learning about this topic. On the one hand, these are sometimes thought of as things children should not have to worry about, but on the other hand, ignorance of sex and sexuality can increase risks such as unwanted pregnancy, sexually transmitted infections, or becoming a victim of sexual abuse or exploitation.

To ensure the issue was addressed in a well-informed and culturally sensitive way, four teams of child researchers interviewed other children in their villages on these topics. After analyzing their data, they produced a report that was published by CESESMA (2012a). Armed with this understanding of what children already knew and what they wanted to know, the CESESMA team was able to develop the new initiative in a way that respected both children's rights and local sensibilities and reduced risks for everyone.

Developing Child Protection Guidelines From the Bottom Up

Before 2009, the issue of child protection was largely ignored in Nicaraguan schools. Still, with growing awareness, not to mention pressure from external funders like Save the Children, schools recognized the need to embrace the idea of safeguarding, which meant new policies and guidelines were needed. Instead of the usual top-down policy process, CESESMA supported local schools and their surrounding communities in developing child protection policies from the bottom up. Children worked in teams to identify the risks they were exposed to—both at school and while traveling to and from school—and propose changes in conditions, practices, attitudes, and abilities that would help safeguard them from these risks. The children's views were written up and published by CESESMA as *Safe and Quality Schools: As Viewed by Children and Adolescents* (CESESMA, 2009). Groups of parents and teachers carried out similar analyses. With this clear vision, smaller working groups involving students, parents, and teachers met to synthesize their findings and develop draft policy documents. Finally, there were joint meetings to review and adopt the policies. Children and adolescents also took a leading role in monitoring and evaluation (Shier et al., 2013, p. 196).

Weekly Radio Show "Children and Adolescents' Voices Heard"

CESESMA also supported a children's radio team, who broadcast their show *Children and Adolescents' Voices Heard* on La Dalia's local radio station every Sunday morning. Young reporters living in the surrounding villages sent in reports on local issues affecting children's rights. Along with these, the show included peer-to-peer messages about preventing, recognizing, and reporting violence, interspersed with music and lighter items (Shier, 2010b). Though there is no data available on the overall reach of the broadcasts, it is interesting to note that many schoolteachers were regular listeners. They told CESESMA that it was the best way to keep abreast of what local children were concerned about.

Conclusion: Lessons Learned

There are six key learnings I want to share after reviewing these examples of children taking action to keep themselves and others safe

No-One Empowers Anyone

Although the above examples can be seen as instances of children and adolescents "empowered," and the work of CESESMA over many years has been praised for the delivery of this empowerment, an important lesson we have learned along the way is that adults cannot "empower" children; specifically, the adult facilitators who supported the processes described here did not "empower" the children and adolescents they worked with. Only children and adolescents can empower themselves.

This is because building capacity and creating enabling conditions for children's authentic participation are not in themselves sufficient to deliver empowerment. Empowerment also requires a transformative process whereby self-esteem, motivation, critical thinking, initiative, perseverance, and solidarity take shape within the person (Sharp, 2014; Shier, 2019a; and see also Freire, 2001, for a similar view).

Thus, true empowerment (as distinct from "enabling" or "capacity building," which are often confused with empowerment) can only be achieved through a transformative process within the person. What adults *can* do, however, is develop and facilitate the kinds of processes that will lead young people toward such transformation. A lot of CESESMA's experience has involved adults rising to this challenge, for example, by supporting, resourcing, and, where needed, facilitating the kinds of activities described in the previous section.

Not "Held Responsible" but Responsible Citizens

Children, especially young children, are *never* responsible for their own protection. It is axiomatic that protecting children from harm is *always* the responsibility of adults. Though it is generally considered a good thing for children to learn to recognize danger, avoid risk, look after themselves, and look out for others, no matter how tough and resilient children become, the responsibility for their protection can never be devolved to the children themselves and always remains with adults. To put it another way, when adults harm children, it is *never* acceptable to blame the victim. Adults must always be held accountable for their actions and omissions in relation to protecting children from violence.

This point must be clearly understood, as failure to understand it can lead to confusion and misunderstanding on the next point. To affirm that children are *never* responsible for the wrongdoing of adults, however, is not to imply that they must therefore be considered irresponsible. As the examples above demonstrate repeatedly, children can assume the role of active citizens and, as such, can unite to undertake appropriate actions that contribute to their own and others' safety: raising awareness, identifying and mitigating risks, practicing assertiveness, denouncing abuse and exploitation, and, through it all, claiming and defending their right to live without violence. In other words, when it comes to the prevention of violence, children can never be *held responsible*, but they can freely choose to *assume responsibilities*, exercising *protagonismo* in ways that correspond to their positive role as active young citizens (Shier, 2018, pp. 774–775).

Cultural Change From Within

Some of the factors that allow the violation of children's right to live without violence to persist in society are linked to belief systems embedded in tradition and culture, including, for example, conceiving of children as the property of their parents; denial of gender equality; denial of children as rights holders; belief that children (particularly girls) should be servile and obedient; belief that violence in the form of corporal punishment is a legitimate part of childrearing; belief that violence and abuse within a family must never be spoken of outside the family; belief that victims, particularly girls, are to blame for sexual violence against them, and worse, that they deserve to be punished for bringing shame on their family; and belief that certain abusive practices are not only sanctioned but also demanded by religious or cultural tradition, female genital mutilation and child marriage being well-researched examples (Hale Reed, 2014; Khosla et al., 2017).

Changing cultural climates that permit such violence and abuse to prevail is one of the toughest challenges in child protection. Bringing about sustainable cultural change is difficult at the best of times, but it can be particularly challenging in the context of postcolonial societies (Girei, 2016). If people associate advocacy for change with the cultural values of the former colonial power (or a notion of "Western values" in general), it may be resisted as an imposition of neocolonial "cultural imperialism" (Wane et al., 2011). It is quite legitimate for the descendants of formerly colonized peoples to question the right of the foreigners who stole their land, enslaved their ancestors, and destroyed their way of life to now tell them that their culture is flawed and that they must adopt the supposedly superior values and practices of their former colonizers (Hickling-Hudson, 2006; Olivier, 2019).

In such situations, there are none better placed than the child activists of Nicaragua to effect significant, sustainable cultural change. These young people are growing up *within* their own local and national culture, and proudly so; yet they see the need for change and the possibility of stimulating and inspiring change. The clearest examples of this are the youth theater groups chipping away at long-standing taboos, the girls' groups demanding gender equity, and the young men arguing for alternative masculinities in communities where such ideas had never previously been countenanced.

In this context, it is important to note that CESESMA, the organization that supported and accompanied them, is solidly Nicaraguan, staffed and run by local people for local people. During my time there, the team numbered around 30, consisting of 28 Nicaraguans, one Irishman (me), and one Swiss. The pressure for change that CESESMA supported was thus not an external force seeking to destroy or diminish local culture, but an alliance of those within the culture, seeking to build on, update, and improve what was already there (Kaime, 2005; Zwart, 2012).

The Power of Creativity and Imagination

Many of the actions undertaken by children and adolescents described above show a high level of creativity and imagination, for example, the Dragon of Violence, youth theater, and festivals against violence. Though prevention of violence and abuse is a deadly serious subject, these vibrant, imaginative actions caught the wider public's attention, communicated key messages, and galvanized responses in ways that somber speeches failed to do. Creative approaches can also get people to question old and outmoded habits of thought, leading to sustainable behavior change. A lesson for adult supporters and facilitators here is that "serious" and "important" are not necessarily synonyms for "tedious" and "boring."

The Power of Children as Researchers

As researchers, children can not only access knowledge about other children's lives that is hidden from adults but also can cast an alternative light on that knowledge from their own distinct perspective and deepen and extend adults' understanding of the issues being investigated (Kellett, 2010, p. 197). Examples of this mentioned above include children's understandings of sex and sexuality and children's experiences of violence on the coffee plantations.

Unfortunately, it is all too common for adults in power to be dubious about children's participation because of previous unsatisfactory experiences. Children are often asked what they want, which means adult decision makers end up with nothing more than a random, fanciful wish list. In contrast, however, when children speak out against violence and back up their recommendations with *robust research findings*, the situation is very different. Instead of telling the adults, "We want A, B, and C," the child researchers will say something like: "Based on our interviews with 150 local children aged 7 to 15 and analysis of the findings, here are our concrete proposals for the changes that are required." When this happens, it is harder for adults in power to ignore or disparage the children's message (CESESMA, 2012b; Young Consultants of Santa Martha, 2009).

We Will Not Silence Children Who Want to Speak Out Against Violence (but We Will Not Put Their Lives at Risk Either)

It is a common occurrence, in both practice and research, for children to be silenced by adults in charge because they fear that they (the adults) will be held responsible for the consequences if the children are allowed to speak out. This silencing of children's voices often happens indirectly through selective exclusion from participation opportunities, which is then rationalized by labeling certain children as "vulnerable" (Tobin, 2015). Once children have been labeled as vulnerable, it is easy for adults to appeal to notions of ethics to justify excluding them from involvement in a participation or research initiative. Skelton (2008, p. 23) shows how "ethical research practice can actually close down participation for children and young people" and how "institutional ethical guidelines can deny children's and young people's competence and ability to make decisions about their own lives." The voices of the supposedly vulnerable children are thus effectively silenced and disappear from the scene.

CESESMA has always taken the view that where children want to speak out about an issue that is of concern to them, and there is a potential risk of adverse consequences, it is the duty of the responsible adults to find a safe alternative, managing the risks so that children can be protected from harm *without* having their voices silenced and their right to speak violated. In the examples above, the clearest instance of this was the research by the children of Yúcul on the relationship between alcohol and violence in their village (CESESMA, 2012b, pp. 37–46). When the children announced their chosen research topic, the CESESMA team had to think long and hard about the implications of letting children go probing into such a contentious issue in a small community. Some felt the easiest solution was to say, "No, we will not let you pursue this; it is too risky." However, taking that approach would have been to silence the children's voices and deny them their right to speak out on an issue that concerned them.

Instead, the CESESMA team took on the challenge. We analyzed the risks and looked at the safeguards we would have to put in place: we talked with parents, teachers, and local community leaders, where we found universal support for the children's initiative and got a commitment to keep an eye on things; we informed the local police; and we made sure someone from our team was always close at hand when the children were doing interviews (but not so close as to hamper conversations between peers). As with every team of child researchers, we discussed and agreed on safety rules. We always worked in pairs, ensuring peers, parents, and a CESESMA team member knew where they were and what they were doing; confirming the interviewee was willing to participate before asking any questions; and politely withdrawing if anyone appeared unhappy about continuing. When we heard that a national television company wanted to interview the children, we discussed options including anonymity or using pseudonyms. However, by then, the children were so proud of what they had achieved that they refused to conceal their identities.

As a practitioner on the ground experiencing these initiatives, the transformative benefits were easy to see. From a researcher's perspective, however, there remains the challenge of demonstrating a causal link from children's social action to concrete social change and finding indicators to evidence and measure this. We have plentiful evidence from the testimonies of children, parents, teachers, and local community leaders, but to shift this from the "anecdotal" realm to the "analytical," we need more focused research. Following a rights-based approach as described above, it is clear that the children's right to speak out and take action is not dependent on them proving the effectiveness of their actions. However, still, this is something we adults (especially social scientists) are keen to know about. It seems only appropriate, therefore, to make a call here for further research in this area.

As mentioned at the start, building children's capacity to claim and defend their right to live without violence is just one aspect of a rights-based approach to keeping children safe. We must also direct our efforts to build the capacity of duty bearers to fulfill their obligations and call those same duty bearers to account when they fail in providing support and solidarity to children whose rights have been violated. What this chapter has set out to demonstrate, however, is that when children are informed and empowered as rights holders and recognized as active citizens, they can not only claim their right to live without violence but also, in doing so, contribute to transformation throughout society.

Acknowledgments

I would like to thank the CESESMA team past and present for welcoming me as one of their own and for the support and *compañerismo* over the years that opened my eyes to a wealth of learning. I would also like to thank the children and adolescents of the rural communities and coffee plantations of San Ramón, Samulalí, and La Dalia, who shared their experiences, who inspired and energized me, and whose struggles and achievements both generated and validated that learning.

Reflection Questions

(1) The experiences described in this chapter come from a specific geographical and cultural setting, namely the remote rural villages and coffee plantations of northern Nicaragua. When we read about these experiences, what are the bigger, universal messages equally relevant in our work or study environment?
(2) Given that the protection of children from harm is essentially an adult responsibility, in what circumstances, and under what conditions, is it appropriate for children to take on responsibilities in relation to keeping themselves and others safe (and for adults to encourage them to do so)?

References

Aronson Fontes, L., & Plummer, C. (2010). Cultural issues in disclosures of child sexual abuse. *Journal of Child Sexual Abuse, 19*(5), 491–518.
CESESMA. (2009). *Escuelas seguras y de calidad* [Safe and quality schools]. http://www.harryshier.net/documentos/CESESMA-escuelas_seguras.pdf

CESESMA. (2012a). *Aprendimos que la sexualidad es pensar, actuar y sentir* [We learned that sexuality is thinking, acting and feeling]. http://www.harryshier.net/documentos/CESESMA-Aprendimos_que_la_sexualidad.pdf

CESESMA. (2012b). *Learn to live without violence: Transformative research by children and young people* (H. Shier, Ed.). University of Central Lancashire and CESESMA. http://www.harryshier.net/docs/CESESMA-Learn_to_live_without_violence.pdf

CESESMA. (2013). *Cuadernillo de trabajo para promotores* [Workbook for promoters]. http://www.harryshier.net/documentos/CESESMA-Cuadernillo_promotores_compartiendo.pdf

Committee on the Rights of the Child. (2003). *General comment no 5: General measures of implementation of the Convention on the Rights of the Child*. United Nations.

Freire, P. (2001). *Pedagogy of the oppressed*. Continuum. (Original work published in 1968).

Girei, E. (2016). NGOs, management and development: Harnessing counter-hegemonic possibilities. *Organization Studies, 37*(2), 193–212.

Greeson, M. R., Campbell, R., & Fehler-Cabral, G. (2016). "Nobody deserves this": Adolescent sexual assault victims' perceptions of disbelief and victim blame from police. *Journal of Community Psychology, 1*(44), 90–110.

Hale Reed, J. (2014). Early marriage as a violation of human rights: A proposal for constructive engagement in non-western communities. *Indonesian Journal of International and Comparative Law, 1*(1), 151–217.

Hernández Méndez, M., & Quintanilla, M. (2016). Retos y aprendizajes sobre participación a partir de la experiencia de Cesesma [Challenges and learning about participation from Cesesma's experience]. In E. Larracoechea Bohigas & A. V. Portocarrero Lacayo (Eds.), *Las resistencias nuestras de cada día* [Our Everyday Resistances] (pp. 249–298). UCA publicaciones. http://www.harryshier.net/documentos/Hernandez_y_Quintanilla-Retos_y_aprendizajes.pdf

Hickling-Hudson, A. (2006). Cultural complexity, post-colonialism and educational change. *International Review of Education, 52*(1–2), 201–208.

Kaime, T. (2005). The Convention on the Rights of the Child and the cultural legitimacy of children's rights in Africa. *African Human Rights Law Journal, 5*(2), 221–238.

Keeping Children Safe. (2011). *Children's participation in child protection*. https://www.keepingchildrensafe.org.uk/sites/default/files/KCSTool4%20-%20English.pdf

Kellett, M. (2010). Small shoes, big steps! Empowering children as active researchers. *American Journal of Community Psychology, 46*(1), 195–203.

Khosla, R., Banerjee, J., Chou, D., Say, L., & Fried, S. T. (2017). Gender equality and human rights approaches to female genital mutilation. *Reproductive Health, 14*(1), 59.

Lavan, D. (2012). *The discourse and practice of child protagonism* (PhD thesis, University of Ottawa).

Lurie, J. (2003). The tension between protection and participation. *IUC Journal of Social Work Theory & Practice, 6*(7).

Moore, T. (2017). *Protection through participation: Involving children in child-safe organisations*. Australian Institute of Family Studies. https://aifs.gov.au/cfca/sites/default/files/publication-documents/protection_through_participation.pdf

Olivier, B. (2019). Decolonisation, identity, neo-colonialism and power. *Phronimon, 20*, 1–18.

Ruiz-Casares, M., Collins, T. M., Tisdall, E. K. M., & Grover, S. (2017). Children's rights to participation and protection in international development and humanitarian interventions. *International Journal of Human Rights, 21*(1), 1–13.

Sharp, R. (2014). Ready, steady, action: What enables young people to perceive themselves as active agents in their lives? *Educational Psychology in Practice, 30*(4), 347–364.

Shemmings, D. (2000). Professionals' attitudes to children's participation in decision-making: Dichotomous accounts and doctrinal contests. *Child and Family Social Work, 5*(3), 235–244.

Shier, H. (2007). *Letters from Matagalpa.* http://www.harryshier.net.http://www.harryshier.net/docs/Harry_Shier-Letters_from_Matagalpa.pdf

Shier, H. (2010a). Children as public actors: Navigating the tensions. *Children & Society, 24*(1), 24–37.

Shier, H. (2010b). "Pathways to participation" revisited: Learning from Nicaragua's child coffee workers. In N. Thomas & B. Percy-Smith (Eds.), *A handbook of children and young people's participation* (pp. 215–227). Routledge.

Shier, H. (2012). *The Nicaraguan children's "Defending our right to play" campaign as it happened, 2009–2011.* CESESMA/Common Threads. http://www.harryshier.net/docs/Shier-Right_to_play_campaign.pdf

Shier, H. (Ed.). (2014). *Children's rights and social justice: Case studies from Nicaragua as a resource for students and teachers.* CESESMA with Leeds DEC. http://www.harryshier.net/docs/CESESMA-Childrens_rights_and_social_justice.pdf

Shier, H. (2015). Children as researchers in Nicaragua: Children's consultancy to transformative research. *Global Studies of Childhood, 5*(2), 206–219.

Shier, H. (2016). *Children's rights in school: The perception of children in Nicaragua.* Queen's University Belfast. http://www.harryshier.net/docs/Shier-Childrens_Rights_in_School.pdf

Shier, H. (2018). Towards a new improved pedagogy of "children's rights and responsibilities." *International Journal of Children's Rights, 26*(4), 761–780.

Shier, H. (2019a). "Empowerment" of children and adolescents: What is it, how does it occur, and what is the adult supporter's role? *Children's Research Digest, 7*(1). https://childrensresearchnetwork.org/files/CRN_Article-4_Final_-Harry-Shier.pdf

Shier, H. (2019b). Student voice and children's rights: Participation, empowerment and "protagonismo." In M. A. Peters (Ed.), *Encyclopedia of teacher education.* Springer Nature. https://rd.springer.com/content/pdf/10.1007/978-981-13-1179-6_27-1.pdf

Shier, H., Padilla, M. L., Molina, N., Barrera, L., Molina, M., Castillo, Z., & Ortiz, K. (2013). Claiming the right to quality education in Nicaragua. In B. Blue-Swadener, L. Lundy, N. Blanchet-Cohen, & J. Habashi (Eds.), *Children's rights and education: International perspectives* (pp. 188–202). Peter Lang.

Skelton, T. (2008). Research with children and young people: Exploring the tensions between ethics, competence and participation. *Children's Geographies, 6*(1), 21–36.

Taft, J. K. (2017). Continually redefining protagonismo: The Peruvian movement of working children and political change, 1976–2015. *Latin American Perspectives, 46*(5), 90–110.

Taft, J. K. (2019). *The kids are in charge: Activism and power in Peru's movement of working children.* NYU Press.

Tobin, J. (2015). Understanding children's rights: A vision beyond vulnerability. *Nordic Journal of International Law, 84*(2), 155–182.

United Nations. (1989). *Convention on the Rights of the Child.*

United Nations Office of the High Commissioner for Human Rights. (2006). *Frequently asked questions on a human rights-based approach to development cooperation.* United Nations. https://www.ohchr.org/Documents/Publications/FAQen.pdf

Van Bijleveld, G. G., Dedding, C. W., & Bunders-Aelen, J. F. (2015). Children's and young people's participation within child welfare and child protection services: A state-of-the-art review. *Child & Family Social Work, 20*(2), 129–138.

Wane, N., Kempf, A., & Simmons, M. (Eds.). (2011). *The politics of cultural knowledge.* Sense Publishers.

Willow, C. (2009). *Children's right to be heard and effective child protection.* Save the Children Sweden.

Wolff, R., Flick, U., Ackermann, T., Biesel, K., Brandhorst, F., Heinitz, S., Heinitz, S., Patschke, M., & Robin, P. (2016). *Children in child protection.* Nationales Zentrum Frühe Hilfen.

Young Consultants of Santa Martha. (2009). The Young Consultants of Santa Martha coffee plantation investigate the problem of violence. In B. Percy-Smith & N. Thomas (Eds.), *A handbook of children and young people's participation* (pp. 228–229). http://www.cesesma.org/documentos/CESESMA-Young_Consultants_of_Santa_Martha.pdf

Zwart, T. (2012). Using local culture to further the implementation of international human rights: The receptor approach. *Human Rights Quarterly, 34*(2), 546–569.

PART II
PARTICIPATORY PROFESSIONAL PRACTICES

PART II
PARTICIPATORY PROFESSIONAL PRACTICES

6
The Participation of LGBTQIA+ Children and Youth in Care in the Netherlands

Rodrigo González Álvarez, Mijntje ten Brummelaar, Kevin R. O. van Mierlo, Gerald P. Mallon, and Mónica López López

Introduction

The United Nations reported that the progress in the achievement of human rights during the last decade was highly uneven (United Nations Human Rights Council, 2016). The 2030 Agenda for Sustainable Development promises to prioritize human rights for groups that are more vulnerable and marginalized, including children. The agenda stresses the importance of preventing discrimination and inequality based on distinctions of any kind (United Nations Human Rights Council, 2016). Member states have made advances to end the discrimination and violence against individuals based on their sexual orientation and gender identity expression (SOGIE). However, much work is still needed, as severe human rights violations are committed against people based on their SOGIE (United Nations Human Rights Council, 2015). Human rights violations based on SOGIE also affect children and adolescents. According to Article 2 in the United Nations Convention on the Rights of the Child (UNCRC), no young person should be discriminated against or excluded based on their age, race, sex, language, religion, political opinion, nationality, ethnic or social origin, disability, or other status (United Nations General Assembly, 1989, n.p.). Although the Dutch government has made significant progress in achieving children's rights over the last 30 years, there is still more work to be done. So far, progress has been uneven and often inequitable, as the most marginalized children are disadvantaged in terms of their material well-being, health and safety, education, behaviors and risks, and housing (UNICEF Office of Research, 2013).

Rodrigo González Álvarez, Mijntje ten Brummelaar, Kevin R. O. van Mierlo, Gerald P. Mallon, and Mónica López López, *The Participation of LGBTQIA+ Children and Youth in Care in the Netherlands* In: *Children and Young People's Participation in Child Protection.* Edited by: Katrin Križ and Mimi Petersen, Oxford University Press. © Oxford University Press 2023.
DOI: 10.1093/oso/9780197622322.003.0006

Children's right to be heard is considered one of the four general principles of children's rights. However, this right is affected by inequality and systemic discrimination. Article 12 in the UNCRC claims that states must ensure to the child who is capable of forming their own views "the right to express those views freely in all matters affecting the child, the views of the child being given due weight in accordance with the age and maturity of the child" (United Nations General Assembly, 1989, n.p.). Unfortunately, children's right to express their views on the wide range of issues that affect them remains unfulfilled due to systemic discrimination based on their identities and statuses (United Nations Committee on the Rights of the Child, 2009). Provisions such as Article 12 are essential elements supporting the children's participation movement.

The children's participation movement has had a strong reverberation within child protection systems (CPSs) in several countries. This movement has resulted in increased interest in research and development of policy and legislation (see, e.g., Bessell, 2011; Cossar et al., 2014; Cudjoe et al., 2019; Healy & Darlington, 2009; Toros et al., 2013; van Bijleveld et al., 2014). Various studies stress the importance and benefits of youth participation in the CPS. Children who participate in decisions affecting their lives experience more connection and commitment to decisions by the CPS (Woolfson et al., 2010) and an increase in self-esteem (Vis et al., 2011). Children's participation is associated with children experiencing agency and feeling in control (Bell, 2002; Leeson, 2007; Munro, 2001). Despite the mounting evidence showing the potential benefits of children's participation, children's involvement does not occur often enough in child protection. There is little evidence pointing to children's views making a difference in the decisions about their lives (Bessell, 2011; van Bijleveld et al., 2015). Several studies highlighted the many difficulties that impede integrating children's participation into practice (Dillon et al., 2016; Gallagher et al., 2012; Healy & Darlington, 2009; Holland, 2001; ten Brummelaar et al., 2018; van Bijleveld et al., 2019; Vis et al., 2012; Woolfson et al., 2010). These researchers have identified challenges at the individual level and the group and system levels. For example, one challenge at the personal level is for children to overcome prior negative experiences with participation. At the group level, prior research found that one challenge was a lack of safe and supportive environments, which are crucial in fostering children's participation. At the system level, one challenge includes the need for laws and policies concerning children's participation and rights. These barriers limit children's opportunities to participate in decision-making processes (Abdullah et al., 2018; Bouma, 2019; Gal, 2017; Horwath et al., 2012; van Bijleveld et al., 2015).

Although most children in the CPS experience the difficulties and barriers of children's participation, specific groups are subjected to substantial disadvantages and marginalization within the system, including lesbian, gay, bisexual, trans, queer, intersex, asexual, questioning, and so on (LGBTQIA+) children and youth. Therefore, they could face challenges to be heard (Horwath et al., 2012; López López et al., 2021; Macpherson, 2008; Mallon, 2021; Shelton & Mallon, 2021). Children's sexual orientation and gender identity expression are potential sources of discrimination for these children. Discrimination might challenge accomplishing their fundamental rights, including their right to participation (Mallon, 2019; McCormick, 2018). Children need a safe, supportive, and friendly environment to participate (Cudjoe et al., 2019; Horwath et al., 2012). It is of utmost importance that child protection caseworkers and other practitioners develop a trusting and positive relationship with children to enable their participation (Cossar et al., 2014; Husby et al., 2018). However, research has recognized the CPS as a mostly unsafe and unwelcoming place for LGBTQIA+ children and youth (Mallon, 2021; McCormick, 2018). Except for some pioneering literature published in the 1990s (Mallon, 1998; Sullivan, 1994), the experiences and lives of LGBTQIA+ children and youth in the CPS have not received attention from social work researchers until recently (Kaasbøll & Paulsen, 2019; McCormick, 2018). Furthermore, most social work research about this topic published in English has been conducted in the United Kingdom and United States (Carr & Pinkerton, 2015; Cossar et al., 2017; McCormick et al., 2017; Wilson et al., 2014; Wilson & Kastanis, 2015). However, no studies explicitly address the participation of LGBTQIA+ children and youth in the CPS in the Netherlands.

This study seeks to fill the gap in the literature by examining how LGBTQIA+ youth and young adults in the Netherlands experience participation while they are involved with the CPS. The findings show that although the Dutch CPS is increasingly oriented toward the recognition and practice of children's and young people's participation, LGBTQIA+ youth experiencing out-of-home care still face challenges to meaningful involvement. This chapter will discuss a positive perspective, where practitioners were affirming and supportive of the needs of LGBTQIA+ youth, and a negative mindset, where they did not hear and consider children's voices and opinions.

LGBTQIA+ Children and Youth in Child Protection Systems

The scarce evidence about the experiences of LGBTQIA+ children and youth in the CPS leads us to four crucial conclusions (Mallon, 2019; McCormick, 2018). First, LGBTQIA+ children and youth seem to be overrepresented in the CPS and overlooked (Mallon, 2019, 2021; McCormick, 2018). Second, there is a systemic inability and unwillingness to recognize the presence of the LGBTQIA+ community in the CPS (McCormick et al., 2017). LGBTQIA+ youth often feel pressured to remain invisible and isolated. They feel like society and its institutions do not want to recognize their presence (Paul, 2018). Paradoxically, LGBTQIA+ youth are overrepresented in child welfare services and out-of-home placements (Baams et al., 2019; Fish et al., 2019; Irvine & Canfield, 2016; Mallon & Perez, 2020; Wilson & Kastanis, 2015). Third, identifying as LGBTQIA+ is often a reason that youths encounter the CPS. Although, at first glance, the reasons that children access the CPS do not seem related to their SOGIE, studies found that the cases involving youth's SOGIE play a significant role in their referrals for services (Mallon, 2001, 2019; Mountz & Capous-Desyllas, 2020; Woronoff et al., 2006). Many of these youth enter the CPS because they have experienced difficulties with their birth families related to their SOGIE (Mountz & Capous-Desyllas, 2020; Capous-Desyllas et al., 2018). Their families' lack of acceptance is one of the reasons LGBTQIA+ leave their birth families and out-of-home placements (Mallon, 1998; Wilber et al., 2006; Woronoff et al., 2006).

Third, LGBTQIA+ children and youth are often exposed to adverse and unwelcoming experiences in the CPS. LGBTQIA+ youth in care frequently need to hide their sexual identity and sexuality; they might become victims of harassment, violence, bullying, discrimination, lack of acceptance, and abuse (Cossar et al., 2017; Gallegos et al., 2011; Mallon, 1998, 2019, 2021; McCormick, 2018; Wilber et al., 2006; Woronoff et al., 2006). Staff and peers perpetuate this exposure to harassment and violence, and at times it is permitted by caretakers who are inclined to blame LGBTQIA+ youth for their mistreatment (Greeno et al., 2021; Mallon, 1998; Wilber et al., 2006; Woronoff et al., 2006). Moreover, LGBTQIA+ youth experience double standards. They are not allowed the same privileges, rights, and relationships as heterosexual youth (McCormick, 2018).

The limited research conducted by professionals in the field suggests that CPSs are frequently not well suited to providing a safe and affirming environment for LGBTQIA+ children and youth. As a result, they fail to protect this group of young people from harassment and violence. For instance, certain states in the United States require LGBTQIA+ youth to participate in reparative or conversion therapies (Estrada & Marksamer, 2006). This creates a double standard that permits disciplining LGBTQIA+ youth for behaviors that hetero and cisgender youths are not accountable for (Mallon, 2019). Overall, the CPS fails to identify community support for LGBTQIA+ youth (Mallon, 1998; Mallon et al., 2006; Mallon & Wornoff, 2006; Wilber et al., 2006). Moreover, the support for LGBTQIA+ young people by CPSs appears limited by professionals' lack of knowledge and confidence in working with LGBTQIA+ children and youth (Cossar et al., 2017).

Lastly, LGBTQIA+ children and youth face permanency challenges. They experience a higher number of placements and instability, a higher likelihood to age out of foster care without adequate preparation for transitioning to adulthood, an overreliance on congregate care or group home settings, and a chronic shortage of competent staff and caregivers equipped to provide affirming care for them (Jacobs & Freundlich, 2006; Mallon, 2011, 2019; Mallon et al., 2002; McCormick, 2018). Therefore, young people's SOGIE affects their pathway into care and the stability of their trajectories in care.

Developing the knowledge base about the experiences of LGBTQIA+ children and youth growing up in out-of-home care is an essential step in creating safe and welcoming environments where children and youth can fully develop and thrive.

Children's Participation in the Dutch Child Protection System

The Dutch CPS is a family service-oriented system that focuses on strengthening family relationships and prefers voluntary out-of-home placements. When a placement is needed, family foster care is preferred above placing the child in a residential setting (López López et al., 2019). One of the most critical features of the Dutch CPS is its growing attention to policies and practices related to the participation of children, young people, and parents in child protection–related decision-making (Bouma et al., 2018; van Bijleveld et al., 2019).

Research shows that the professionals working in the Dutch CPS value children's participation, although they face challenges to implement it fully

(Bouma, 2019; Rap et al., 2019; van Bijleveld et al., 2014, 2019). First, there is a lack of clarity among professionals about what full participation entails and the specific ways in which the child should be provided with information, heard, and involved in care services. In addition, there are no clear guidelines in Dutch legislation and policy about how to engage children in decisions, and a coherent participation policy is still lacking (Bouma et al., 2018). Second, possibilities for children's participation differ depending on several factors and contexts; for example, there are more legal opportunities (via court orders) for children's participation in the cases of compulsory youth care when compared to voluntary youth care services (Rap et al., 2019). Additionally, older children seem to have more possibilities to participate than younger children (Bouma et al., 2018).

Third, professionals' views are vital in determining the implementation of children's participation. Professionals often see children's participation as a means to ensure the child's cooperation (as instrumental participation), while young people think that professionals should consider their opinions and explain their decisions clearly (van Bijleveld et al., 2014). Furthermore, professionals' image of children as vulnerable can hamper the participation process, although this vulnerability can also be a reason to advocate for child participation (Bouma et al., 2018; van Bijleveld et al., 2019). Finally, child protection conferences are still in development, and the whole process depends heavily on the organization in each municipality and professionals' commitment (Rap et al., 2019). Thus, despite the Netherlands introducing progressive legislation and policies to encourage children's and youth participation in care, and nongovernmental organizations and academia actively advocating for children's participation, there is still a long way to go for its full implementation in the CPS (Bouma et al., 2018; van Bijleveld et al., 2019).

LGBTQIA+ Children and Youth in the Dutch CPS

The Netherlands is considered an LGBTQIA+ friendly country, yet LGBTQIA+ communities experience discrimination and marginalization in Dutch society (ILGA-Europe, 2019). Regarding young people, research shows that LGBTQIA+ youth still have a marginalized position compared to their peers and experience discrimination and other forms of oppression (Bos & Sandfort, 2015; Felten et al., 2010; Kuyper, 2015; Pizmony-Levy, 2018). Within the CPS, the absence of a systematic registration makes it difficult to know the number of LGBTQIA+ individuals growing up in care (de Groot et al., 2018; Emmen et al., 2014). According to different studies conducted in the Netherlands, professionals in the CPS usually do not register or discuss the young person's SOGIE (de Groot et al., 2018; Emmen et al., 2014; Taouanza & Felten, 2018). Systematic registration can be a controversial measure: on the one hand, it can make visible and normalize SOGIE. On the other hand, if not done sensitively, it could lead to more stigmatization. Furthermore, research suggests that professionals are not sensitive enough toward LGBTQIA+ young people and do not offer LGBTQIA+ youth affirmative practice (de Groot et al., 2018; Emmen et al., 2014).

In summary, the research evidence indicates that the Dutch CPS remains a relatively unwelcoming place for LGBTQIA+ children and youth, which could create additional barriers for the participation of this group in care. However, studies exploring the impact of their disadvantaged position and vulnerability on their participation and decision-making in the Dutch CPS are lacking.

Research Methods

This chapter explores the challenges and prerequisites associated with the participation of care experienced by LGBTQIA+ young people using data gathered from the Audre project (see also López López et al., 2021; González-Álvarez et al., 2021). The Audre project took a reflexive, flexible, and participatory approach. It included care-experienced LGBTQIA+ young people and stakeholders as project advisors throughout the research process (see, e.g., Bramsen et al., 2019; Schofield et al., 2019). The project sought to cast light on the experiences, needs, and wishes of Dutch LGBTQIA+ youth growing up in care. In addition, the project explored the opportunities and challenges for their participation while in care.

The ethics committee of the Department of Pedagogy and Educational Sciences at the University of Groningen approved the study in November 2017. The salient ethical elements were informed consent, privacy and anonymity, termination and withdrawal, the component of choice, compensation (gift card and travel cost), what happened after the interview, and data storage. One member of the research team was a trained care professional whom the Audre team relied on for consultation. After each interview, the group reflected as much as possible on how the interview process went. Later, the team reached out to see how the youth were doing. The research team informed all participants that they could contact the research team after the interview if they wished to do so.

The Audre team consisted of a group of people (care-experienced young people, students, practitioners, and researchers) across the spectrums of SOGIE brought together by a moral commitment to reduce social inequality. The research team began recruiting participants in 2017 and finalized the interviews in 2019. The team utilized multiple recruitment techniques, including snowball sampling, recruitment via social media, personal contacts, youth care organizations, youth groups, and LGBTQIA+ advocacy groups to identify youth who were willing to participate in an in-depth interview about their experiences with the CPS. These efforts allowed the researchers to find 13 young people willing to share their life stories. The sample consisted of youth ages 15 to 28 years. Only one participant, who was 15 years old, required parental consent to participate in the study, which the team obtained. The young people had experienced different out-of-home services, including foster care, secure residential care, group homes, and independent living programs. Some participants were born into care or had been in care from a very young age; others entered care as adolescents.

Of the 13 youths we interviewed, four were transwomen, one a transman, one sometimes identified as a woman, and one was nonbinary. The other six young people did not discuss their gender identity in the interview. Additionally, regarding sexual orientation, four young people were gay, one was lesbian (she sometimes also referred to herself as gay), two were bisexual, one was pansexual, one was questioning, one "liked women,"[1] and one liked both men and women. Three did not disclose their sexual orientation. To our knowledge, no young person in the study identified as intersex or asexual.

Other characteristics of the sample included four young people having a bicultural background, one an unaccompanied migrant person who only stayed shortly in an asylum seekers' center, one of them dealing with a chronic illness, and another young person having autism. The study participants possessed a range of educational backgrounds, such as vocational education, secondary education, higher vocational education, higher professional education, and university education.

The research team used a semi-structured interview guide that included questions about the period before the CPS, the participants' time in care, coming out, contact with family and their social support network, experiences of discrimination, and their future perspectives. With a focus on flexibility in their interviewing style, the research team remained open to following the young persons' topics during the interview. The researchers used open-ended questions such as these: Can you tell us something about why you left your home or were placed into care (focus on: did gender identity or sexual orientation play a role in this process)? Are people around you aware of your sexual orientation/gender identity? If so, how did they deal with it (family, network, wider environment)? Have you ever been discriminated against? If so, how did you experience it? Have you had negative experiences? How do you deal with it? What does your social network look like (friends and broader social environment)?

The interviewers conducted all but one interview (which took place via telephone) face to face. Each interview averaged 81 minutes. One participant was interviewed twice and shared multiple documents with the team, such as autobiographical writing. The research team asked the young people to choose where the interview should occur (e.g., at home, a park, or a restaurant). All the interviews were recorded with the participants' consent. After the interviews, the recordings were transcribed verbatim using the audio transcription program T4 and uploaded to Atlas.ti, version 8.4. Finally, the research team performed a reflexive thematic analysis. The team members met multiple times to discuss their analyses (Braun & Clarke, 2019). In the analyses, the team focused on the young person's stories about their participation in decision-making while in care, especially receiving information, being heard, and being involved.

Findings

In this section, we will discuss four main themes around the participation of LGBTQIA+ young people in care. The first theme is the importance of a supportive and affirmative environment for LGBTQIA+ young people and how this acts as a prerequisite for participatory practices. Second, we identified the youth's need to connect with practitioners (caseworkers or other staff members) to participate. The third theme that emerged from our data was how participation could occur by professionals preparing and informing young people before decisions. The fourth theme is the request of young people to have their own space and be supported by practitioners trained to address the needs of LGBTQIA+ youth. It important to note that the following information refers to youths' lives while in care, not their experiences before or after they were in care.

An LGBTQIA+ Affirmative, Supportive Child Welfare Practice

It is a prerequisite for the participation of LGBTQIA+ youth that practitioners in social work and education affirm their SOGIE. For instance, many young people expressed the need for an open, knowledgeable, and affirming social climate within their out-of-home care and school settings. One young person described it this way: "Some foster families, they don't know, and they cannot help you. My foster parents also didn't know, they couldn't help me, but they did their best to make me happy. They treated me as a real child. That is the most beautiful thing about them."

Some youths experienced supportive environments where they could be themselves, felt respected, and had "casual conversations" about SOGIE. Quite often, these affirmative environments were provided by affirmative practitioners, as this young person suggests:

> That woman, I had a woman there [name of woman], and she, with her it was really, she was like "okay, we have to change your name in the system right now to a woman and to [own name]. I just don't see a man in you, so we have to do it now." And that has really helped me. If she hadn't been there, I wouldn't have come this far. And she has really, you know, she has really helped me a lot.

Despite these caring and supportive environments, some young people expressed that some caregivers and organizations did not provide the support they needed and showed a lack of awareness, knowledge, and sensitivity toward LGBTQIA+ youth. For example, this youth stated, "They're often not used to it" or "Those people don't know better, they just don't think about it." Practitioners did not know how to react appropriately, such as thinking in prejudicial ways, for example, thinking that every LGBTQIA+ person is the same. Alternatively, some professionals made heteronormative cisgender assumptions. The youths said, "They assumed I was a boy" or "They thought I wasn't sexually interested." The practitioners did not intervene when other youths made inappropriate or discriminatory remarks or inappropriate jokes and negative comments, like homophobic slurs. One of the participants had this suggestion about how professionals should react in this situation:

Interviewer: How should it be done better [responding to negative comments by other kids in the group]?
Young person: Be stricter towards this. Just like bam! If they make a comment, bam, go directly to their room, you know. For half an hour, directly. Then, they know instantly, yeah, this is not possible. This is not possible.

Practitioners' lack of awareness, knowledge, and sensitivity impacted youths' openness about their SOGIE and the care they received. Children sometimes were not allowed to be or chose not to be open about their SOGIE with peers or practitioners. The former was especially the case for young trans people living in group care. Their caseworkers did not allow some of them to be themselves and forced them to sign a contract that stipulated they could not be open about their gender identity. If they were, caseworkers would take away their toys because they were not considered gender appropriate. Sometimes staff justified these actions by saying that other kids "cannot handle it" or that "it wasn't allowed by the church." One young person provided this illustration:

I wasn't allowed to talk about being a girl. I wasn't allowed to dress this way. Otherwise, I had to go back to my parents, where I was maltreated. Yes, I was allowed to talk about it with my supervisors, but they were like, yeah, they didn't entirely believe it. So, they denied it, and I wasn't allowed to be [a girl].

The young people felt that their lives were "put on hold." They found themselves either acting out or conforming. They had difficulties being themselves around caseworkers and making meaningful connections and did not feel "at home" or wanted to leave the care settings. One young person highlighted this dilemma with the following quote:

So with everything, in the group, I was someone else. And upstairs, in my room, I was myself. I was in my room every day after school. After dinner, I was upstairs, even after breakfast. I went to breakfast, and after that, I went upstairs again . . . just because, I mean, because I didn't want any difficulties with the head of the staff. I mean, I didn't want any problems with her, so I stayed upstairs.

Some participants suggested that practitioners be open about their lack of knowledge and expertise. The youths believed that the caseworker should then refer them to LGBTQIA+ organizations or support groups. The participants mentioned it was necessary to provide LGBTQIA+ children and youth training to caseworkers and social work programs. Universities should add courses introducing human values to their curriculum. One young person observed:

> And then again, some subjects within the humanistic, philosophical courses, here and there a course should be added in [students'] education, I would really say that that would really be a good thing. . . . I think it would really achieve something good, that more people would benefit from it [courses] than they thought in advance. Anyway, it helped me a lot. I think it really helps to find peace within yourself. And by dealing with certain life questions in an academic setting, especially in the context of youth care, . . . or something like that, also by creating your own image of how you feel about it, that you can find more tranquility and respect for the person you are treating. To offer room for that, because again, it's not just about what you want to do with your life. But also, how do you stand in life.

Positive Connections With Caseworkers

The young people felt it was crucial to connect with a caseworker who takes time for them and shows interest, makes an effort on their behalf, advocates for them, and sees them for who they are. This is how one of the participants described one of the social workers she had a meaningful relationship with: "And she was so sweet. . . . [W]e always talked and laughed and laughed and laughed." Most of the meaning and impact of their relationships with caseworkers only emerged when we examined the youths' personal stories in more depth. Some young people talked highly about practitioners who "stuck their neck out for them" or "went the extra mile," as this participant noted:

> It was just like, like yeah, I had to, it [my placement] kept being extended and extended, and otherwise I had to go to a residential group somewhere in [name province], or [name province], or something like that. And then my foster dad said something like, "Yes, we're not going to do that so you can stay here."

When young people knew social workers for a more extended period, they felt more comfortable opening up to them. One of the participants told us: "One of them I've known for eight years, and the other one I've known for ten years, so I've known them already quite long. So, then talking about stuff goes easier." In addition, finding a caseworker who openly identified as LGBTQIA+ was helpful, as this young person pointed out: "[The caseworker] is also gay, coincidentally. I only figured that out about half a year ago.... So in that way, I really can talk with him about this, about everything, everything I had surrounding me, you know. My environment was very suitable for this."

Not all young people we interviewed felt that the caseworkers or decision makers "heard" them or took them seriously in decisions while they were in care. When they did not have a good connection with their caseworkers, youths felt that some decisions were made for them as if they did not have a genuine choice. Some young people expressed that they did not dare to speak up because they felt powerless, they feared the consequences, or caregivers told them not to. Other young people indicated that they felt heard when they spoke up or stood up for themselves.

> Back then, I didn't dare to say what I wanted. It was like everything I wanted to say was in my head and I, if I said something, it was something else. Now that I have matured, I have learned a lot of things. I have learned to give my opinion.

Most young people experienced multiple practitioners and environments before and during care: "The staff comes and goes," one of the participants said. The different contexts differed in restrictiveness, influencing the decision-making space the young person enjoyed. Some young people had experienced these changes from a young age. The instability resulted in a lack of trust in people or in becoming selective about whom to trust. For example, one young person suggested using the staff turnover to his advantage by telling them "what they wanted to hear."

Information and Preparation

Many of the study participants expressed that they were not sufficiently informed or prepared for decisions about their lives. They said there was a lack of information about why caseworkers made decisions about their care trajectory or life course. Often, the youths did not feel well prepared for the next step in their care trajectory, such as being placed out of home, being placed into a new facility or foster family, or transitioning from out-of-home care because these decisions felt sudden or abrupt to them. One of them recalled: "It didn't go well at my mother's place. It also didn't go well at my father's place. So they placed me in a secure facility. I'm like, well, that's quite a dramatic turn of events." A lack of information and preparedness often led to the young person's lack of understanding about what motivated the caseworkers to make certain decisions. One of the young people who had just recently transitioned out of foster care felt betrayed by her social worker and foster parents. She felt like the social worker did not give much thought to her decision's impact and "stepped over" her feelings. She said, "It's like . . . being stabbed in the back with a knife. It came completely out of nowhere. . . . Go and live on your own, have fun, goodbye! Yes, that's weird."

Young people had different experiences with receiving information on the topic of their sexual orientation and gender identity expression. Some of them did not express the need to receive information. They said that they had their resources, figured it out themselves, or felt "comfortable in their skin." Others would have found it helpful to have been able to select useful resources. For instance, according to one of the young people who stayed in residential care, it would have been helpful if practitioners of the facility would have taken the time to provide information or explore the information about the topic of gender identity together. She stated, "Just informing [me] about, looking for [information] together on identity, also what is healthy information and that sort of stuff." Another young person explained that he received information about sexual orientation from his therapist after he transitioned out of foster care. Some young people expressed frustration about being on a "waiting list" or having to wait for others to make decisions, such as receiving mental health care or starting their transition process while in care. "So yeah, shitty [names of the medical experts who helped with transitioning] to move on things. However, yeah, I have to wait for that. Furthermore, nothing special. Just waiting, waiting, and waiting."

Space for LGBTQIA+ Youth to Be Themselves

Another way young people expressed their need to have their views taken into consideration was by having "their space" and being supported to be themselves. As one young person said: "Give me my pride." The youths also stated that they wanted two things: deciding what personal information to disclose and deciding what the timeframe looked like when disclosing that personal information. "They should have given me space, to be myself, to support me in this, to build a trusting relationship." For instance, some young people sometimes felt pushed by caseworkers. One of the participants said:

> You should, I mean, give them [children] the chance a bit to say it themselves. And not, I mean, push them, like "how are you?", and okay, it can come from a good heart, but you shouldn't push them. And that is what they did with me. They really pushed me, and it was like, they knew, they didn't know what to do with it. So, I had to explain while I just started figuring things out myself. And I didn't know everything yet, exactly, so I had to explain to them.

Conclusion

Based on our interviews with LGBTQIA+ youth in care, we suggest four critical prerequisites for enabling participatory practices that have a notable impact on these youth: an LGBTQIA+ affirmative and supportive environment; a positive connection between caseworkers or peers and LGBTQIA+ youth; information and preparation for decision-making processes, and giving LGBTQIA+ youth space to be themselves while having informed and trained caseworkers, or at least caseworkers who are willing to be trained.

Although LGBTQIA+ youth in the child welfare system have experienced greater acceptance and understanding in the past 30 years, many CPSs still actively discriminate against LGBTQIA+ youth (Cossar et al., 2017; Mallon, 2019; McCormick, 2018). In other cases, the inattentiveness of the systems to the needs of LGBTQIA+ youth will send a clear signal that they are not welcome or that the caseworkers are not fully competent to address their needs. As our findings suggest, although some LGBTQIA+ youth in care in the Netherlands encounter experiences of affirmation and acceptance, others still face negative experiences while in care, from denial of their identity to overt acts of aggression against them. Besides directly adversely affecting the well-being of youths, these experiences impede their participation in the CPS.

A public CPS's commitment to LGBTQIA+ youth involves more than quick and shallow solutions, such as one-off training sessions, affirming posters, and books. It is critical to recognize that the internal structure of the system, as reflected in its written policies and public information materials, needs to be evaluated and changed (Estrada & Marksamer, 2006; Mallon, 2019; Wilber et al., 2006). Training and educational efforts may assist practitioners in developing their competence in working with a particular population. However, written policies, supportive supervision of child welfare practitioners, and the outside community's knowledge about the organization must change to effect genuine and long-lasting change for LGBTQIA+ youth.

Regardless of the systemic changes that must occur, the most potent influence in LGBTQIA+ youth's life is the personal contact with the people around them, including caseworkers, peers, and other competent and caring adults. The structure of the CPS can set the stage for an LGBTQIA+ affirming environment, where young LGBTQIA+ people can heal from trauma, socialize, learn, and find a safe place to be themselves. However, it is the LGBTQIA+ competent caseworkers who ensure that LGBTQIA+ youth experience an affirming setting. The youth will engage, connect with, and possibly disclose the most personal information to their caseworker. As previous research demonstrated, nurturing and enduring connections are fundamental to allowing meaningful participation (Cossar et al., 2014; Husby et al., 2018).

CPSs seeking to improve their services by removing barriers to meaningful participation can do so by cultivating LGBTQIA+ affirming environments where youth can be most fully and authentically themselves. This mission is vital for supporting LGBTQIA+ youth in care who have often experienced trauma within their family systems and communities so they will never have to undergo additional trauma from the system designed to protect them.

Reflection Questions

(1) What are the barriers to participation that LGBTQIA+ youth might face?

(2) How would you work with LGBTQIA+ youth to assist them in dealing with the issue of "not being heard"?
(3) What two things could a CPS do to address the negative experiences reported by the youth who were part of this study?
(4) What interventions would you encourage the CPS, education system, and mental health system to undertake to support youth and address the stress or trauma they have experienced from hiding their sexual orientation and/or gender identity expression from foster care providers?

Note

1. All the translations in this chapter are by the authors.

References

Abdullah, A., Cudjoe, E., & Frederico, M. (2018). Barriers to children's participation in child protection practice: The views and experiences of practitioners in Ghana. *Children Australia*, *43*(4), 267–275. https://doi.org/10.1017/cha.2018.41

Baams, L., Wilson, B. D. M., & Russell, S. T. (2019). LGBTQ youth in unstable housing and foster care. *Pediatrics*, *143*(3), 1–9. https://doi.org/10.1542/peds.2017-4211

Bell, M. (2002). Promoting children's rights through the use of relationship. *Child & Family Social Work*, *7*(1), 1–11.

Bessell, S. (2011). Participation in decision-making in out-of-home care in Australia: What do young people say? *Children & Youth Services Review*, *33*(4), 496–501. https://doi.org/10.1016/j.childyouth.2010.05.006

Bos, H., & Sandfort, T. (2015). Gender nonconformity, sexual orientation, and Dutch adolescents' relationship with peers. *Archives of Sexual Behavior*, *44*(5), 1269–1279.

Bouma, H. (2019). *Taking the child's perspective. Exploring children's needs and participation in the Dutch child protection system* (Doctoral dissertation, University of Groningen).

Bouma, H., López López, M., Knorth, E. J., & Grietens, H. (2018). Meaningful participation for children in the Dutch child protection system: A critical analysis of relevant provisions in policy documents. *Child Abuse & Neglect*, *79*, 279–292. https://doi.org/10.1016/j.chiabu.2018.02.016

Bramsen, I., Kuiper, C., Willemse, K., & Cardol, M. (2019). My path towards living on my own: Voices of youth leaving Dutch secure residential care. *Child and Adolescent Social Work Journal*, *36*(4), 365–380.

Braun, V., & Clarke, V. (2019). Reflecting on reflexive thematic analysis. *Qualitative Research in Sport, Exercise and Health, 11*(4), 1–9. https://doi.org/10.1080/2159676X.2019.1628806

Capous-Desyllas, M., Pourciau, E., & Mountz, S. (2018). "Because we're fighting to be ourselves": Voices from former foster youth who are transgender and gender expansive. *Child Welfare, 96*(1), 103–126.

Carr, N., & Pinkerton, J. (2015). Coming into view? The experiences of LGBT young people in the care system in Northern Ireland. In J. Fish & K. Karban (Eds.), *Lesbian, Gay, Bisexual and Trans health inequalities* (pp. 99–112). Policy Press.

Cossar, J., Brandon, M., & Jordan, P. (2014). "You've got to trust her and she's got to trust you": Children's views on participation in the child protection system. *Child & Family Social Work, 21*(1), 103–112. https://doi.org/10.1111/cfs.12115

Cossar, J., Schofield, G., Belderson, P., Ward, E., Keenan, J., Larsson, B., Dodsworth, J., & Cocker, C. (2017). *SpeakOut: A study of the experiences and identity development of lesbian, gay, bisexual, transgender and questioning young people in care - and the support they receive.* Research Briefing. Centre for Research on Children and Families, University of East Anglia.

Cudjoe, E., Abdullah, A., & Chua, A. A. (2020). Children's participation in child protection practice in Ghana: Practitioners' recommendations for practice. *Journal of Social Service Research, 46*(4), 462–474. https://doi.org/10.1080/01488376.2019.1596196

De Groot, N., Vijlbrief, A., & Emmen, M. (2018). *Out on the streets. Onderzoek naar de hulp aan Amsterdamse lhbti-jongeren die thuisloos zijn* [Research into help for LGBTQI youth who are without a home]. Research Briefing. Movisie.

Dillon, J., Greenop, D., & Hills, M. (2016). Participation in child protection: A small-scale qualitative study. *Qualitative Social Work, 15*(1), 70–85. https://doi.org/10.1177/1473325015578946

Emmen, M., Addink, A., & Felten, H. (2014). *Jong en anders. Onderzoek naar aandacht voor lesbische, homo-en bi-jongeren, transgenderjongeren en jongeren met een intersekse conditie (LHBTi) in jeugdwelzijn, jeugdzorg en jeugd-(L)VB* [Young and different: Research into attention for lesbian, gay and bi youth, transgender and intersex youth in child welfare]. NJi en Movisie.

Estrada, R., & Marksamer, J. (2006). The legal rights of LGBT youth in state custody: What child welfare and juvenile justice professionals need to know. *Child Welfare, 85*(2), 171–194.

Felten, H., Hoof, J., & Schuyf, J. (2010). Weesjezelfmaarweesnietanders: heterojongeren over homo- en biseksualiteit [Be yourself but don't be different: hetero youth about homosexuality and bisexuality]. In S. Keuzenkamp (Ed.), *Steeds gewoner, nooit gewoon. Acceptatie van homoseksualiteit in Nederland* [More and more ordinary. Never ordinary. Acceptance of homosexuality in the Netherlands] (pp. 54–75). Sociaal en Cultureel Planbureau.

Fish, J. N., Baams, L., Wojciak, A. S., & Russell, S. T. (2019). Are sexual minority youth overrepresented in foster care, child welfare, and out-of-home placement? Findings from nationally representative data. *Child Abuse & Neglect, 89*, 203–211. https://doi.org/10.1016/j.chiabu.2019.01.005

Gal, T. (2017). An ecological model of child and youth participation. *Children & Youth Services Review, 79*, 57–64. https://doi.org/10.1016/j.childyouth.2017.05.029

Gallagher, M., Smith, M., Hardy, M., & Wilkinson, H. (2012). Children and families' involvement in social work decision making. *Children & Society, 26*(1), 74–85.

Gallegos, A., White, C. R., Ryan, C., O'Brien, K., Pecora, P. J., & Thomas, P. (2011). Exploring the experiences of lesbian, gay, bisexual, and questioning adolescents in foster care. *Journal of Family Social Work, 14*, 226–236.

González Álvarez, R., ten Brummelaar, M., Orwa, S., & López López, M. (2021). "I actually know that things will get better": The many pathways to resilience of LGBTQIA+ youth in out-out-of-home care. Children & Society, *36*(2), 234–248. https://doi.org/10.1111/chso.12464

Greeno, E., Matarese, M., & Weeks, A. (2021). Attitudes, beliefs, and behaviors of child welfare workers toward LGBTQ youth. *Journal of Public Child Welfare, 16*(5), 555–574. https://doi.org/10.1080/15548732.2021.1940415

Healy, K., & Darlington, Y. (2009). Service user participation in diverse child protection contexts: Principles for practice correspondence. *Child & Family Social Work, 14*, 420–430. https://doi.org/10.1111/j.1365-2206.2009.00613.x

Holland, S. (2001). Representing children in child protection assessments. *Childhood, 8*(3), 322–339.

Horwath, J., Kalyva, E., & Spyru, S. (2012). "I want my experiences to make a difference": Promoting participation in policy-making and service development by young people who have experienced violence. *Children & Youth Services Review, 34*(1), 155–162. https://doi.org/10.1016/j.childyouth.2011.09.012

Husby, I. S. D., Slettebø, T., & Juul, R. (2018). Partnerships with children in child welfare: The importance of trust and pedagogical support. *Child & Family Social Work, 23*(3), 443–450. https://doi.org/10.1111/cfs.12435

ILGA-Europe. (2019). *Annual review of the human rights situation of Lesbian, Gay, Bisexual, Trans and Intersex people in Europe*. Brussels, Belgium. Retrieved January 31, 2020, from https://ilga-europe.org/sites/default/files/Attachments/annual_review_final2018_web.pdf.

Irvine, A., & Canfield, A. (2016). The overrepresentation of lesbian, gay, bisexual, questioning, gender nonconforming and transgender youth within the child welfare to juvenile justice crossover population. *Journal on Gender, Social Policy, and the Law, 24*(2), 243–261.

Jacobs, J., & Freundlich, M. (2006). Achieving permanency for LGBTQ youth. *Child Welfare, 85*(2), 299–316.

Kaasbøll, J., & Paulsen, V. (2019). What is known about the LGBTQ perspective in child welfare services? A scoping review protocol. *BMJ Open, 9*(9), n.p. https://doi.org/10.1136/bmjopen-2019-030675

Kuyper, L. (2015). *Jongeren en seksuele oriëntatie. Ervaringen van en opvattingen over lesbische, homoseksuele, biseksuele en heteroseksuele jongeren* [Youth and sexual orientation. Experiences and views of lesbian, gay, bisexual and heterosexual youth]. Sociaal en Cultureel planbureau.

Leeson, C. (2007). My life in care: Experiences of non-participation in decision-making processes. *Child & Family Social Work, 12*(3), 268–277.

López López, M., Bouma, H., Knorth, E. J., & Grietens, H. (2019). The Dutch child protection system: Historical overview and recent transformations. In L. Merkel-Holguin, J. D. Fluke, & R. D. Krugman (Eds.), *National systems of child protection: Understanding the international variability and context for developing policy and practice* (pp. 173–192). Springer. https://doi.org/10.1007/978-3-319-93348-1

López López, M., González Álvarez. R., ten Brummelaar, M., van Mierlo, K. R. O., & Wieldraaijer-Vincent, L. (Eds.). (2021). *Working with LGBTQIA+ youth in the child* welfare system. Perspectives from youth and professionals. University of Groningen Press. https://doi.org/10.21827/60e5a36110a9

Macpherson, S. (2008). Reaching the top of the ladder? *Policy & Politics, 36*(3), 361–379.

Mallon, G. P. (1998). *We don't exactly get the welcome wagon: The experiences of gay and lesbian adolescents in child welfare systems.* Columbia University Press.

Mallon, G. P. (2001). *Lesbian and gay youth: A youth worker's perspective.* CWLA Press.

Mallon, G. P. (2011). Permanency for LGBTQ youth. *Protecting Children, 26*(1), 49–57.

Mallon, G. P. (2019). *LGBTQ youth issues: A practical guide for youth workers serving lesbian, gay, bisexual, transgender, & questioning youth.* CWLA Press.

Mallon, G. P. (2021). *Strategies for child welfare professionals working with transgender and gender expansive youth.* Jessica Kingsley.

Mallon, G. P., Aledort, N., & Ferrera, M. (2002). There's no place like home: Achieving safety, permanency, and well-being for lesbian and gay adolescents in out-of-home care settings. *Child Welfare, 81*(2), 407–443.

Mallon, G. P., Lakin, D., & Lyons, N. (2006). Facilitating permanency for youth. In A. Khoury (Ed.), *Achieving permanency for adolescents in foster care: A guide for legal professionals* (pp. 45–62). American Bar Association.

Mallon, G. P., & Perez, J. (2020). The experiences of transgender and gender expansive youth in juvenile justice systems. *Journal of Criminological Research, Policy and Practice, 6*(3), 217–229.

Mallon, G. P., & Wornoff, R. (2006). Busting out of the child welfare closet: Lesbian, gay, bisexual, and transgender affirming approaches to child welfare. *Child Welfare, 85*(2), 115–122.

McCormick, A. (2018). *LGBTQ youth in foster care. Empowering approaches for an inclusive system of care.* Routledge.

McCormick, A., Schmidt, K., & Terrazas, S. (2017). LGBTQ youth in the child welfare system: An overview of research, practice, and policy. *Journal of Public Child Welfare, 11*(1), 27–39. https://doi.org/10.1080/15548732.2016.1221368

Mountz, S., & Capous-Desyllas, M. (2020). Exploring the families of origin of LGBTQ former foster youth and their trajectories throughout care. *Children & Youth Services Review, 109*, 104622. https://doi.org/10.1016/j.childyouth.2019.104622

Munro, E. (2001). Empowering looked-after children. *Child & Family Social Work, 6*(2), 129–137.

Paul, J. (2018). *Under the radar: Exploring support for lesbian, gay, bisexual transgender, queer and questioning (LGBTQ) young people transitioning from foster care to emerging adulthood* (Doctoral dissertation, University of Wisconsin-Madison).

Pizmony-Levy, O. (2018). *The 2018 Dutch national school climate survey report.* Research Report. Teachers College, Columbia University.

Rap, S., Verkroost, D., & Bruning, M. (2019). Children's participation in Dutch youth care practice: An exploratory study into the opportunities for child participation in youth care from professionals' perspective. *Child Care in Practice, 25*(1), 37–50. https://doi.org/10.1080/13575279.2018.1521382

Schofield, G., Cossar, J., Ward, E., Larsson, B., & Belderson, P. (2019). Providing a secure base for LGBTQ young people in foster care: The role of foster carers. *Child & Family Social Work, 24*(3), 372–381. https://doi.org/10.1111/cfs.12657

Shelton, J., & Mallon, G. P. (Eds.). (2021). *Social work practice with transgender and gender variant youth* (3rd ed.). Routledge.

Sullivan, T. R. (1994). Obstacles to effective child welfare service with gay and lesbian youths. *Child Welfare, 73*(4), 291–304.

Taouanza, I., & Felten, H. (2018). *Hulpverlening voor iedereen? Verkennend onderzoek naar hulpverleners met een negatieve houding ten aanzien van LHBT's* [Help for everyone? An exploratory study of care practitioners with a negative attitude towards LGBT's]. KIS.

Ten Brummelaar, M. D. C., Harder, A. T., Kalverboer, M. E., Post, W. J., & Knorth, E. J. (2018). Participation of youth in decision-making procedures during residential care: A narrative review. *Child & Family Social Work, 23*(1), 33–44. https://doi.org/10.1111/cfs.12381

Toros, K., Tiko, A., & Saia, K. (2013). Child-centered approach in the context of the assessment of children in need: Reflections of child protection workers in Estonia. *Children & Youth Services Review, 35*(6), 1015–1022. https://doi.org/10.1016/j.childyouth.2013.03.011

UNICEF Office of Research. (2013). *Child well-being in rich countries: A comparative overview. Innocenti Report Card 11.*

United Nations Committee on the Rights of the Child. (2009, July 20). *General comment No. 12 (2009): The right of the child to be heard.* CRC/C/GC/12. Retrieved January 31, 2020, from https://www.refworld.org/docid/4ae562c52.html

United Nations General Assembly. (1989, November 20). *Convention on the Rights of the Child.* United Nations, Treaty Series, vol. 1577. Retrieved January 31, 2020, from https://www.refworld.org/docid/3ae6b38f0.html.

United Nations Human Rights Council. (2015, May 4). *Discrimination and violence against individuals based on their sexual orientation and gender identity.* A/HRC/29/23. Retrieved January 31, 2020, from https://www.refworld.org/docid/5571577c4.html

United Nations Human Rights Council. (2016, December 15). *Protection of the rights of the child in the implementation of the 2030 Agenda for Sustainable Development.* A/HRC/34/27. Retrieved February 3, 2020, from https://www.refworld.org/docid/58ad86d44.html

Van Bijleveld, G. G., Bunders-Aelen, J. F. G., & Dedding, C. W. M. (2019). Exploring the essence of enabling child participation within child protection services. *Child & Family Social Work, 25*, 286–293. https://doi.org/10.1111/cfs.12684

Van Bijleveld, G. G., Dedding, C. W. M., & Bunders-Aelen, J. F. G. (2014). Seeing eye to eye or not? Young people's and child protection workers' perspectives on children's participation within the Dutch child protection and welfare services. *Children & Youth Services Review, 47*, 253–259. http://dx.doi.org/10.1016/j.childyouth.2014.09.018

Van Bijleveld, G. G., Dedding, C. W. M., & Bunders-Aelen, J. F. G. (2015). Children's and young people's participation within child welfare and child protection services: A state-of-the-art review. *Child & Family Social Work, 20*, 129–138. http://dx.doi.org/10.1111/cfs.12082

Vis, S. A., Holtan, A., & Thomas, N. (2012). Obstacles for child participation in care and protection cases—Why Norwegian social workers find it difficult. *Child Abuse Review, 21*(1), 7–23. https://doi.org/10.1002/car.1155

Vis, S. A., Strandbu, A., Holtan, A., & Thomas, N. (2011). Participation and health—A research review of child participation in planning and decision-making. *Child & Family Social Work, 16*(3), 325–335. https://doi.org/10.1111/j.1365-2206.2010.00743.x

Wilber, S., Reyes, C., & Marksamer, J. (2006). The Model Standards Project: Creating inclusive systems for LGBT youth in out-of-home care. *Child Welfare, 85*(2), 133–149.

Wilson, B. D. M., Cooper, K., Kastanis, A., & Nezhad, S. (2014). Sexual and gender minority youth in foster care: Assessing disproportionality and disparities in Los Angeles. UCLA, The Williams Institute. Retrieved January 31, 2020, from https://escholarship.org/uc/item/6mg3n153

Wilson, B. D. M., & Kastanis, A. A. (2015). Sexual and gender minority disproportionality and disparities in child welfare: A population-based study. *Children & Youth Services Review, 58*, 11–17. https://doi.org/10.1016/j.childyouth.2015.08.016

Woolfson, R. C., Heffernan, E., Paul, M., & Brown, M. (2010). Young people's views of the child protection system in Scotland. *British Journal of Social Work, 40*(7), 2069–2085.

Woronoff, R., Estrada, R., & Sommer, S. (2006). *Out of the margins: A report on regional listening forums highlighting the experiences of Lesbian, Gay, Bisexual, Transgender, and Questioning youth in care*. Research Briefing. CWLA.

7
Children's Participation in Foster Care in Germany

Daniela Reimer

Introduction

Social work research and practice are highly developed in Germany. In social work practice, it is undisputed that clients should participate in decisions. Practitioners and scholars agree that this aspiration extends to children who have become social work clients (Blandow et al., 1999; Hansbauer & Kriener, 2000; Kriener, 1999). Participation by children in out-of-home care is a normative guideline and can be justified on several levels (Blandow et al., 1999). From a legal perspective, children's participation is crucial because children have the right to participate in all important matters concerning their lives, according to the United Nations Convention on the Rights of the Child (UNCRC; United Nations, 1989) and its implementation under national law. A social work perspective underlines that children's development is something they achieve themselves—a process that social workers can stimulate and promote if the children are independent actors who share responsibility for it. Children's education and emotional and social development are inconceivable without participation (Wolf, 2006, 2013). Participation is important in terms of child welfare as well. When child welfare workers involve children so they can participate appropriately in decisions about their lives, this can help shield children from stressors and experiences of powerlessness, which could cause them suffering. Children's participation is likely to make their living conditions in care more stable and enables care arrangements that align with children's wishes and fears. Children can then experience more viable foster care arrangements and achieve the stability they need for their development (Reimer & Wolf, 2011).

As this chapter shows, while "participation" is a broad term that is supported by law and professional practice, its implementation is complex.

Daniela Reimer, *Children's Participation in Foster Care in Germany* In: *Children and Young People's Participation in Child Protection*. Edited by: Katrin Križ and Mimi Petersen, Oxford University Press. © Oxford University Press 2023.
DOI: 10.1093/oso/9780197622322.003.0007

If child welfare workers are to apply the concept of children's participation effectively in professional practice in a way that is useful for children, the term must be operationalized for all practice fields and contexts. In the German foster care system, children and professionals make many decisions in one-on-one meetings. A definition of participation that is suitable for this context needs to be sufficiently nuanced to avoid an either-or approach: without this nuanced definition, participation would only distinguish between participation and nonparticipation instead of recognizing the levels and types of participation necessary in different contexts. (The term "participation" here refers to the balance of power between children and adults.)

On a societal level, children's participation has been shifting. For the past decades, children in Western countries have increasingly been placed in positions of power. For instance, studies in Germany and neighboring countries have shown that children are progressively more involved in decisions about school and family matters and considered relevant discussion partners (see, e.g., Büchner, 1989; Waterstrad, 2015). If the foster care system deliberately aims to achieve participatory practice, it remains in sync with the general debate about children's rights in society and how adults and children should ideally interact with each another.

The practical implementation of children's participation in foster care can prove complex and demanding and raises many questions: What does participation specifically mean to children? At what age can a child be involved? What is the degree to which children can participate? Are children able to sufficiently grasp the scope of decisions that will have a major effect on their lives? What decisions should and can children make for themselves in situations when adults need to accept and take responsibility for decisions consciously? What is the relationship between the child's best interests and wishes? It is worth examining how child welfare agencies should implement participation in practice and how children themselves experience participation in foster care, or the lack of it. These insights can serve as a strong foundation on which to build and fortify the practice of children's participation in foster care.

With its 83 million inhabitants, including 13.4 million children younger than 18 years, Germany is the most populated country in the European Union. In 2016, 74,120 children and young people were placed in foster care, and 92,122 children were placed in residential care (Destatis, 2018a, 2018b). In 2017, more than 50% of young people in residential care and 31% of young people in foster care had at least one parent with a migration background (Tabel, 2020). All of them were in contact with several social work professionals. It is common knowledge in German youth welfare research that most parents of children in care have experienced considerable biographical risks, suffer from poverty and economic deprivations, possess low educational capital, and have a poorly developed social network (Faltermeier, 2004).

I will first introduce the studies on which this chapter builds, including the research methods and data. Next, I will present a brief literature review, pointing out the relevant literature on participation and foster care. I will embed the topic in international research and briefly examine the implementation of children's participation rights established by the UNCRC. I will then present the research findings. Finally, I will use my findings to draw conclusions about implementing foster children's participation rights and discuss implications for future research.

Children's Participation Rights in Germany

Participation is a normative guideline in the German child welfare system that does not match children's actual circumstances (Münder, 2006). As Liebel (2013) argues, the German child welfare system continues to be very paternalistic: it mainly assumes a protective role. A genuinely participatory practice would, by contrast, view children as central actors and take them seriously as agents, as Liebel (2013, p. 95) notes:

> The crucial issue for a non-paternalistic concept of child protection that sees protection as the children's right and takes it seriously is supporting and empowering children. This views children from the viewpoint of actual and potential threats and sees them as subjects with a varied range of characteristics and within the whole context of their lives. This concept of child protection is thus not only aimed at averting risks to children but—whenever possible—tries to make things easier for children and perhaps puts them in a position to counter and resist any potential dangers themselves. This includes the idea that children not only have a say in how they are protected but are also involved in deciding against which risks they want to be protected. This does not mean leaving children to their own devices; it means developing and encouraging a relationship with them that respects their views and abilities.[1]

Germany ratified the UNCRC in 1992, albeit initially with the proviso that German immigration law should supersede the UNCRC. (The government dropped the proviso in 2010.) Since 2010, the UNCRC has been the central guideline behind all child-related legislation in Germany (Wapler, 2017). Nonetheless, there is still a broad debate among social work and legal scholars and professionals about the importance of children's rights and implementing them appropriately.

Previous scholarship examines the extent of paternalistic ideas on children's rights and asks whether they should be understood as rights belonging to children or as rights designed for children (Liebel, 2013). The legal discourse asks whether implementing the UNCRC requires that Germany change the law in various domains or whether it would suffice to merely recognize children's rights in every field, such as medical law, urban development, and others (Wapler, 2017). Only the domains of family law and legislation on children and youth welfare services (CYWS[2]) currently address participation rights for children. (The legislation on the CWYS falls under the Social Services Code [*Sozialgesetzbuch*], SGB VIII.) The SGB VIII legislation primarily ensures that a child's guardians are legally entitled to support from the state, not the children themselves (Sozialgesetzbuch, 2021). These are the children's rights as established by the SGB VIII:

- Article 1 (1): "Every young person has the right for his or her development to be promoted and brought up as a person with individual responsibility, capable of living in a community."
- Article 1 (3), Clause 1: "(To fulfill the law under Section 1, the youth welfare services should, in particular) promote young people's individual and social development and play a part in averting or reducing disadvantages."
- Article 4 (3), Clause 1: "(To fulfill the law under Section 1, the youth welfare services should, in particular) play a part in maintaining or creating a positive living environment for young people and their families, along with a child and family-friendly environment."
- Article 8 (1): "Children are to be involved in all decisions regarding them which are made by the public youth welfare services, per their stage of development...."
- Article 9, Clause 2: "(When designing the services and carrying out the tasks, it is necessary to) take into account the increasing ability and

growing need of the child to act in an independent, responsible manner." (Sozialgesetzbuch, 2021, n.p.)

Article 11, Clause 1 states that youth welfare services should take their "'clients'" interests into account and enable them to help design and decide on the services based on those interests (Sozialgesetzbuch, 2021).

In legal terms, participation rights for children whose families are very disadvantaged are (theoretically) regulated. However, children cannot directly demand that their rights be enforced, and these provisions are merely prescriptive and optional, not required. As a result, social workers and planners must take on the role of lawyers for children. Given this situation, there is a broad-ranging debate in social work on how professionals can implement these rights. For example, most children are placed in out-of-home care facilities without a court decision, which is not required (see Destatis, 2018a, 2018b). If the parents agree to their child being taken into care, and if there is no need to intervene with the parents' custodial right, the parents' consent is often given at the professionals' insistence. This is often regarded as parental pseudo-participation (Schäfer et al., 2015, pp. 55–56).

For the children, being taken into care without a court decision means being spared what can often be a lengthy, exhausting process involving many different parties. On the other hand, the lack of a court decision means that the only points at which children's voices are heard are when they can consent to or reject the intervention in conversation with the social work professional and during the planning process of support services. Thus, children depend on professionals to put their participation rights into practice. According to Münder (2006, p. 485), "It is a specialist task that falls to social work professionals in the child welfare agency to create children's capacity to participate and help children achieve that goal." That role frequently strains professionals because they do not have the time or skills to have the conversations with children that would be required to implement their participation rights. The following quote by a professional illustrates a feeling that may be widespread among child welfare professionals: "'Co-determination, inclusion, participation—they only work in theory. Cases pile up on my desk, and I don't have a whole lot of time for participation'" (Müller, 2006, p. 72).

Prior Literature on Children's Participation in Foster Care

The scholarly debate places the concept of participation in different theoretical contexts that lead to different connotations with implications for child welfare practice (see, e.g., Clark, 2005; ten Brummelaar et al., 2018; van Bijleveld et al., 2013). These connotations can sometimes lead to confusion about the term "participation." Eberitzsch et al. (2021) show that many authors situate the concept of participation in theories of democracy; accordingly, participation is understood as a characteristic of democratic societies and then means sharing and involvement in the community. The frequently cited ladder models of participation (e.g., Hart, 1992) stem from this understanding and can be used to gauge the level of children's participation in decision-making processes. These models are often linked to childhood theories that emphasize children's subjectivity and status as social actors (ten Brummelaar et al., 2018). This understanding of children's participation promotes democracy-centered ideas of institutional councils and other forms of children's participation in residential care settings. Where such forms of participation are implemented, children participate in shaping institutions through voting, having opportunities to criticize and formulate praise. In a grassroots democratic sense, the children in these institutions may also have to subordinate themselves to the democratically expressed will of the majority. Children learn the meaning of participation in settings that follow this understanding of participation, especially in a group context. They know to convince others, be diplomatic, and compromise and adapt.

More pedagogically oriented attempts at theorizing participation have emerged that differ from this democratically based understanding of participation but are undoubtedly compatible with it. They view participation as an overall concept consisting of rights, contexts, and factors influencing participation (Moos, 2012). From this perspective, participation becomes sociopedagogical empowerment whose demands the CYWS can meet through children's co-responsible self-determination (Hörmann, 2013). Participation then occurs in interactive pedagogical processes between children and adults.

Backe-Hansen (2018) developed an interesting, multidimensional approach to foster children's participation. She distinguishes four rationales that support a more thorough participation of foster children: (1) the enlightened rationale: "children have important information which may change decisions adults make on their behalf, again an important issue in relation to children as service users in the child welfare system" (Backe-Hansen, 2018, p. 229); (2) the empowerment agenda: "in countering ideas about children as 'incompetent', this rationale positions children as complete individuals or citizens with adult-sized rights and responsibilities" (Backe-Hansen, 2018, p. 230); (3) the ambiguity of citizenship principle: "this rationale argues that children's preparation for and participation in civic activities help them develop a sense of responsibility and obligation to society" (Backe-Hansen, 2018, p. 230); and (4) outcomes for children and adults: although there is not much research, from the existing literature it can be surmised that participation can improve relationships between young people and adults. Children want to participate and want their voices heard, even though they know their wishes cannot always be met (Backe-Hansen, 2018).

Backe-Hansen states that "the three first rationales can all be understood as instances of an individualistic approach to children's participatory rights.... [C]riticism of these approaches . . . underlines how grown-ups play an important role in facilitating or limiting children's possibilities. Thus, it can be argued that it is not possible to leave the unequal power relationship between children and adults out of the equation" (Backe-Hansen, 2018, p. 230). Other authors also emphasize the importance of the issue of the fit between foster children and families and the unequal distribution of power between children and adults (Barth & Olsen, 2020; Gal, 2015). Child welfare scholars and practitioners need to take it seriously to understand (failed) participation processes in research and practice and develop adequate conditions for children's participation in practice. Gal (2015) points out that adults can be gatekeepers and facilitators for children's participation. Professionals' attitudes toward children, childhood, and participation influence how they implement participation (Bessell & Gal, 2009; Gal, 2015; Graham et al., 2015; Križ & Skivenes, 2017).

Backe-Hansen's (2018) overview shows the interplay of democratic and pedagogical understandings of the meaning of participation. The rationale related to civil society and the need for individuals to learn and experience the effectiveness of participation are fundamental prerequisites for co-creation in democratic societies. Decisions need to have a chance to improve when the CYWS incorporate foster children's experiences and perspectives. It is crucial that foster relationships can succeed through good relationships between children and adults that were enabled by participatory experiences. Participation is a child's right and important because it can support good outcomes for young people in care (Bessell, 2011).

The value of participation seems undisputed. Nevertheless, studies that focus on children's perspectives continuously show that children do not feel they can sufficiently participate in important decisions in their lives (Bessell, 2011; Eberitzsch et al., 2021; Gal, 2015; Križ & Roundtree-Swain, 2017; Reimer & Wolf, 2011). Bessell (2011, p. 500) points out that "the absence of participation created a sense [among children] of being ignored or disregarded, with damaging consequences for children's sense of dignity and self-worth." Several studies show how children react to a lack of participation opportunities by creating participation opportunities for themselves, but they are not always viewed positively by adults (Bessell, 2011; Gal, 2015).

Research Methods

This chapter is based on several studies about children's experiences in foster care conducted in Germany by the author and their colleagues from the Foster Care Research Group, based at the University of Siegen, Germany, between 2007 and 2019. All projects went through peer review processes and ethical reviews. (These processes depended on the funders.[3]) In all projects, the researchers conducted "biographical interviews" with a total of 100 young people who had grown up in foster families. Biographical interviews are a suitable means of giving individuals the opportunity to tell their life stories from their (very subjective) viewpoint. They allow researchers to gain a unique insight into clients' experiences and the narratives that point toward the interviewees' perceptions and how they construct their identity (see Schütze, 1981, 1983, for a more detailed description of biographical interviews).

Each interview lasted between 2 and 3 hours. The interviewers initiated the first part of the interview with an open question like this: "I am interested in the life stories of young adults who have spent time living in a foster family. If you would like to, you can now tell me your life story." The sample of participants consisted of young people, primarily between 18 and 25 years of age. Young women were slightly overrepresented in our sample of study participants. About one third of the interviewees had a migration background, and the families of origin of most study participants were economically deprived, according to the participants. Many of the parents of origin experienced mental health problems or a history of substance abuse. Their biographies were subjectively and objectively partly successful, partly problematic. Some participants came to live in foster care as infants or as very young children, and some in adolescence. Some lived permanently in a foster family, and some only for a short time. Some participants had lived in various residential care institutions and foster families, and some were placed together with siblings, while others were separated. The sample thus represents German foster care in its broadness and diversity.

Some of the interviewees had many problems and challenges, and some were happy and had successful careers. The latter tends to challenge the stereotypes professionals might have of foster children as particularly vulnerable and needy. In almost all the interviews, the participants delved deeply into their memories and recounted very emotional stories. They returned to very early childhood, and some started with their life story before foster care. It often became clear that the participants did not just report on their past but often relived the situations in their narratives.

In the second part of the interview, the researchers asked the participants about specific experiences, including their first birthday, their first vacation in the foster family, meeting siblings, contact sessions, conflict in or with the foster family, and leaving their birth family. The interviewers asked the participants to visualize the most critical events on a timeline and evaluate them above that timeline in the form of a line representing good times and bad times (for more details, see Reimer, 2017). This process resulted in more intense narratives, evaluations, and interpretations of children's life stories.

The interviews were recorded digitally and listened to several times. They were transcribed and analyzed in detail. This analysis involved a mix of a theme-centered comparative method and an approach based on grounded theory (for more information, see Reimer, 2017). We sorted the interviews into themes based on their content and at the same time recontextualized and placed them in a theoretical setting, including normality theory or turning points (Reimer, 2014, 2017).

Although the sample of study participants represents much of foster care in Germany, the interviews are only from one subjective perspective—that of the young adults. The empirical material based on these interviews creates an opportunity to listen carefully to the young adults and understand their perspectives. At the same time, the interviews are limited in that they do not convey any information about structures, adult behavior, or what young people learned from their experiences.

In two projects (see Pierlings, 2011; Reimer, 2011), a total of 28 one-day workshops were conducted using the interview analyses with foster parents (Reimer, 2011) and then with foster care professionals (Pierlings, 2011). The workshops aimed to compare the foster children's perspectives to the perspectives of foster parents and foster care professionals. The foster parents and the foster care professionals were volunteers interested in research on foster care. Based on the interview material and the results of the workshops with foster parents, I published a book on counseling foster carers (Reimer, 2011). The foster care professionals were from a German region called Rhineland. During the workshop, they aimed to develop standards and guidelines for foster carers in the area. The combined material from the interviews and the results of the workshops were also published in a book (Pierlings, 2011).

During the workshops, the researchers presented findings on several topics from the interviews and discussed them extensively. This approach gave the researchers the chance to elicit the perspectives of the former foster children and the foster parents' and professionals' reactions to children's views. The professionals' intensive engagement with the foster children's perspectives during the workshops and the openness with which the foster parents discussed taboo issues were impressive. The workshops were all documented in detail and became another data source, which I will use for this chapter in addition to the children's points of view expressed in the interviews.

The study itself did not (only) focus on the young people's experiences with participation and their opportunities or obstacles to participation. However, the analysis of the biographical narratives and the workshops showed when participation was possible. It elucidated at what points participation is necessary or would have been essential and illustrated what existing or missing opportunities for participation mean for the experiences of the young people. It demonstrated what hinders participation from the points of view of the young people, foster parents, and professionals. This chapter examines children's participation to understand how foster children's participatory opportunities affect their biographies, narratives, experience, and life chances.

Participation in Children's Biographies

How is the goal of children's participation as stated in the law translated into participatory practice? Children who enter foster families have all kinds of stories. Children's ages, experiences before coming into care, wishes for another family, experiences in the foster family, and assessments and interpretations of foster care range widely. Accordingly, children have very different experiences of participation and insufficient or nonexistent participation. In the following, I will go through various biographical stages, show how the issue of participation is relevant to each case, and give examples of how the participants remembered their experiences of participation. I will discuss which questions this raises for research and practice and analyze data from the workshops (observations and quotes) and interviews.

Parental Needs Over Children's Participation

Children and their families often find themselves in difficult situations long before children are placed in care or the CYWS step in. In the biographical interviews, children described widely differing situations. Parents' mental illness or alcohol or drug use compounded difficult family situations. In the worst-case scenarios, the children experienced neglect, violence, and other ill treatment in their families. The children often did not know what was happening to them. They felt powerless and, at the same time, believed that what was happening to them was normal. It was frequently the siblings who supported one another and at times also cared for their parents.

In family situations of this kind, the children faced contradictory parental expectations on top of the many tasks they would normally undertake. They were left to their own devices, with hardly anyone listening to their wishes, hopes, fears, and worries. Yet many of them assumed a great deal of responsibility: they took care of themselves, their siblings, and sometimes their parents. The extent of responsibility the study participants assumed, including making decisions, was far more than expected of children in our society. For instance, Kusuma,[4] who lived with her birth family and two younger and two older half-siblings, described challenging circumstances. The context the children lived in assigned them a lot of responsibility at a very young age. This included taking care of basic needs themselves. The family members created a shared family culture, defined as a common system of meanings and symbols. Everything that a family uses can be viewed as a symbol that communicates these meanings, whether substantial, such as furniture, or nonsubstantial, such as time management and communication. A family culture may vary in its strength and consistency, depending on the length of time family members lived together, the intensity of their interactions, and their cultural backgrounds (Reimer, 2010). In Kusuma's birth family's case, the family culture was dominated by the adults and their needs. Kusama told us:

> We really went through lots and lots during that time. My two older siblings hit and punched each other. For example, Steffen went through a window, and then I went to the doctor's office with him. Or we went hungry, and we found things outside to eat. We ate plants, we picked flattened lumps of old chewing gum off the street and chewed them, and we went begging to the neighbors. And when my mother was passed out drunk on the sofa, things were always the same at home. Sometimes we tried to steal food from the fridge, and one time she caught us. David and I took a slice of salami from the fridge, and she jumped up like something had bitten her and demanded to know where the piece of salami was. She'd seen it, and we'd hidden it in a gap under the door, and then she took the slice of salami and chucked it in the trash can. She took it away from us and chucked it in the trash can.

Dennis lived with his brother and mother, who suffered from a mental illness, until he was 6. He remembered a situation that was slightly less drastic yet equally as desperate as Kusuma's:

> Even though I was still quite young then, I felt very responsible for my brother. He's two years younger than me. [I felt responsible] for making sure we had bread to eat. Just little things I did just because my mother couldn't manage to do anymore. Things like making sandwiches for me and my brother. Because my mother, she was simply out of it. She didn't hit us or anything. She wasn't a really horrific mother, but she was simply far too busy with her own problems.

The participants in our projects reported that it was not easy to gain access to supports. They stated that their critical situation and their signals were only recognized relatively late. They were often only recognized when they acted out and drew attention to themselves through behavior that was considered atypical, as Kusuma explained: "They only realized that something was wrong with my family situation when I misbehaved in kindergarten and became aggressive; when they noticed I never had my own backpack, which we were supposed to come with."

Lack of Participation in the Transition to Care

The topic of participation becomes highly charged once children are in contact with the CYWS, which have made decisions about where they will live. Professionals make decisions that are significant for children's lives, so children have a right to participation. Our analysis of the biographical interviews revealed that participation is essential during the transition stage so children can be well matched with their foster families. Kusuma described how she was placed in a family where she could not stay but later found a family that was a good fit:

> I was first taken to a family with many children. I did not feel good there. Finally, I asked the social worker to find a new family for me. When I met my new foster mother first, she kneeled, and we spoke about hairstyles, and even today, she is an important person to me.

When young adults were involved in decision-making, they were more likely to view foster care experiences as a helpful intervention in their biographies. They told stories about their memories of caring adults around them, and they seemed more capable of finding an unbroken thread running through their life stories. Iris stated: "I got to know my foster mum, and I knew it would be a fit. During the first couple of months, I felt very controlled by her, but I really wanted to stay there. It was my place to be. So, I did a lot to make sure I can stay there." However, transition situations in which children reported genuine instances of participation were the exception, not the norm. The children mainly experienced the transition as an intervention that was partially incomprehensible to them. For example, Marcel was in the hospital with a broken leg when he was placed into care. He spent years not understanding why he was in his foster family's care:

> That day in the hospital—I don't think I'll ever forget it—this family came in. It was Gerlinde, Fritz, and a child, I think, and then Gerlinde said, we're packing up your things, we're taking you with us. And I didn't understand it at all, and I actually always wanted to stay with my mum. Well, then I had to go to their family. I thought I was visiting or something, but somehow that wasn't it. It was really weird—a family you don't know comes and picks you up and you've never seen them in your life. Then I kind of only understood

it two years later. For a long time, I didn't know why I was there. When the doorbell rang, I always thought, here comes my mum to pick me up.

There was no direct participation in Marcel's case: he felt at the mercy of the adults' decisions. Matteo's case was even more dramatic. Matteo, who lived in a foster home against his wishes for years, described how he was denied the opportunity to participate in important decisions in his life. The following scene described a planning discussion about support services between foster care professionals and the foster family:

> Then the professionals arranged stuff behind my back . . ., and then I was supposed to do this and go to this club and all that even though I didn't want to. Then what happened was that during that time, I was sent out of the room. I was supposed always to be there, really, but then I often got sent out, even as long as an hour, and then they talked. I think the professionals also spoke about my development. That's fine, but of course, I eavesdropped and heard lots of things, and then suddenly they were saying residential home and that a foster family definitely wouldn't work. And to my face, the lady responsible for me said, yeah, sure, we'll find something, and then at some point I burst in, and I said right, I know you're not meant to eavesdrop, but I can't believe what I'm hearing, and I think it's terrible and all that, so tell me, tell me to my face. I mean, I might still be a child, but I'm not stupid.

The two situations of Marcel and Matteo are in stark contradiction to participatory practice. In the case of these two study participants, their lack of participation, or its denial, had severe consequences for their later biography. Both pointed out that they found it difficult to build trust with state institutions and stated that they wanted to prevent any state intervention into their own families at all costs in the future. They therefore preferred to live inconspicuously.

The transition to foster care can be understood as a change of family culture (Reimer, 2008, 2010, 2015). This change subjects children to various experiences of alienation and confusion. My analysis showed that it is imperative to give children the opportunity to participate in their foster family on an everyday basis. Participation allows them to make decisions about everyday things and how they want to live their lives, such as what to eat, how to decorate their room, hobbies, and leisure activities to pursue. This also needs to be considered when the CYWS select and prepare the foster family (Reimer, 2010, 2015).

Token Participation in Ongoing Case Support

The participatory processes initiated by professionals cannot stop when a child is living in a foster family. The central issues here are: Is it taken for granted that professionals will regularly talk with the child alone? Who receives support—the child, the foster family, or both? Ideally, the foster child should have a personal contact person in the social services agency to stay in touch regularly, both openly and privately.

The law specifies that children must participate in the support planning meetings, which occur at least once a year. However, the young adults we interviewed who had no or minimal contact with the professionals responsible for them outside these meetings saw their participation in the support planning process as token (or staged) rather than genuine participation. One way to improve children's involvement in practice might be to support more trusting connections between professionals and children if their lives with their foster families become difficult. It would be vital for children to have a contact person with the foster care services they already know and can contact spontaneously. Children should have at least one familiar contact person in the child welfare system to discuss their wishes, dreams, or fears when the CYWS plan new transitions for children in care. These transitions include children returning to their original families, children moving to another setting, or foster care formally coming to an end upon children reaching the age of majority.

Stressful Visitations With Family

Children's visitations with members of their biological family play a central role in their eyes. The study participants frequently described visitation sessions as stressful for everyone involved. Children reported feeling agitated and having psychosomatic symptoms before and after visitations. At the same time, contact meetings were an essential resource in the children's lives

(Reimer & Pierlings, 2015). In Germany, unless there is evidence that contact will harm the child's well-being, the biological parents have a right to see the child regularly (Reimer & Pierlings, 2015). The interview material shows that contact meetings are taxing for children if they do not have a say in how often the meetings will take place and what form they will take. The meetings might then not be child-friendly, or they could overstep the child's personal boundaries. Some examples include the amount of physical contact between the child and parents that is appropriate in the child's eyes or the child receiving gifts from their parents.

In the biographical interviews, many children reported having experienced a deficient level of participation and feeling stressed by the contact meetings. For example, Lena said:

> There were just always contact meetings. But I never really got into it, like I often reacted by feeling sick. And I had a bit of an advantage in that my biological father is in a wheelchair, so I could always hide away in my bunk bed, and he couldn't get near me. And then, like my parents [the foster parents] always really helped make sure they were at a bit of a distance, so they didn't get on my nerves too much or anything, but you can't avoid it entirely.... But [in the visitation meetings] I always managed to get really worked up and really queasy, and always felt sick. And then that always had an after-effect for a week, really.

Lena had no say in determining the visitation parameters, and she reacted with symptoms to them. Her behavior could be interpreted as a way for her to gain some degree of control over the situation.

The biographical narratives demonstrated how crucial participation is. At the same time, they showed how often the young adults felt retrospectively that they had not participated. One caveat of our data material is that there is no way to tell whether the foster parents and professionals promoted children's participation how I defined it. Children often felt retrospectively as if they did not participate, leaving them feeling powerless, ignored, and unheard. These feelings indicate that, from their point of view, participatory processes have failed them. The failure of participatory approaches is problematic because it violates a child's rights and limits and, in some cases, severely curtails their developmental opportunities.

Stumbling Blocks to Participation in Foster Care

Here I will consider the conditions that adults need to meet to promote participatory processes. For this purpose, I will use excerpts from the biographical interviews and observations from workshops with professionals and foster parents. During the workshops, professionals and foster parents jointly examined and interpreted the biographical interviews about successful and unsuccessful participatory processes and discussed the implications for practice.

Professional Attitudes Closed to Participatory Practice

The fundamental requirement in promoting participatory processes is that professionals understand their role as open to participatory practice. In this context, it is highly relevant how professionals view their work. When young people discuss their experiences with professionals, it becomes clear that there are professional attitudes that preclude any opportunity for children's participation. I want to illustrate this point based on the statements made by a young man called Dave. Dave was a foster child who was later adopted by a foster family. During adolescence, he moved to a residential home when living with his adopted family grew enormously difficult. When I interviewed him, Dave was 20 years old and had just moved into a granny flat in his adopted parents' house. He received support from a social worker who visited him regularly to provide case-by-case support. Dave reported witnessing a high staff turnover since most professionals could not deal with him for long and he could not deal with them. Dave's case was passed from one worker to the next. Dave described his social workers as follows:

> Yes, it's always like that with them, you have to be careful with social workers, it's always the people in care's fault, right? . . . [T]he social workers never look in the mirror. . . . [T]hey always pass the blame onto the clients because it's they who have the problem—they have problems from the start and not the social workers, and that's the problem that I think that's no good, right?

Here Dave depicted professionals as being responsible for labeling their clients based on problems that professionals have ascribed to them. He described professionals as judging and controlling people who offer or refuse support depending on what they are willing to do. Dave stated:

And then a guy came where I thought, whoa, what kind of a moron have they sent me now, big, strict, and wanted to construct a whole new Dave, help build me right up from the bottom, change my personality, like if you wanted to shift a great rock with a really flimsy crowbar, you know? He fell flat on his face with that approach. Yeah, and then, everything [in my room] was cleaned, there was just some dust left on the door frame that I'd forgotten. [He said to me,] "Mr. Spiker, I should now inform the youth welfare department that you can't clean the flat yourself, right?" I said, "What? I dusted all the furniture here, the floor and everything is clean. There's just a bit of dust up there." [The worker said,] "No I'm not going to discuss this with you. I'm filling it in right now, right? Here— D minus!" and I'm like "Uh? What's going on today? And your personality is also an F, right?" [Dave said.] . . . [A]nd then I didn't even open the door to him anymore when he was there coz then I thought, nah, before I get an F again or something right? . . . I'm like I'm not opening the door anymore, right? To protect myself because I couldn't deal with that.

Dave used a metaphor in his description of what had happened. He did so deliberately, to some extent, to highlight his opinion of the social worker labeling him. The labeling and unwarranted presumptions by a professional about someone they were working with hindered participation. As Dave did not open the door to the social worker, he, of course, participated in the process in his way and took back control of the situation. However, this act was not a form of participation that resulted from the social worker aiming for more involvement by Dave. Dave had to participate in this way, illustrating the problem with a paternalistic and controlling CYWS system (and maybe also with a controlling social worker). One could say that the only way in which Dave can "participate" is by refusing to comply with the rules. This should not be the goal of professional child welfare work because it thwarts the idea of professionals creating opportunities for participation.

Similarly, the interviews and workshops showed that another problematic professional self-image is that of the social worker as a bureaucrat. This type of attitude lends itself to professionals making decisions based on paperwork rather than individual cases and peculiarities. Some young people described the bureaucratic mindset of their social workers in ways that showed that they followed a fixed set of rules and routines rather than listening to the children. The young people felt frustrated by this type of behavior because they thought practitioners perceived them as "cases" or "numbers," not children.

Another professional attitude that hinders children's participation is professionals perceiving themselves as problem finders and solvers. This type of attitude is problematic because the professionals place more significance on their actions than on the personal initiative of their clients, whose responsibility for their lives should be the focus of attention. This is taken even further when professionals see themselves as all-knowing doctors or even healers. In these cases, the social workers view their clients as needing therapy or medication to get better—a thoroughly absurd notion considering the complex problems that social workers encounter.

The kind of child welfare practice where participation happens requires practitioners to see their profession like social work rather than medical intervention. Western societies view it as abnormal when children do not grow up with a biological parent. (For a detailed discussion of the concept of normality, see Reimer, 2017.) Many foster children reported severe experiences of stigmatization because of being a foster child, especially at school or when applying for jobs, in relationships, or with potential parents-in-law. The lack of normality, or at least the precarious state of normality in the family, which applies to children who do not grow up with their biological parents, may be extended to their entire personality as a (pathological) characteristic and stigma (see Goffman, 1963).

When child welfare workers see children as predominantly lacking normality, as pathological or disturbed, this may imply that they cannot make good decisions for themselves because of their condition. It may also suggest that they cannot participate appropriately in everyday life and must be treated by "experts." The literature on foster care might quickly convey that all foster children are traumatized and need therapy, and are perhaps unwell, disturbed, and undoubtedly anomalous. (For a detailed literature review, see Reimer, 2017.) In the *Practical Guide for Professionals and Foster Parents* (Zwernemann, 2007), which practitioners widely use, the following can be read under the heading "How Does a Child Become a Foster Child?":

> A large percentage of foster children have been maltreated, neglected, and rejected. . . . The longer the children are exposed to this heavy burden, the more clearly the *unhealthy* attachment patterns can be seen. The children are *deeply lonely and suspicious*. . . . The children have *low self-esteem*. They feel *rejected and unlovable*. *They barely allow themselves feelings*. Experiences of violence, neglect, or rejection result in *behavioral anomalies*.

Aggressive impulses and the *repetition of violent patterns* make *life with peers difficult*. (Zwernemann, 2007, p. 37, emphases by the author)

It is noteworthy that this quote contains no conjunctive, restrictions, or relativizations. The guide locates the problem only with the child who becomes a foster child. It does not describe the problem as a (surmountable) phase but conceptualizes it as a permanent feature of a child's character.

In the biographical interviews with former foster children, the participants frequently reported so-called diagnoses that they had received, such as fetal alcohol syndrome, attention deficit disorder, and attention deficit/hyperactivity disorder. When the child left a foster family for various reasons, they may have received a so-called diagnosis of "incompatibility with family life." The question arises of whether professionals can achieve participation when they view foster children predominantly in this way. Several study participants had experienced not being taken seriously and involved because of these professional views. Nina, who was diagnosed as suffering from a borderline personality disorder, expressed it with this hyperbole: "Sometimes I do feel like a person with some kind of disability that ... can't do anything. I mean, that's how I'm being treated." This view of foster children contrasts sharply with the wishes and self-image of the young adults I interviewed. They wanted to be normal children and be seen and treated as such, including possibilities to participate, being taken seriously, and having a say.

Discussion

The interview-based findings show that children frequently feel that they do not participate, they only participate to a small extent, and participation is only possible when they act out. It is not enough for participation to be recognized in the professional and legal guidelines. Children in care need participatory options at every stage: in difficult life situations, in transitions, and in decisions about visitations. They need to feel listened to, informed, and valued and have the opportunity to be part of the decision-making process.

Based on the initial impressions from the biographical interview material, a definition of participation for children in foster care can be summarized as follows (see Reimer & Wolf, 2011, p. 154):

"Participation means that:

- children have the experience of adults listening to them in a favorable conversational situation,
- children are properly informed,
- they are valued, even if they cause difficulties,
- decisions can be negotiated with them as partners, or can be taken by them autonomously, and
- if a decision must be made which goes against their wishes, children's forgiveness and retroactive consent are sought."

This definition clarifies that the basis for participation is that adults listen to children and value them. They inform children about their situation in life, interventions, and what is happening to them. Additionally, during child protection interventions, conditions can occur in which adults must make decisions without the child's permission; for example, a child might be separated from a parent they love if the parent cannot care for the child. In these cases, participation means that adults ask children for their retroactive consent, again and again, if needed. Adults must explain the reasons for the decision and listen to and value children's opinions. The aim must be that children feel that there are benevolent and caring adults even if consent is difficult to achieve, and the decision must lead to more emancipation and freedom for the child in the long run (see Brumlik, 2017).

According to my findings, the crucial contact points concerning participation that arise before children enter care are the contact persons for children in difficult family situations. The children and youth welfare agencies need to provide answers to the question of who children can turn to. Linked to this is how society can become more responsive to children's signals about being taken seriously by their environment. How can social workers and other professionals who children encounter in institutional settings, such as daycare and schools, be sensitized to taking them seriously about their difficult circumstances and skills and strengths?

In transitions to foster care, there must be someone who will ask the children and young people what they want and attends to them and their wishes. Children's wishes may be ambivalent, but adults need to take them seriously. Children need to feel supported during the transition. At least one professional will need to explain their situation (perhaps repeatedly) and spell out and work on possible options with them. Child welfare services need to be flexible to take children's wishes and ideas seriously and react to them. Professionals need to approach groups of siblings in a way where they can openly discuss whether they come into care together or separately. Professionals cannot fully consider children's wishes in all processes. Child welfare services need to find good ways to communicate with children about decisions that differ from the child's wishes.

In the context of visitation meetings, it is essential to give children a significant say in how the meetings occur, prepare them for the contact sessions, and discuss them afterward to reduce or altogether avoid stress. Some critical questions for professionals are: Who prepares the child? Who offers support for the contact meetings? Who will take the time to decide with the children how the contact session should be designed so that children can have a positive experience?

Children and youth welfare agencies can only achieve children's participation in foster care if professionals carefully re-examine their self-image, professional attitudes, and image of foster children. At the same time, professionals need time to encourage and supervise participatory processes and gain knowledge and experience in having conversations with children. The CYWS must ensure that professionals can continuously develop participatory attitudes and conditions as a step forward in foster care—from the children's point of view and on their behalf. Professional training, continuing education, and targeted, practical projects involving discussions with professionals about their attitudes to participation are sorely needed. Professionals ought to examine their self-image and reflect on their perceptions of foster children. An alternative, nonstigmatizing, and nonpathologizing view of foster children could involve the following aspects: Foster children are children who have had difficult experiences in their biography. Their position as children in foster families places them beyond the boundaries of family "normality." They have a right to protection. They have frequently proved to be competent actors under challenging situations and circumstances, and they want to be perceived as capable actors when working with professionals.

Professionals need time and skills to put participation into practice. Even if they embrace a self-image that is fundamentally conducive to participation and a helpful view of children, the success of participation will always depend significantly on professionals' skills. Foster care professionals must be able to talk with children in a manner that suits their age and level of development. Foster care professionals must be aware of how they can negotiate good solutions with the children, especially if they express themselves ambiguously. Discussions of this kind, which are often complex, take time, empathy, and skills and include knowing creative ways to talk with children.

Professional practice and research on child welfare practice are called upon to promote children's participation. Research involving children must explore the different ways professionals treat and react to children and the procedures they use. Child welfare scholars need to conduct more research on whether children see professionals as promoting or preventing participation. It is not sufficient for research to ask young adults to look back at their experiences and draw inferences from them. Research is also needed to analyze foster children's experiences throughout their lives and conduct ethnographic observations on their everyday lives in foster families and their interactions with professionals. These different types of research would help professionals understand how and when children fall through the cracks in participatory processes and decision-making.

Reflection Questions

(1) What are the essential capacities social workers need to possess so they can put participation into practice? How can they acquire these capacities?
(2) What can social work organizations and professionals do to develop helpful attitudes toward children's participation?

Notes

1. All the translations from German are mine.
2. The public child welfare services are called "Aid for Children and Youth" (*Kinder- und Jugendhilfe*) in Germany. I will use "children and youth welfare services (CYWS)" throughout the chapter.
3. In Germany, research projects that are financed by funding agencies do not typically undergo an institutional review by the university but are subject to the review process of the funder.
4. I have used pseudonyms throughout the chapter to protect the study participants' confidentiality.

References

Backe-Hansen, E. (2018). Formal and everyday participation in foster families: A challenge? In A. Falch-Eriksen & E. Backe-Hansen (Eds.), *Human rights in child protection. Implications for professional practice and policy* (pp. 227–244). Springer Nature.

Barth, R., & Olsen, A. N. (2020). Are children oppressed? The timely importance of answering this question. *Children & Youth Services Review, 110*, 104780. https://doi.org/10.1016/j.childyouth.2020.104780

Bessell, S. (2011). Participation in decision-making in out-of-home care in Australia: What do young people say? *Children & Youth Services Review, 33*(4), 496–501. https://doi.org/10.1016/j.childyouth.2010.05.006

Bessell, S., & Gal, T. (2009). Forming partnerships: The human rights of children in need of care and protection. *International Journal of Children's Rights, 17*, 283–229.

Blandow, J., Gintzel, U., & Hansbauer, P. (1999). *Partizipation als Qualitätsmerkmal in der Heimerziehung. Eine Diskussionsgrundlage* [Participation as a quality characteristic in residential care. A platform for discussion]. Votum.

Brumlik, M. (2017). *Advokatorische Ethik. Zur Legitimation pädagogischer Eingriffe* [Advocatory ethics. About the legitimation of educational interventions]. Europäische Verlagsanstalt.

Büchner, P. (1989). Vom Befehlen und Gehorchen zum Verhandeln. Entwicklungstendenzen von Verhaltensstandards und Umgangsformen seit 1945 [From commanding and obeying to negotiating. Trends in behavioral standards and manners since 1945]. In U. Preuss-Lausitz, P. Büchner, & M. Fischer-Kowalski (Eds.), *Kriegskinder, Konsumkinder, Krisenkinder. Zur Sozialisationsgeschichte seit dem Zweiten Weltkrieg* [Children of war, children of consumption, children in crisis. On the history of socialization since the Second World War] (pp. 196–212). Beltz.

Clark, A. (2005). Listening to and involving young children: A review of research and practice. *Early Child Development and Care, 175*(6), 489–505. https://doi.org/10.1080/03004430500131288

Destatis. (2018a). *Statistiken der Kinder- und Jugendhilfe. Erzieherische Hilfe, Eingliederungshilfe für seelisch behinderte junge Menschen, Hilfe für junge Volljährige - Heimerziehung, sonstige betreute Wohnform* [Statistics about child and youth welfare. Educational assistance, integration assistance for young people with a mental illness, assistance for young adults: Residential care and other assisted living arrangements]. Statistisches Bundesamt.

Destatis. (2018b). *Statistiken der Kinder- und Jugendhilfe. Erzieherische Hilfe, Eingliederungshilfe für seelisch behinderte junge Menschen, Hilfe für junge Volljährige—Vollzeitpflege* [Statistics about child and youth welfare. Educational assistance, integration assistance for young people with a mental illness, assistance for young adults: Fulltime care]. Statistisches Bundesamt.

Eberitzsch, S., Keller, S., & Rohrbach, J. (2021, April). Partizipation in der stationären Kinder- und Jugendhilfe—Theoretische und empirische Zugänge zur Perspektive betroffener junger Menschen: Ergebnisse eines internationalen Literaturreviews. [Participation for children in care – theoretical and empirical approaches to you people's perspectives: finding of an international literature review]. *Österreichisches Jahrbuch für Soziale Arbeit, 3*, 113–154. https://doi.org/10.30424/OEJS2103113

Faltermeier, J. (2004). Herkunftseltern und Fremdunterbringung: Situation, Erleben, Perspektiven [Birth Parents and out of home placements. Situation, Experience,

Perspectives]. In Sozialpädagogisches Institut im SOS Kinderdorf (Eds.), *Herkunftsfamilien in der Kinder- und Jugendhilfe. Perspektiven für eine partnerschaftliche Zusammenarbeit* [Families of origins in child- and youth welfare. Perspectives for a cooperative partnership]. München: SOS (pp. 44–60). https://www.sos-kinderdorf.de/resource/blob/8584/326f5c0670b9e163fab4b02a02f954ea/dokumentation3-data.pdf

Gal, T. (2015). From social exclusion to child-inclusive policies: Toward an ecological model of child participation. In T. Gal & B. Duramy (Eds.), *International perspectives and empirical findings on child participation: From social inclusion to child-inclusive policies* (pp. 451–463). Oxford University Press.

Graham, A., Fitzgerald, R., & Cashmore, J. (2015). Professionals' conceptions of "children," "childhood," and "participation" in an Australian family relationship services sector organization. In T. Gal & B. Duramy (Eds.), *International perspectives and empirical findings on child participation: From social exclusion to child-inclusive policies* (pp. 257–281). Oxford University Press.

Goffman, E. (1963). *Stigma: Notes on the management of spoiled identity*. Simon & Schuster.

Hansbauer, P., & Kriener, M. (2000). Partizipation von Mädchen und Jungen als Instrument zur Qualitätsentwicklung in stationären Hilfen (§ 78b SGB VIII) [Participation of girls and boys as an instrument to improve quality for children in care]. In J. Merchel (Ed.), *Qualitätsentwicklung in Einrichtungen und Diensten der Erziehungshilfe. Methoden, Erfahrungen, Kritik, Perspektiven* [Quality development in out-of-home care institutions and services. Methods, experiences, critiques, and perspectives] (pp. 219–246). IGfH-Eigenverlag.

Hart, R. (1992). *Children's participation: From tokenism to citizenship*. UNICEF International Child Development Center. http://www.unicef-irc.org/publications/pdf/childrens_participation.pdf.

Hörmann, K. (2013). *Partizipation von Kindern und Jugendlichen. Beteiligungsmöglichkeiten in Fremdunterbringungseinrichtungen* [Participation of children and young people. Opportunities to participate in residential care homes]. Retrieved on March 17, 2021, fromwww.partizipation.at/fileadmin/media_data/Downloads/Forschungsplattform/MA_Hoermann_2013_Beteiligung_von_Jugendlichen.pdf

Kriener, M. (Ed.). (1999). *Beteiligung in der Jugendhilfepraxis. Sozialpädagogische Strategien zur Partizipation in Erziehungshilfen und bei Vormundschaften* [Participation in youth welfare practice. Social work strategies for participation in out-of-home care and guardianship]. Votum.

Križ, K., & Roundtree-Swain, D. (2017). "We are merchandise on a conveyer belt": How young adults in the public child protection system perceive their participation in decisions about their care. *Children & Youth Services Review, 78*, 32–40. https://doi.org/10.1016/j.childyouth.2017.05.001

Križ, K., & Skivenes, M. (2017). Child welfare workers' perceptions of children's participation: A comparative study in England, Norway and the USA (California). *Child & Family Social Work, 22*(S2), 11–22. https://doi.org/10.1111/cfs.12224

Liebel, M. (2013). *Kinder und Gerechtigkeit. Über Kinderrechte neu nachdenken* [Children and justice. Rethinking children's rights]. Beltz Juventa.

Moos, M. (2012). *Beteiligung in der Heimerziehung. Einschätzungen aus Perspektive junger Menschen und Einrichtungsleitungen* [Participation in residential care homes. Assessments from the perspective of young people and managers]. Retrieved on March

17, 2021, from www.ism-mz.de/fileadmin/uploads/Downloads/Beteiligung_in_der_Heimerziehung_Moos.pdf

Müller, D. (2006). *Partizipation im Hilfeplangespräch. Eine Einzelfallstudie* [Participation in case management meetings. A case study]. Universität Siegen. Retrieved on June 5, 2021, from https://www.bildung.uni-siegen.de/mitarbeiter/wolf/files/download/wisdiplom/danielle_mueller.pdf

Münder, J. (2006). *Frankfurter Kommentar zum SGB VIII: Kinder- und Jugendhilfe* [Frankfurt commentary about SGB VIII: Child and youth welfare] (5th ed.). Juventa (Reihe Votum).

Pierlings, J. (2011). *Leuchtturmprojekt Pflegekinderdienste* [Light house project on foster care services]. ZPE-Schriftenreihe. Retrieved on July 18, 2021, from https://www.lvr.de/media/wwwlvrde/jugend/service/arbeitshilfen/dokumente_94/jugend_mter_1/allgemeiner_sozialer_dienst/pflegekindeiifsrdienst/LeuchtturmProjekte.pdf

Reimer, D. (2008). Pflegekinder in verschiedenen Familienkulturen. Ressourcen und Belastungen im Übergang [Foster children in different family cultures. Ressources and liabilities in transitions]. ZPE.

Reimer, D. (2010). "Everything was strange and different": Young adults' recollections of the transition into foster care. *Adoption and Fostering, 34*(2), 14–22. https://doi.org/10.1177/030857591003400204

Reimer, D. (2011). *Pflegekinderstimme. Arbeitshilfe zur Begleitung und Beratung von Pflegefamilien* [The foster child's voice. Working guidelines for supporting and advising foster families]. PAN e. V.

Reimer, D. (2014). Subjective and objective dimensions of turning points. *Social Work and Society, 12*(1), 1–19. Retrieved on July 26, 2021, from https://ejournals.bib.uni-wuppertal.de/index.php/sws/article/view/385

Reimer, D. (2015). Übergänge als Kulturwechsel und kritische Lebensereigniss [Transitions as cultural change and critical life events]. In K. Wolf (Ed.), *Sozialpädagogische Pflegekinderforschung* [Social work research on foster children] (pp. 61–84). Klinkhardt Verlag.

Reimer, D. (2017). *Normalitätskonstruktionen in Biografien ehemaliger Pflegekinder* [Constructions of normality in the biographies of former foster children]. Beltz Juventa.

Reimer, D., & Pierlings, J. (2015). Belastungen und Ressourcen im Kontext von Besuchskontakten [Burdens and resources in the context of visitations]. In K. Wolf (Ed.), *Sozialpädagogische Pflegekinderforschung* [Social work research on foster children] (pp. 245–262). Klinkhardt Verlag.

Reimer, D., & Wolf, K. (2011). Beteiligung von Pflegekindern [Participation of foster children]. In H. Kindler, E. Helming, T. Meysen & K. Jurzyk (Eds.), *Handbuch Pflegekinderhilfe* [Handbook of foster care] (pp. 506–515). DJI e.V.

Schäfer, D., Petri, C., & Pierlings, J. (2015). *Nach Hause? Rückkehrprozesse von Pflegekindern in ihre Herkunftsfamilie* [Back home? Foster children's process of returning home to their families of origin]. ZPE-Schriftenreihe 41. Retrieved on July 18, 2021, fromhttps://dspace.ub.uni-siegen.de/handle/ubsi/949

Schütze, F. (1981). Prozessstrukturen des Lebenslaufs [Structures of the processes in the life course]. In J. Matthes, A. Pfeifenberger, & M. Stosberg (Eds.), *Biographie in handlungswissenschaftlicher Perspektive. Kolloquium am Sozialwissenschaftlichen Forschungszentrum der Universität Erlangen-Nürnberg* [Biography from the perspective of applied science. Colloquium at the Social Science Research Center at the University Erlangen-Nürnberg] (pp. 67–156). Verlag der Nürnberger Forschungsvereinigung.

Schütze, F. (1983). Biographieforschung und narratives Interview [Biography research and narrative interviews]. *Neue Praxis, 13*(3), 283–293.

Sozialgesetzbuch. (2021). *Kinder- und Jugendhilfe* [Social Services Code: Child and youth welfare]. Retrieved on July 7, 2021, from https://www.sozialgesetzbuch-sgb.de/

Tabel, A. (2020). Hilfen zur Erziehung [Supports for caring for children]. In DJI (Ed.), *DJI-Kinder- und Jugendmigrationsreport 2020. Datenanalyse zur Situation junger Menschen in Deutschland* [2020 German Youth Institute's report on the migration of children and youth. Data analyses about the situation of young people in Germany] (pp. 169–189). https://www.dji.de/fileadmin/user_upload/dasdji/themen/Jugend/DJI_Migrationsreport_2020.pdf

Ten Brummelaar, M. D. C., Harder, A. T., Kalverboer, M. E., Post, W. J., & Knorth, E. J. (2018). Participation of youth in decision-making procedures during residential care: A narrative review. *Child & Family Social Work, 23*(1), 33–44. https://doi.org/10.1111/cfs.12381

United Nations. (1989). *Convention on the Rights of the Child. Adopted and opened for signature, ratification and accession by General Assembly resolution 44/25 of 20 November 1989.* https://www.ohchr.org/en/professionalinterest/pages/crc.aspx

Van Bijleveld, G. G., Dedding, C. W. M., & Bunders-Aelen, J. F. G. (2013). Children's and young people's participation within child welfare and child protection services: A state-of-the-art review. *Child & Family Social Work, 20*(2), 129–138. https://doi.org/10.1111/cfs.12082

Wapler, F. (2017). *Umsetzung und Anwendung der Kinderrechtskonvention in Deutschland. Rechtsgutachten im Auftrag des Bundesministeriums für Familie, Senioren, Frauen und Jugend* [Implementation and application of the Child's Rights Convention in Germany. Legal opinion on behalf of the Ministry for Families, Seniors, Women and Youth]. Mainz. Retrieved on June 5, 2021, from https://www.bmfsfj.de/blob/120474/a14378149aa3a881242c5b1a6a2aa941/2017-gutachten-umsetzung-kinderrechtskonvention-data.pdf

Waterstrad, D. (2015). *Prozess-Soziologie der Elternschaft: Nationsbildung, Figurationsideale und generative Machtarchitektur in Deutschland* [Process-Sociology of parenthood: nation building, figurative ideals, and generative power architecture in Germany]. M&V-Verlag Münster.

Wolf, K. (2006). Bedeutung pädagogischer Gestaltung gelingenden Aufwachsens [The importance of pedagogical design in children growing up successfully]. *Gilde Rundbrief, 60*(1), 7–16.

Wolf, K. (2013). Subjektkonstitution oder Erziehung von Menschen? [Constitution of subjects or education of people?] In U. Buchmann & E. Diezemann (Eds.), *Subjektentwicklung und Sozialraumgestaltung als Entwicklungsaufgabe* [Subject development and social space as a developmental task] (pp. 71–104). G. A. F. B. Verlag.

Zwernemann, P. (2007). *Praxisbuch Pflegekinderwesen: Wir gehen gemeinsam in die Zukunft* [Practical Book for Foster Children]. Bundesarbeitsgemeinschaft für Kinder in Adoptiv- und Pflegefamilien e. V.

8
Creating and Crossing Age-Related Participation Boundaries in Child Protection in the United States (California)

Megan Canfield, Emma Frushell, Jenna Gaudette, and Katrin Križ

Introduction

Child protection caseworkers can play a vital role in creating participatory opportunities for children and youth who encounter public child protection agencies (Križ, 2020; ten Brummelaar et al., 2018; van Bijeleveld et al., 2014). However, they can also stifle children's involvement in decisions about removal from home, placement in out-of-home care, services, visitations with family members, and other decisions (Arbeiter & Toros, 2017; Bessell, 2011, 2015; Bouma et al., 2018; Križ & Roundtree-Swain, 2017; Križ & Skivenes, 2015; Paulsen, 2016; Vis & Thomas, 2009; Willumsen & Skivenes, 2005). Professionals' views of children's age, vulnerabilities, authenticity, trustworthiness, and rights may determine the degree to which they create participatory conditions in administrative decisions (Križ, 2020; Križ & Roundtree-Swain, 2017; Magnussen & Skivenes, 2015; Vis et al., 2012). This chapter analyzes the views of child protection caseworkers employed by public child protection agencies in California about children's participation in child protection–related decisions depending on their age. It aims to add to the scholarly knowledge base about age as a determinant of children's involvement in child protection.

The term "children's participation" spans different types of involvement that denote various degrees of power for children to influence or make decisions about their lives. For example, at the front end of a child protection case, children might provide and receive information and express opinions during an investigation. It is child protection caseworkers' responsibility to assess the risk to the child and determine what should happen to keep the child safe. In other

Megan Canfield, Emma Frushell, Jenna Gaudette, and Katrin Križ, *Creating and Crossing Age-Related Participation Boundaries in Child Protection in the United States (California)* In: *Children and Young People's Participation in Child Protection*. Edited by: Katrin Križ and Mimi Petersen, Oxford University Press. © Oxford University Press 2023.
DOI: 10.1093/oso/9780197622322.003.0008

situations, children might collaborate with child protection caseworkers to decide about safety plans, out-of-home placements, types of services, extracurricular activities, contact with family members, and so on. Thus, collaborations involve equalizing power relations between children and adults in decision-making. Hart (1992) depicted cooperation between youth and adults as the highest rung on the ladder of youth participation. Lansdown (2010) referred to it as "genuine participation," and Shier (2001) described collaboration as the fifth level of children's empowerment, where children and adults share power and responsibility. For this chapter, the characteristics of genuine participation are for children to have their opinion heard *and* be taken seriously in decision-making (Archard & Skivenes, 2009).

We address these questions: Which age groups do child protection caseworkers distinguish when discussing children's participation? How does the involvement of children in child protection–related processes vary by children's age? How do child protection caseworkers justify including some children and excluding others from genuine participation based on their age? These questions have been influenced by the sociological concept of "symbolic boundaries," "the conceptual distinctions made by social actors to categorize objects, people, practices, and even time and space" (Lamont & Molnár, 2002, p. 168). These boundaries help create an individual's or group's reality and influence the power dynamics between individuals (Lamont et al., 2015). Drawing on this theoretical concept, we will show how experienced child protection caseworkers in California create symbolic boundaries between those children they think should participate because of their age and those who should not. We will describe the effects of their boundary drawing on how they involve children.

We will first provide some background information about the U.S. child protection system before discussing prior literature on children's age and participation in child protection. We will subsequently describe our research methods and findings. Lastly, we will discuss the implications of our findings on child protection practice and research.

The U.S. Child Protection System and Children's Participation

There were over 73 million children in the United States in 2019 (Children's Defense Fund, 2021), out of a total population of 328 million (U.S. Census

Bureau, 2019). In 2019, half of the children in the United States were children of color (Children's Defense Fund, 2021). Approximately 424,000 children were in foster care in 2019. Forty-six thousand children were in congregate care (institutional care such as group homes), and 138,000 children were in the care of relatives in 2018 (Children's Defense Fund, 2021). Black and American Indian/Alaska Native children were overrepresented in foster care in 2018 (Children's Defense Fund, 2021). According to survey data from 1999–2000, foreign-born immigrant children were underrepresented among children who encounter the child protection system. Among the children of immigrant parents, Hispanic and Black children were overrepresented, and non-Hispanic, Asian, and White children were underrepresented (Dettlaff & Earner, 2012).

The child protection system in the United States is a protection-oriented (investigative-legalistic) system (Berrick, 2011) in the context of a liberal or residual welfare state (Arts & Gelissen, 2002; Esping-Andersen, 1990). The policy aims of the U.S. system are children's safety, permanency, and family well-being (Berrick, 2011). An analysis of the policy vision stated by the same sample of U.S. caseworkers as studied in this chapter showed that the principles of safety and family preservation were most prominent (Križ & Skivenes, 2014). The intervention threshold in U.S. child protection is high compared to child protection systems focusing on preventing maltreatment (Gilbert et al., 2011). Children do not fare as well in the United States as children in many other global northern countries: the United States is ranked low on UNICEF's well-being index, which gauges children's material well-being, health, safety, and education (UNICEF, 2013). Among 29 countries, it occupied rank 26 (UNICEF, 2013).

Overall, children in the United States do not have legal participation rights that are as solid as children in other global northern countries, such as the United Kingdom, Netherlands, and Norway. It is up to individual states and local child protection agencies to decide how to include children (Peters, 2007). The 2006 amendment of the Social Security Act stipulates that in court and administrative hearings, child protective services consults children 16 and older about their permanency and transition plans (Social Security Act, 2006; Weisz et al., 2011). In California, where the interviews for this study occurred, judges will inquire whether a child 10 years and older had the chance to attend the hearing if they did not appear for it (Advokids, 2018). All children are assigned an attorney in court proceedings, and children may work with a court-appointed special advocate (CASA) during the court process (Berrick, Peckover, et al., 2015; Berrick et al., 2018). The United States is the only United Nations member state that has not ratified the United Nations Convention on the Rights of the Child (UNCRC). U.S. delegates contributed to drafting the UNCRC, but Republican senators opposed ratification in the 1990s, and conservative groups are still opposing it out of a concern that it would undercut national sovereignty by allowing international law to influence domestic law and diminish parental sovereignty by increasing children's individual rights (Attiah, 2014; Rothschild, 2017).

While statutory participation rights for children are not substantial in the United States, many counties in California utilized a practice approach called team decision-making (TDM) at the time of this research that has the potential to promote children's genuine participation. TDM (or family team) meetings are a structured way of involving children, family members, professionals, and others involved with the child to discuss the child's safety and placement (Berrick, Dickens, et al., 2015). Since 2014, California has embraced Safety Organized Practice (SPO), a strengths-based, collaborative practice model that involves the child, family, caseworker(s), and the community (Casey Family Programs, 2019). Research on family group decision-making in Vermont (a state in the United States) has shown that this practice model positively affects children's participation. Still, not all families have access to it (Burford & Gallagher, 2015). Many U.S. states are implementing family group decision-making, either statewide or in some jurisdictions (Children's Bureau, 2021).

Prior Literature on Children's Age and Participation

Previous scholarship demonstrates that older children are more likely to be involved in child protection processes; however, this literature does not delve deeply into caseworkers' justifications for providing different participatory opportunities for children *because of their age*. We know that children's age determines their participation in administrative processes in child protection agencies and courts: older children (children older than 8 or 10 years) are more likely to participate. Child protection caseworkers, judges, and other decision makers in child protection are more likely to give older children information, invite them to meetings, hear them in court in care order decisions, and appoint spokespersons for them (Archard & Skivenes, 2009; Berrick, Dickens, et al., 2015; Križ, 2020; Križ & Roundtree-Swain, 2017; Križ

& Skivenes, 2015; Magnussen & Skivenes, 2015; Paulsen, 2016; Shemmings, 2000; Skivenes, 2015; Vis & Thomas, 2009).

Križ's (2020) study on child protection caseworkers' understanding of children's participation used some of the same interview data as this chapter. It showed that the study participants discussed preteens or teens when they were asked to describe a situation in which a child's opinion mattered significantly to their decision. The participants weighed the opinions of children older than 10 more because they thought older children could articulate their views more clearly, forcefully, and effectively than younger children (through verbal communication or their acts, e.g., by running away from home). Older children could also resist child protection interventions they did not want. Overall, many study participants said they consulted with preteens and teens, took their opinions seriously, and even collaborated with them. At the same time, several participants considered teens more manipulative, which appeared to preclude their genuine participation (Križ, 2020).

Skivenes's (2015) study linked Norwegian caseworkers' attitudes toward children's vulnerability with age. Skivenes's research demonstrated that Norwegian caseworkers embraced a more protective and paternalistic attitude toward younger children and supported older children's autonomy and self-determination. Berrick, Dickens et al. (2015) gathered survey information about child protection caseworkers' attitudes toward children's participation in England, Finland, Norway, and the United States (California) with the help of a case vignette. The survey asked caseworkers about the extent to which they would involve a 5-year-old boy. The agency had started care order proceedings for the boy (to place him outside the home), who was considered a high-risk case. The survey inquired to what extent the respondents would gather information from the child, provide information about the care order proceedings, and involve the child in decision-making. The respondents in California were more likely to gather than provide information and ask about the child's placement preferences. The authors linked this finding with the rise of TDM and family group decision-making (Berrick, Dickens, et al., 2015).

The researchers then asked the child protection services caseworkers how they would react if the child were 11, and not 5. Most Californian respondents answered that they would involve both the 5-year-old (89%) and the 11-year-old (91%) early in the child protection process. Workers in California were more likely to state that they would gather information from the child than provide it and less likely to discern the child's needs for help and support than, for example, the Norwegian respondents (Berrick, Dickens, et al., 2015). These findings echo the legalistic-investigative orientation of the U.S. child welfare system (Berrick, 2011) and the time constraints that Californian workers face during child protection investigations (Berrick, Peckover, et al., 2015).

We know very little about the participation of babies, toddlers, and young children in decision-making in child protection. Recent research has shown that court processes tend to neglect the experiences of very young children. Križ et al.'s (2022) study on how court decision makers in eight European countries consider the child's perspective when deciding about newborn children's removal from home revealed that the children remain largely overlooked in the judgments made on their behalf. However, there are clear country differences (Križ et al., 2022). A recent study by Helland et al. (forthcoming) on the extent to which (young) children's views are heard in adoption proceedings in seven European countries demonstrated a similarly high level of invisibility of young children in adoption proceedings. (The children were 6 years old on average when adoption proceedings occurred.)

Methods

For this chapter, we analyzed 40 in-depth, semi-structured interviews with child protection caseworkers in two public child protection agencies in California that Katrin Križ and Marit Skivenes conducted in California in 2010.[1] This data material was part of a larger, 10-year-long research project called CHILDPRO that the Norwegian Research Council funded. The research project, which the Norwegian Research Ombudsperson approved, compared the child protection systems of England, Norway, and the United States. Marit Skivenes, the project's principal investigator, recruited study participants from emergency response units in California's two public child protection agencies.[2] Caseworkers in these units assess the risk to the child after a referral of child maltreatment has reached the agency and provide services for up to 30 days (Reed & Karpilow, 2002). Križ and Skivenes conducted most of the interviews face to face. (Skivenes conducted most of the interviews. A few interviews were on the phone.) We obtained informed consent from the study participants before each interview. The interviews lasted between 1 and 1.5 hours and were digitally recorded and transcribed verbatim. We de-identified the data and assigned each participant a code number to maintain the study participants' anonymity.

The interview protocol contained four sections, one of which focused on children's participation. Some of the interview questions in this section were: "What is your understanding of participation for children in child protection cases?" "In your opinion, why is it useful to let children participate in decision-making processes?" "At what stages in a case do you involve the child?" "Can you describe a situation in which the child's opinion mattered a lot in your decision-making?" and "In your work, how do you give the opinion of the child due weight in accordance with age and maturity of the child?" For this chapter, we selected the interview material that contained the words "age," "teenage," "maturity," and "old" from the entire section on children's participation. Next, the chapter authors read the data material and discussed the themes emerging in response to our research questions. Based on these themes, we first established several thematic categories and engaged in a second-round coding (see Lofland et al., 2006). The categories we developed were "children younger than 10 years," "children older than 10 years," and "children's ability to articulate (verbally)." Other categories were "children's ability to understand and developmental stage," "laws, procedures and participation," "participatory practices with older children," and "other" (for data that did not fit into any of the other categories). We then used the software program Atlas.ti to code the data based on these categories.

Most of the study participants were female and were experienced social workers who had work experience at the front end of child protection cases as well as with ongoing case support. On average, the study participants had 16 years of work experience in child protection. Thirty of the 40 participants held a graduate degree in social work. (The remaining participants had obtained an undergraduate degree.) The skew toward highly educated, senior caseworkers resulted from the hiring pattern of one of the agencies and the 2008 economic recession, which led to the dismissal of junior-level caseworkers because of severe budget cuts. The advantage of this senior and highly educated sample was the depth of knowledge of the study participants and their experience practicing in several child protection roles. The main limitation of the sample was its bias toward caseworkers who practiced in emergency response units at the time of the interview.

Symbolic Age Boundaries and Children's (Non-)Participation

In this section, we will summarize our findings and provide evidence from our interview material. We found that most of the study participants drew a symbolic boundary between three age groups. They distinguished between "very young children" (babies); "young children" or "little children" (4- or 5-year-old children) or simply "children" (versus youth); and "older children," "teens" (children older than 10 years), or (less frequently) "adolescents." Babies and children aged 5, 10, and 12 were most mentioned. The study participants seldom mentioned 2-year-old children, toddlers, and children older than 15. Table 8.1 summarizes our research questions and findings.

Babies and Younger Children's Participation

Overall, caseworkers viewed babies and younger children and involved them differently than older children. For caseworkers investigating child maltreatment, participation of young children mostly involved gathering information about the risk to the child. Some participants thought that young children did not understand and could not articulate what was happening. Some felt that young children were more honest than older children, who were perceived by several participants as more manipulative. At the same time, some participants perceived younger children as more fickle and emotional and thought their information was not reliable.

Many of the study participants were caseworkers investigating the risk to a child at the front end of child protection cases. When they discussed how they involved babies, the participants said they would see them and assess their behaviors. Several participants mentioned that babies' and younger children's inability to speak prevented the participants from involving them in decisions. CA (acronym for study participants in California) 39[3] said that "if you have a baby, of course, they're not going to talk to you, but you have to look at their injuries and also take into consideration where the injuries are and that kind of thing." According to CA 4, "A six-month-old, you eyeball them, and you see, you look at them and see that they're OK, but you're not going to interview them." CA 36 replied, "Even babies, you would still go out and see the baby." CA 29 stated:

Table 8.1. Research Questions and Findings

Research Questions	Findings
Which age groups do child protection caseworkers distinguish?	• They distinguish between "babies" and "younger" or "little" children (usually children who are under 10) and "older" children (children older than 10 years) • Missing ages: infrequent mention of 2-year-old children and children older than 15
How does child protection caseworkers' involvement of children in child protection–related processes vary by children's age?	"Babies": • Seen during investigations "Little children" and "young children": • Heard but child's opinion not typically sought or weighed "Older children": • Heard in TDM meetings and opinions taken seriously depending on child's ability to articulate, worker's safety concerns and perception of child's honesty (corroborated by other evidence) • Encouraged to participate in court proceedings and consult with legal counsel • Involved in decisions in independent living programs • Given more responsibility and offered resources
How do child protection caseworkers justify including some children and excluding others from genuine participation based on their age?	Justifications for inclusion: • Older children can better understand and speak (but it depends on maturity) • Young children are more honest • Older children can be controlled less than younger children • The law stating that children 10 years and older need to be invited to court hearings • The practice approach of involving children 9, 10, and older in TDM meetings Justifications for exclusion: • Babies and young children do not understand what is going on and are unable to communicate verbally • Younger children are typically less mature • Young children are too vulnerable to be involved in meetings • The information from young children is less reliable • Older children may be trying to manipulate the system

With an infant, a lot of times, the mother will make a disclosure to somebody in the hospital, or the baby's failure to thrive, the pediatrician will call, or [there are] bruises or explanations for injuries that don't match the injury. So you go by the evidence that you see, and what the people that are around . . . say that they've heard disclosed to them or seeing the child's behavior.

Only one participant, CA 2, mentioned "talking with" a baby:

> I try to spend time talk with the kids. When I'm doing an investigation, I talk to all the kids. If they're only six months old, I talk to them because it gives me an opportunity... because a six-month-old, if you're smiling and laughing, they respond to you, you know. And they'll smile back. If they're listless, I can see that. If they're unable to hold their head up, or if they don't have a good grasp.

Many study participants said they talked with 3-, 4-, and 5-year-old children during a child protection investigation to gather information but did not seek their opinion about what they thought should happen. Several participants mentioned that young children did not understand what was going on and that their information was unreliable. Many said that young children's involvement depended on their maturity and stage of development. A few participants reported involving young children in discussing safety plans and said they let young children weigh in on decisions. None of the participants mentioned involving children younger than 9 years in TDM meetings.

CA 11 said that she treated children 5 and under differently from children 7 and older: "Five and under, [that] takes a very different stance from me, because five and under, they're children. They can tell me what's going on, and their bodies will either match what's going on or not going on. It isn't until seven and up through about 12, 13, that they have a better idea of exactly what's going on." CA 21 said that they would be truthful with children about why they were removed from their family, then said, "I wouldn't necessarily have that conversation, I would have a simpler version of it with a three-year-old or a four-year-old but not so much ask them what do you want?"

CA 35 said, "The child doesn't necessarily have much of a say at a young age." CA 25 felt that children younger than 12 did not "have any participation. They just go with the flow. So whatever the adults decide. When children are older than 12, there should be an effort to bring them to the table and ask how they would like to see their life through the child protection system." When the interviewer asked CA 25 why they thought 12 years was the cut-off between participation and nonparticipation, CA 25 responded:

> Because of maturity. A lot of the children, and let's say that a lot of 12-year-olds that I know are really immature, but mainly maturity that they feel like

they can say something and people will listen to them. Before they are 12, they are just like little kids. And they have to do whatever the adults are saying. And there's a lot of fight with that. I see a lot of younger children who are very mature, but unfortunately, they're never, they're interviewed and everything, but they're never asked what do you think about what should happen next? I've never seen it around this table.

Unlike teens, who caseworkers sometimes describe as likely to "vote with their feet" (running away from a placement they do not like or acting out), younger children were viewed as more cooperative, pliable, and less likely to rebel. CA 37 explained that they would tend to give a younger child's opinion less weight than a teenager's: "We can't put our hands on children to keep them running out the door at our shelter, but if [a] seven-year-old tries to run out the door, we're going to try and physically stop them. . . . Now, if a 15-year-old tries to run out the door, we're not allowed to put our hands on them. They can go." CA 22 declared:

> Little children, under ten, if you can still pick them up, you can pretty much control them. You just have to talk to them about "I know you don't agree, you're sad, this hurts you, blah, blah, blah, but we have to make this decision for you, and you're not going to like it, but I promise it'll get better." You just try to smooth it over.

Justifications for Babies' and Younger Children's (Non-)Participation

Many participants mentioned that younger children's lack of ability to understand, speaking ability, maturity, focus, judgment, and reliability precluded participation.[4] CA 4 said that "when I do interviews, children under five, they're really, really sketchy, developmentally, and also with speech." The participant then qualified their statement by saying, "Some [young children] are very precocious and can tell you everything. I've honestly met some three-year-olds that were like that. And then sometimes, I'll have a five-year-old that is maybe not as outgoing . . . and their speech is not as advanced." CA 19 told us that they talked with children as young as 4 or 5 "when the child can articulate what he or she wants." CA 19 then said, "It depends on their developmental maturity, because some at age five, they don't want to talk to us, they say, 'I don't know. I don't know.' All they do is cry or get mad. Then it's really hard. But some kids I've seen at age five, they can say, 'I don't want this, but I want this.'" CA 18 thought that little children's "attention tends to be drifting a little bit more than teenagers." CA 16 was asked how they take the child's age and maturity into consideration when investigating. They replied: "You take it from whence it comes. A four-year-old isn't going to tell you much more than what he ate for breakfast. But they will tell you if they're scared, too." CA 7 thought that "we need to remember they're a five-year-old and listen to them as a five-year-old. Five-year-olds often tell you what they want it to be versus what it really was."

CA 38, who defined younger children as "maybe like nine and under or ten and under," explained why caseworkers take older children more seriously than younger children:

> I think we value the teens' participation, the older kids because we really take into account their opinion and really try to work with them because I just don't believe that things will work out right if they don't buy into it. The younger kids, I think we tend to, I mean, we take their opinion into account, but we also make a lot of decisions . . . just independent of what they think might be the best plan for them. And it's not necessarily to say that they don't have a good plan or whatever, but they're younger, so maybe their views are a little skewed when it comes to certain things, and they're not able to weigh the pros and cons.

One reason that caseworkers started limiting younger children's participation is to protect them. For example, CA 14 believed that "for little children, I think it's more difficult because I want to keep them as much out of the process as possible. I want to make sure that they're safe." CA 14 believed young children to be too vulnerable to be involved. Similarly, CA 37 recounted that "things are going to be said at these meetings that would not be appropriate for a child to be hearing, especially a young child."

CA 12 was in the minority in explaining that children as young as 5 should participate in decisions. When asked why CA 12 thought it is helpful to let children participate in decision-making processes, CA 12 responded:

> It's about them, and as they get older, from about five years on, they have opinions. They're the ones that have watched and experienced what's happened with their parent, whether it's abuse, or neglect, or domestic

violence. And oftentimes, in those risk situations, the way they deal with them is to internalize it. And I think them being able to participate gives them an opportunity to verbalize how it's affecting them and what they want to see happen. I think children, for the most part, are very, very wise about what needs to happen. And so, I think they do need to participate in the situation.

CA 37 explained why they thought even a child as young as 5 or 6 should be involved in decision-making:

Just because you want to make sure you're making the right decision. If you're weighing two things and they're equally as good, and you could go either way, I would ask for buy-in from the child. Because the more buy-in you get from any child, the more success you're going to have if a child really knows what they're even talking about.

CA 20 thought that they would take children's opinions seriously if they were "cognitively ready." The participant said:

If I see that they're cognitively ready, I would definitely talk to them and get them involved. Maybe not two or three, you know. It would be difficult to get their involvement. But I can, I mean not so much them giving me an opinion, but really considering what's best for this child from the perspective of what's best for this child. But I think in terms of active involvement, I would say, if cognitively they're ready to give me their opinion, their ideas, talk to me or give me some direction, I will take it because they're the victim.

CA 34 told us that the youngest child they experienced participating in a TDM meeting was 7. We asked at what ages the worker included children in TDM meetings. The participant replied, "It's usually ... according to how mature they are. We can have a child like seven—the youngest I think I had once—where they wanted to share what happened to them and what they wanted to see happen. So it can vary according to their development, stage, and level of maturity and emotional state."

Some participants mentioned taking younger children seriously because they thought they were honest and could take their statements at face value. For example, CA 33 reported, "Younger ones are very believable." Nine participants cited younger children as honest and truthful. CA 28 explained, "If it's a younger child, my experience is that the younger kids don't lie, and the younger kids don't necessarily distort or exaggerate." Two participants believed that young children could not distinguish between truth and lies, and four mentioned working with young children coached by their parents. Thus, the participants' statements about age and participation reveal huge differences in their views on children.

Older Children's Participation

Most of the participants thought that older children or teens were more capable of understanding their situation and articulating their opinions and wishes than younger children. CA 2 encapsulated this by explaining, "The older kids, definitely from 10 on up, we have a clear list of things for them.... The older they get, definitely, they're in a position that they can participate more." A few participants were reluctant to encourage older children's participation due to concerns about an older child's maturity and traumatization.

The study participants granted older children more power in decisions. They gave them the more significant opportunity to be active, vocal participants in decision-making. The participants thought it was important to grant decision-making power to children as they get older because otherwise, children would "vote with their feet." Several participants mentioned that older children could run away from home or placement if they were not taken seriously or disagreed with decisions being made on their behalf. However, this would put them at greater risk. Participants stated that they were more likely to ask older children questions about what they envisioned as an outcome. In some cases, a child's opinion could significantly influence a case's overall trajectory. For example, CA 24 described the case of a 16-year-old male teenager: "And I asked him, 'How do you want me to help you? What do you think you need?' So we worked together on a plan. And eventually, the child chose to be out of the home." This case emphasized the weight an older child's voice carries and the possibility of genuine participation.

The study participants mentioned granting more control to older children over the extent to which they participate. CA 22 emphasized, "With a teenager, I tell them straight out and straight forward, this is how it is. You can decide to walk away, do this, not participate, whatever. This is your life. So I just tell them that you do have the control in this situation." The participants said they facilitated participation among maturing teenagers by directly granting them more ownership and autonomy in the participation process. They reported promoting children 10 years and older in two ways: First, they invited them to TDM meetings, involved them in independent living programs (ILPs), and encouraged them to take advantage of their right to attend court proceedings. Second, they offered information and practical resources, such as business cards, phone numbers, and transportation.

The most frequently cited method of promoting participation with older children was through inviting them to TDM meetings. CA 5 stated, "They're [children] often not invited, but sometimes if they're teenagers, it might make sense once in a while for them to be able to say what they want to say at one of those meetings." TDM meetings can provide older children with the opportunity to voice their opinions or concerns in front of their parents or caregivers. CA 4 emphasized the value of such meetings: "We've had teen decision-making meetings where ... the mom's like, 'Oh, yes, I'm going to do this or do that.' And the child will say, 'No, you're not,' and sometimes they're the ones that have the right to confront the parents on it. So, I think, depending on how old they are, they're a very important piece of that process." Another caseworker (CA 40) described the weight and importance that personal accounts carry in TDM meetings. The following occurred when a 12-year-old boy living with his physically abusive father asked to participate in a TDM meeting:

> [The boy] described how his father has the shades pulled down, he didn't use the word depression, but the illustration and description said it. He was able to tell his father that he didn't want to be hit in such a manner with a hanger or be abused, and he was in a safe place because we were there. His father couldn't retaliate. So in that situation, his opinion mattered a whole lot.

In this case, the child could directly address his father and express how he wanted the situation to proceed. Other study participants emphasized the importance of promoting teenage participation at these meetings because they make children feel that their voices have been heard, even if their opinions are not decisive to the outcome. The participants thought that older children might be more likely to accept the result of a decision if they had a say. When asked why it is useful to let children be a part of decision-making, CA 10 responded:

> If you don't listen to them and just say, hey, I'm going to make this decision, you really disempower them, and to me, that's not going to help them in the long run anyway. . . . Like when we have a decision meeting, if you can at least include them as part of the decision, tell them what's going on, explain and then listen to them, I think, eventually, what decision you make, they will understand it a lot better, and I think in the long run, psychologically, whatever decision you make, they will settle with that.

Other participants concurred with the value that TDM meetings offer. CA 8 pointed out: "I think it's important for prevention, if all else fails, that children feel that they are being listened to because if they do, then they will be more likely to let us know if something happens in the future."

Many participants stated that they valued older children's opinions and that they are invited to court. CA 20 discussed how a child's participation evolves with age and moves in the direction of more genuine participation: "I think it gets more and more as they grow older, because they will choose to be in court, they will choose to be in meetings, they will choose to represent themselves and express their opinion." The participants mentioned that while older children's voices are heard in courtrooms, they did not indicate that older children's opinions are consistently included in the final decision-making process. The legal age to participate in court-related processes is 10. A few study participants appeared unaware of the specific legal age of court participation or disagreed with the age limit because they thought 10 years was too young. CA 6, for example, said, "For court, I think, to legally ask if they want to come, if they're ten years or older, which I'm not quite sure I agree with that, but it's legal." CA 6 explained why she thought the age threshold was too low: "I think ten years old is young for a child to come to court, because the court, you know, can be kind of a threatening experience, or it can be a traumatic experience because there's attorneys for everybody." Some participants mentioned that while children could voice their opinion in court, it had little sway. CA 19 explained:

> I cannot say anything about participation for children who are under the age of 10 and can't speak for themselves. Because there is an age, I think, not cut-off, but the starting point is, if they are age ten and above, they can

go to court and share their cases. So they have some say, not a whole lot, but they have some say because they have representation. They have a lawyer, they can say, "You know, I want whatever, and I don't want to visit" or "I don't want to go home," or whatever it is that they tell their attorneys. Their attorneys could represent them. So that's the level of their participation. And maybe it's good; I think it's good that they have a voice, and no matter how little it is, they have a voice.

Similar to CA 19, CA 34 thought that children 10 and older, while invited, often had limited decision-making power in court. When an interviewer asked whether they thought the state of California was committed to children's participation in child protection, CA 34 replied:

Not so much. There's legal mandates for participation, but there's no mandate that a kid appears in court. They're invited. There's no mandate that not just the attorney but the judge meets with kids. There's mandates obviously that the workers meet with kids. And I think we're moving, once again, the economy hasn't helped, we're moving towards putting supports in place, particularly for older kids, that takes what they want and need, and what they say they want and need rather than what we want them to want and need, more into account. So there's, I think, a movement towards doing that, but I think we have a ways to go.

From what CA 34 emphasizes above, it is clear that while there is more in place for older children, ultimately the decision-making power rests with the child protection caseworkers. Similarly, CA 35 draws attention to the influence and role attorneys play in the court process:

Depending on how old they are, they can appear in court; their opinions are valued. There are occasions where they do have an attorney who represents their opinion. Fortunately, a lot of attorneys are very clear to [say], they will express their client's opinion to the court, but they will also say what their feeling is because occasionally, that will be different.

In addition to participating in TDM meetings and being invited to and attending court hearings, there are more future-oriented programs offered to older children. ILPs assist teenagers in transitioning from adolescence to adulthood, allowing them to be self-sufficient and stable in the future. Older children's involvement in an ILP will enable children to take a leading role in their future. The participants revealed that case outcomes appeared to have greater compromise when they took a back seat and allowed the older child to be more involved in their ILP. In one case of a 16-year-old girl, CA 2 explained, "She actively went and advocated for herself to get into an independent program at school. And all this because I didn't tell her what to do. Yeah, that's when it becomes really important. In that situation, she took responsibility for herself, and I was just, basically, I was just a car." As CA 35 established, "Teenagers with independent living skills, we have all of these programs that offer them everything, and some of them are really good." Children 10 years and older who become involved in an ILP are given additional support starting at the age of 18 up until the age of 23. CA 2 explained, "The [workers who transition children to independent living] work with them basically from age 18, 19 up until 23. And, usually, they're the ones who'll help them do the college, do the armed forces, do, you know, employment, get an apartment, help them get their I.D.s and checking account, all that stuff."

Less frequently mentioned but still relevant, child protection workers said they promoted the participation of children older than 10 years by offering practical resources and knowledge to their clients. This degree of involvement takes form in providing business cards, giving work phone numbers and hotline information, being a source of transportation, recommending legal counsel, and encouraging older children to seek out child protection services. CA 2 stated, "If they're ten and over, I give them my card, and I say, 'If you need to talk to me, if you have any questions, here. Call me directly.'" Some participants said they encourage their clients to talk with their lawyers to clear up confusion, advise and make children aware of their rights, and advocate for their interests in court. Acquainting a client with their legal counsel can, in some cases, provide a child with another adult who can promote their interests. This support is especially crucial when a caseworker and a child disagree and cannot reach a compromise. CA 12 discussed the importance of being a resource and ally to a child even in the event of a disagreement: "'You have an attorney, and I will get you an appointment with your attorney, and I will take you to his office if you want me to. And I'll let him know that you and I disagree about this, and you can tell him because he's your voice in the courtroom.'" By providing such information, offering additional referrals, and making oneself readily available to the child,

child protection caseworkers hope to move to a greater level of participation among older children.

Justifications for Older Children's (Non-)Participation

Many caseworkers discussed the idea that preteens' or teens' decision-making abilities often overlook certain risk factors that may put their safety in jeopardy. CA 25 addressed a case where a 12-year-old girl wanted to be placed with a best friend she had met on the Internet. While CA 25 did acknowledge the child's wishes, the participant emphasized that "we need to be more specific, more real.... [CA 25 told the child], 'that doesn't sound like it's the best way to go, and we try, we're directing them.'" Several participants made it clear that, ultimately, the final decisions lie with them (child protection caseworkers), as CA 23 underlined: "You don't have to represent to the best degree of what the child's opinion is. What you need to do is help represent the child so that the child is taken care of. That's my position." CA 31 reiterated this idea by stating, "You have a voice, but you are a child." In this way, children 10 and older are often presented with the appearance of more choices than younger children; however, their options remain within the boundaries of what child protection workers consider to be in the child's best interests, especially in regard to their safety.

Several participants contended that age and the child's developmental stage influenced whether they believed children would lie and try to manipulate the caseworkers to achieve what they wanted. Participants made a distinction between the two types of dishonesty that surfaced based on a child's age. The participants generally described younger children as more honest and believable, and when they were dishonest, it was likely from a parent's coaching. Some participants thought that teens were more likely to lie for various reasons, such as wanting more freedom at home. (In the context of lying, child protection workers would usually refer to older children as "teenagers" or "teens.")

Teenagers, however, were more likely to lie for their benefit, according to some of the participants. These participants discussed how they would enter their conversations with skepticism and gauge the likelihood a teenager would lie based on factors such as motivation, language (verbal and physical), and whether they had previously lied. CA 14 described, "For little kids, I don't read into it, I just take it for face value. But older kids is where I have to do a lot of negotiations."

The likelihood that a teen would lie during their initial interaction would influence how participants would engage with the teen later and offer opportunities to participate. When asked about listening to the opinion of older children, CA 21 stated, "You have to be careful with teenagers." Six participants described instances when older children exaggerated when discussing their situation to influence the outcome of their case. The participants sometimes referred to these children in negative terms. For example, CA 4 answered, "And oftentimes it's a narcissistic teenager who's like, 'my parents are totally horrible.'" Some participants believed their clients would lie because they were "system savvy" teenagers who used their experience of the child protection system to manipulate their caseworkers. When asked about children's participation, CA 14 reported, "I think as children get a bit older, it gets a little bit more complicated because some of our kids are very savvy, and so they manipulate the system." Participants reported that the number of opportunities to participate they presented to teenagers was influenced by how long they had been in the system because "institutionalized children know how to manipulate the system" (CA 40).

Not all participants who identified lying teenagers revoked their opportunities to participate. CA 6 described her approach: "We just pretty much talk with them honestly and open, and tell them, 'What you're telling us doesn't match what's going on, and we're not really believing this, so what can we do to make this situation better?'" CA 10 stated it was essential to give children who manipulate a chance to participate and not to disempower them

> because there are some teenagers that are acting out, they do have out-of-control behavior, they do want to manipulate, to tell you where they want to live and where they don't want to live. But if you don't listen to them, just say, "Hey, I'm going to make this decision," you really disempower them.

Discussion and Conclusion

This study aimed to add to prior literature on children's age as a determinant of their genuine participation in child protection–related processes. "Genuine participation" refers to children's views being heard *and* weighed in decision-making processes about children's lives. We analyzed 40 in-depth interviews with child protection caseworkers in California to discover how their perceptions of children differed by age group and how these perceptions affected how they involved children. How did they draw the symbolic boundaries between different age groups? How did their boundary drawing create inequalities between children who experienced genuine participation and those who did not? The process of boundary drawing is a way of sorting individuals into different categories and creating hierarchies. This process can translate into power differentials between people and create social inequalities (Lamont & Molnár, 2002; Lamont et al., 2015).

We analyzed the age-related boundary drawing that child protection caseworkers engaged in and the effects of their classifications on how they provided the conditions for children's involvement. We found that the study participants distinguished between three age groups: babies, young children, and older children (preteens and teens). There were "missing age groups" too: some age groups remained mainly outside the participants' consciousness; they did not frequently mention toddlers or older teens when discussing children's participation.

While participants' responses about age and participation varied, many participants associated the three age groups with characteristics that qualified or disqualified them from genuine participation in decision-making processes about children's lives. The starkest distinction was between children who could express their experiences and opinions (older children) and those who could not (babies and younger children). Many caseworkers linked participation to a child's ability to express their experiences and opinions verbally. There were other age-related boundaries: between children who were too vulnerable to participate (typically babies or younger children) and those who were not (typically preteens and teens); between children who could resist child protection interventions (usually older children) and could participate and those who could not (typically younger children); between children who attended meetings because of the TDM practice model that brought older children to the table and those who did not (primarily children younger than 10); between children who, by law, were invited to attend court hearings (children 10 and older) and those who were not. (Table 8.1 provides a more exhaustive list of the age boundaries and caseworkers' reasonings.)

We would like to conclude with an observation that has significant implications for child protection practice, policy, and research. Our findings suggest that it is vital to apply an intersectional approach (Crenshaw, 1989,

1991; Collins, 1993) to assess how street-level bureaucrats like child protection caseworkers facilitate children's participation. Such an approach can emphasize the intersections of age and ability, which are crucial to creating inequalities in participation that children may experience in child protection. There was ageism (between older children and younger children, not only between children and adults) when it came to child protection workers' involvement in child protection practice: babies and younger children were said to be granted less influence in decision-making than older children. Ageism is connected to ableism because a child's ability to express themselves verbally (and do so clearly) appeared to be a precondition for children's genuine participation for many participants in this study.

Our vision of equal opportunity to participate for all children regardless of their age, ability, and so on, has implications for child protection practice, law, policy, and research. In child protection practice, it could mean that babies and younger children and children who cannot express themselves because of age or a disability are given independent representation by a spokesperson who practices anti-oppressive law or social work (Dominelli, 2002). It could mean that curricula and education and training programs for child protection caseworkers teach about biases toward babies and young children and children who cannot verbally express themselves. It could involve domestic legal and policy language similar to the UNCRC that ensures nondiscrimination for children of different ages, levels of maturity, and abilities. Lundy (2007) explains how Articles 2, 3, 5, 13, and 19 of the UNCRC and the General Comments support Article 12 to safeguard children's right to express a view and have it given weight. Article 2 on nondiscrimination ensures participation rights for marginalized children by requiring states to ensure Article 12 regardless of a child's race, ethnic or social origin, ability, and so on, or other social status (Lundy, 2007). According to Lundy (2007, p. 937), "The Committee has emphasised that in the case of younger children (which it defines as those up to eight years of age), the achievement of participation rights 'requires adults to show patience and creativity by adapting their expectations to a young child's interests, level of understanding and preferred ways of communicating'" (2005, para. 11(c)). It could mean researching how public administrations currently prevent babies' and young children's participation. Together, these types of efforts could be influential in ensuring that all children, regardless of their age and ability to articulate, can have a say in decisions in child protection.

Reflection Questions

(1) What are your views of the capacities and rights of children of different age groups?
(2) How can you ensure that you hear and take seriously the opinions of newborn children, babies, and toddlers in your practice and research?
(3) What do you think are effective ways to overcome participatory challenges related to children's ability to communicate verbally?

Notes

1. Križ & Skivenes (2015) and Križ (2020) provide a more detailed description of our data collection, analysis, and sample.
2. California was chosen because of Skivenes's prior professional contacts and access to study participants.
3. The researchers assigned each study participant a code number to maintain participants' anonymity.
4. Regardless of age, children who did not have the opportunity to participate were the ones who did not meet the criterion of a child's "ability to articulate and understand." The participants described this group of children as developmentally delayed or children with a disability, such as deafness. (Five participants cited a child's disability as justification for not involving them.) Some participants explained that they sought the child's perspective in other ways than through verbal communication, for example, through observation.

References

Advokids. (2018). *Dependency court process*. https://www.advokids.org/legal-tools/juvenile-court-process/

Archard, D., & Skivenes, M. (2009). Hearing the child. *Child & Family Social Work, 14*, 391–399. https://doi.org/10.1111/j.1365-2206.2008.00606.x

Arbeiter, E., & Toros, K. (2017). Participatory discourse: Engagement in the context of child protection assessment practices from the perspectives of child protection workers, parents and children. *Children and Youth Services Review, 74*, 17–27. https://doi.org/10.1016/j.childyouth.2017.01.020

Arts, W., & Gelissen, J. (2002). Three worlds of welfare capitalism or more? A state-of-the-art report. *European Journal of Social Policy, 12*(12), 137–158. https://doi.org/10.1177/0952872002012002114

Attiah, K. (2014, November 21). Why won't the U.S. ratify the UN's child's rights treaty? *Washington Post*. Retrieved on August 12, 2021, from https://www.washingtonpost.

com/blogs/post-partisan/wp/2014/11/21/why-wont-the-u-s-ratify-the-u-n-s-child-rights-treaty/

Berrick, J. D. (2011). Trends and issues in the U.S. child welfare system. In N. Gilbert, N. Parton, & M. Skivenes (Eds.), *Child protection systems. International trends and orientations* (pp. 17–35). Oxford University Press.

Berrick, J. D., Dickens, J., Pösö, T., & Skivenes, M. (2015). Children's involvement in care order decision-making: A cross-country analysis. *Child Abuse & Neglect, 49*, 128–141. https://doi.org/10.1016/j.chiabu.2015.07.001

Berrick, J. D., Peckover, S., Pösö, T., & Skivenes, M. (2015). The formalized framework for decision-making in child protection care orders: A cross-country analysis. *Journal of European Social Policy, 25*(4), 366–378. https://doi.org/10.1177/0958928715594540

Berrick, J. D., Dickens, J., Pösö, T., & Skivenes, M. (2018). International perspectives on child-responsive courts. *International Journal of Children's Rights, 26*, 251–277. https://doi.org/10.1163/15718182-02602011

Bessell, S. (2015). Inclusive and respectful relationships as the basis for child inclusive policies: The experience of children in out-of-home care in Australia. In T. Gal & B. Faedi Durami (Eds.), *International perspectives and empirical findings on child participation: From social exclusion to child-inclusive policies* (pp. 183–205). Oxford University Press.

Bessell, S. (2011). Participation in decision-making in out-of-home care in Australia: What do young people say? *Children & Youth Services Review, 33*(4), 496–501. https://doi.org/10.1016/j.childyouth.2010.05.006

Bouma, H., López López, M., Knorth, E., & Grietens, H. (2018). Meaningful participation for children in the Dutch child protection system: A critical analysis of relevant provisions in policy documents. *Child Abuse & Neglect, 79*, 279–292. https://doi.org/10.1016/j.chiabu.2018.02.016

Burford, G., & Gallagher, S. (2015). Teen experiences of exclusion, inclusion and participation in child protection and youth justice in Vermont. In T. Gal & B. F. Duramy (Eds.), *International perspectives and empirical findings on child participation: From social exclusion to child-inclusive policies* (pp. 227–255). Oxford University Press.

Casey Family Programs. (2019). *Strategy brief: Healthy organizations. How was Safety Organized Practice implemented in San Diego County?* https://www.casey.org/safety-organized-practice/

Children's Bureau. (2021). *Family and group decision-making: State and local examples.* Retrieved on August 23, 2021, from https://www.childwelfare.gov/topics/famcentered/decisions/statelocal-examples/

Children's Defense Fund. (2021). *The state of America's children 2021.* Retrieved on August 23, 2021, from https://www.childrensdefense.org/wp-content/uploads/2021/04/The-State-of-Americas-Children-2021.pdf

Collins, P. H. (1993). Toward a new vision: Race, class, and gender as categories of analysis and connection. *Race, Sex & Class, 1*(1), 25–45.

Crenshaw, K. (1989). Demarginalizing the intersectionality of race and sex: A Black feminist critique of antidiscrimination doctrine, feminist theory and antiracist politics. *University of Chicago Legal Forum, 1*, 139–168.

Crenshaw, K. (1991). Mapping the margins: Intersectionality, identity politics, and violence against women of color. *Stanford Law Review, 43*, 1241–1299.

Dettlaff, A., & Earner, I. (2012). *Children of immigrants in the child welfare system: Findings from the National Survey of Child and Adolescent Well-being.* Migration and Child

Welfare National Network Research Brief. Retrieved on January 3, 2013, from http://www.americanhumane.org/assets/pdfs/children/pc-childofimmigrantpdf.pdf

Dominelli, L. (2002). *Anti-oppressive social work theory and practice*. Palgrave Macmillan.

Esping-Andersen, G. (1990). *The three worlds of welfare capitalism*. Polity Press.

Gilbert, N., Parton, N., & Skivenes, M. (2011). Changing patterns of response and emerging orientations. In N. Gilbert, N. Parton, & M. Skivenes (Eds.), *Child protection systems: International trends and orientations* (pp. 243–257). Oxford University Press.

Hart, R. (1992). *Children's participation: From tokenism to citizenship*. UNICEF International Child Development Center. http://www.unicef-irc.org/publications/pdf/childrens_participation.pdf

Križ, K. (2020). *Protecting children, creating citizens: Participatory child protection practice in Norway and the United States*. Policy Press.

Križ, K., Krutzinna, J., Skivenes, M., & Pösö, T. (2022). The invisible child: A comparative study of newborn removal judgments from a Child Equality Perspective (CEP). *The International Journal of Children's Rights*, 30(3), 644–674. brill.com/view/journals/chil/30/3/chil.30.issue-3.xml

Križ, K., & Roundtree-Swain, D. (2017). "We are merchandise on a conveyer belt": How young adults in the public child protection system perceive their participation in decisions about their care. *Children & Youth Services Review*, 78, 32–40. doi:10.1016/j.childyouth.2017.05.001

Križ, K., & Skivenes, M. (2015). Child welfare workers' perceptions of children's participation: A comparative study of England, Norway and the USA. *Child & Family Social Work*, 11(S2), 11–22.

Križ, K., & Skivenes, M. (2014). Street-level policy aims of child welfare workers in England, Norway and the United States: An exploratory study. *Children & Youth Services Review*, 40, 71–78. https://doi.org/10.1016/j.childyouth.2014.02.014

Lamont, M., & Molnár, V. (2002). The study of boundaries in the social sciences. *Annual Review of Sociology*, 28, 167–195. https://doi.org/10.1146/annurev.soc.28.110601.141107

Lamont, M., Pendergrass, S., & Pachucki, M. (2015). *Symbolic boundaries* (2nd ed., pp. 850–855). International Encyclopedia of the Social & Behavioral Sciences. https://doi.org/10.1016/B978-0-08-097086-8.10416-7

Lansdown, G. (2010). The realization of children's participation rights: Critical reflections. In B. Percy-Smith & N. Thomas (Eds.), *A handbook of children and young people's participation: Perspectives from theory and practice* (pp. 11–23). Routledge.

Lundy, L. (2007). "Voice" is not enough: Conceptualising Article 12 of the United Nations Convention on the Rights of the Child. *British Educational Research Journal*, 33(6), 927–942.

Lofland, J., Snow, D., Anderson, L., & Lofland, L. H. (2006). *Analyzing social settings: A guide to qualitative observation and analysis*. Wadsworth.

Magnussen, A.-M., & Skivenes, M. (2015). The child's opinion and position in care order proceedings: An analysis of judiciary discretion in the County boards' decision-making. *International Journal of Children's Rights*, 23(4), 705–723.

Paulsen, V. (2016). Ungdommers erfaringer med medvirkning i barnevernet. *Fontene Forskning*, 1, 4–15.

Peters, J. (2007). *Representing children in child protection proceedings*. LexisLexis.

Reed, D., & Karpilow, K. (2002). *Understanding the child welfare system in California: A primer for service providers and policy makers.* California Center for Research on Women and Families. http://www.fiscalexperts.com/pdf_files/CWS_Primer.pdf

Rothschild, A. (2017, May 2). Is America holding out on protecting children's rights? *The Atlantic.* Retrieved on August 12, 2021, from https://www.theatlantic.com/education/archive/2017/05/holding-out-on-childrens-rights/524652/

Shemmings, D. (2000). Professionals' attitudes to children's participation in decision-making: Dichotomous accounts and doctrinal contests. *Child & Family Social Work, 3,* 235–243. https://doi.org/10.1046/j.1365-2206.2000.00160.x

Helland, H. S., Križ, K., & Skivenes, M. (Forthcoming). Gauging the child's presence and voice in adoption proceedings of children from care in seven European countries: Applying a Child Equality Perspective. In N. Lowe QC (Hon) & C. Fenton-Glynn (Eds.), *Research handbook on adoption.* An Edward Elgar Research Handbook in Family Law Series.

Social Security Act. (2006). Amended title IV-B reauthorizing the promoting safe and stable families program. Sec. 475 [42 U.S.C 675].

Shier, H. (2001). Pathways to participation: Openings, opportunities and obligations. *Children & Society, 15*(2), 107–117. https://doi.org/10.1002/chi.617

Skivenes, M. (2015). The space for children's participation (in Norwegian). *Tidsskrift for Velferdsforskning, 1,* 48–60.

Ten Brummelaar, M. D., Knorth, E. J., Post, W. J., Harder, A. T., & Kalverboer, M. E. (2018). Space between the borders? Perceptions of professionals on the participation in decision-making of young people in coercive care. *Qualitative Social Work, 17*(5), 692–711.

UNICEF. (2013). *Innocenti report card 11. Child well-being in rich countries: A comparative review.* http://www.unicef.org.uk/Images/Campaigns/FINAL_RC11-ENGLO RES-fnl2.pdf

U.S. Census Bureau. (2019). *Population.* Retrieved on August 23, 2021, from https://www.census.gov/quickfacts/fact/table/US/PST045219

Van Bijleveld, G. G., Dedding, C. W., & Bunders-Aelen, J. F. (2014). Children's and young people's participation within child welfare and child protection services: A state-of-the-art review. *Child & Family Social Work, 20,* 129–138. https://doi.org/10.1111/cfs.12082

Vis, S. A., Holtan, A., & Thomas, N. (2012). Obstacles for child participation in care and protection cases: Why Norwegian workers find it difficult. *Child Abuse Review, 21,* 7–23. https://doi.org/10.1002/car.1155

Vis, S. A., & Thomas, N. (2009). Beyond talking—Children's participation in Norwegian care and protection cases. *European Journal of Social Work, 12*(2), 155–169. https://doi.org/10.1080/13691450802567465

Weisz, V., Wingrove, T., Beal, S., & Faith-Slaker, A. (2011). Children's participation in foster care hearings. *Child Abuse & Neglect, 35*(4), 267–272. https://doi.org/10.1016/j.chiabu.2010.12.007

Willumsen, E., & Skivenes, M. (2005). Collaboration between service users and professionals: Legitimate decisions in child protection - A Norwegian model. *Child & Family Social Work, 10,* 197–206. https://doi.org/10.1111/j.1365-2206.2005.00371.x

9
Arts-Based Research With Children in Program Evaluation in Spain

Nuria Fuentes-Peláez, Ainoa Mateos, M. Àngels Balsells, and María José Rodrigo

Introduction

Children's right to participation is widely recognized in the Spanish legislation on child protection (Organic Law 8/2015) in Articles 2[1] and 9.[2] Article 2 defines the child's best interest, and Article 9 discusses children's right to be heard. However, in practice, children's participation in child protection continues to be inconsistent and depends on the age and maturity of the child. Children's participation in public services is meager (Montserrat et al., 2016). The Spanish child protection services (CPS) often recommend interventions in families but do not involve children. For example, research on children's participation in child protection in Spain by Balsells et al. (2017) found that the information provided to children in out-of-home care is inaccurate and incomplete at all stages of the decision-making process. During the assessment and removal processes, children's participation was limited. Child protection caseworkers did not give information to children before they separated them from their parents. The CPS also did not provide information to children before reunifying them with their parents (Balsells et al., 2017). Recent public debates have addressed whether social services can appropriately care for children without including them (Montserrat et al., 2016; Pösö, 2022).

This chapter will describe an approach to including children in evaluating child protection programs called arts-based research (ABR). ABR is an innovative and promising approach designed to include young children's voices in program evaluation. This methodology, which is based on conversations with children about their art, can be used for inquiring about a particular topic by asking them to produce representations, usually visual, of the subject and then discuss the pictures they created with researchers. It is crucial to examine how children can participate in child protection program evaluation because, to date, research about how children, especially children younger than 8 years, can participate in evaluating child protection services in Spain is scarce. It is essential to consider children's views about programs designed for their benefit because they contribute to a broader view of program assessment in general. This methodology also allows children to make valuable contributions to program evaluations based on their experiences and teaches adults an evidence-based means to capture children's experiences in a program that aims to protect children.

This chapter describes how we employed ABR with children in Spain to ensure their participation in evaluating a parental education program called "Learning Together, Growing as a Family." The program is an example of a preventative family preservation intervention that seeks to promote children's welfare by avoiding high-risk situations that result in out-of-home placements. We provide examples from the Spanish national evaluation of the program from 2015 to 2016 (Amorós et al., 2011, 2015). We will show that children's participation in program evaluation contributes to empowering children because they are at the center of child welfare services. Adults can use the knowledge children provide to improve service effectiveness. Our chapter calls for promoting a child-centered focus in all services, interventions, and evaluations of programs that support children. All services that care for and support children in child protection and other domains should include children's perspectives in their program evaluations since children are the experts of their experiences.

We will first describe the Spanish child protection system before providing background information about the Learning Together, Growing as a Family program, the social services program for children and families that we evaluated with ABR. We will then describe the origins and ethical aspects of ABR and discuss how it promoted children's participation. We will provide examples of children's illustrations and words from the ABR we conducted. We will end the chapter by discussing ABR's benefits and limitations when including children in evaluating social services programs that support vulnerable children and families.

Child Protection in Spain

The European and North American child protection systems have embraced two different orientations to child protection. One approach focuses on protecting children from possible harm or risk of harm and the other promotes children's welfare (Fargion, 2014). These approaches have traditionally been known as "child protection systems" and "child welfare systems." Although scholars have used both terms interchangeably on many occasions, the nuances are important because they have clear implications in practice. The first approach aims for professional objectivity by using standardized means of evaluation of a risk situation. This approach is concerned with dealing with the challenges of evaluating signs of risk. The second approach seeks to understand children's and families' challenges to find ways of providing support with the help of public services (Fargion, 2014).

These orientations affect the types of intervention by child protection agencies. The first system focuses on the individual, and the second is more communal. The Spanish CPS's perspective lies between these orientations. The CPS is increasingly including a collective mindset and working with families to promote child protection. Its interventions start by strengthening families. It offers them different kinds of support in the context of communal, social, educational, and psychological interventions. The intervention continues by activating the protection system in families where the child has been harmed or is at risk of harm. Thus, the interventions evolve depending on the risk to the child and the family's situation (Rodrigo, 2016).

In Spain, 49,985 children between the ages of birth and 18 were at risk and in out-of-home care in 2018. Out of those 49,985 children, 53% were in residential care, and 47% in foster care (Ministry of Health, Consumption, and Social Welfare, 2020). The number of children in care represents 0.56% of Spain's child population. Before an out-of-home placement is needed, CPS has already started intervening. We do not have sufficient overview data about children in Spain regarding the point when the state starts intervening in the lives of vulnerable children and families (before CPS makes an out-of-home placement). We know that the rate of children at risk of poverty and exclusion (the so-called At-Risk of Poverty and Exclusion [AROPE] rate) was 31.30% of the child population. (The term "children" here includes anyone younger than 18 years.) In 2017, the AROPE rate was 29.50%. According to Eurostat's 2017 report, the European average was 24.9% in 2018. Immigrant families have been particularly affected by the economic downturn in Spain and are overrepresented among families in poverty. Unaccompanied children and children of immigrant origins with disabilities are highly vulnerable to social exclusion (López Peláez & Segado Sánchez-Cabezudo, 2015).

The "Learning Together, Growing as a Family" Program

The Learning Together, Growing as a Family program (*Aprender Juntos, Crecer en Familia*; Amorós et al., 2011, 2015) targets families with children ages 6 to 12 years who are in vulnerable situations because of their disadvantaged socioeconomic status and high psychosocial risks. The program aims to help families who rely on social services and parents who need to improve their parenting skills. It supports children and parents. Learning Together, Growing as a Family follows the initiative of the Council of Europe Recommendation 2006/19 on the policy to support positive parenting (Council of Europe, 2006). That policy understands positive parenting as "parental behaviour based on the best interests of the child, that is nurturing, empowering, non-violent, and provides recognition and guidance which involves the setting of boundaries to enable the full development of the child" (Council of Europe, 2006, p. 2).

The program is similar to family protection projects that seek to prevent risk to the child and develop positive parent-child relationships that place the child at the center of the family (Rodrigo, 2016). By putting children at the center, the program ensures that they are heard as individuals with the right to be protected, have a voice, and express their viewpoints. The program aims to build a positive family context for children, which, according to Recommendation 2006/19, is the best way to protect them, guarantee their rights, and ensure their development.

Learning Together, Growing as a Family differs from previous programs. These programs focused on parents' responsibilities to nurture and provide security, education, and affection for their children while ignoring children's rights and the role they play in the family. The program's new focus is a significant turn in child protection professionals' work with families by moving services away from solving problems to preventing them. The program seeks to engage in preventative work by improving parental capabilities, identifying existing weaknesses, and developing strengths. Providing supports to help families face today's parenting responsibilities on all levels of society is vital not only for parents but also, first and foremost, for children (Council of Europe, 2006). The idea behind the program is that services offered to families benefit children, their parents, and society in general.

Local public administrations and nonprofit organizations have implemented the program across Spain with the help of the Social Integration Branch of the La Caixa Foundation. The program started in 2011 and has reached 12,953 children to date. Regarding the children who have participated in the program, 57.7% were boys and 47.3% were girls; 46.39% had a migrant family background. The mean age was 8.8 years (standard deviation [SD] 2.44), and they had lived in families with 2.4 (SD 1.14) children.

The key issues the program targets are the child's emotional bonds in the family, the family's norms and values, intellectual stimulation, shared leisure activities, emotional regulation, communication and conflicts, healthy peer relationships, coping with daily stress, social support, the collaboration between the family and school, and restriction of Internet use (Rodrigo, 2016). The program occurs in a group setting and introduces activities that offer a learning experience of cooperative knowledge building between children and parents. It involves 16 two-hour sessions. In the first hour, the group is divided (parents in one group, children in another). The second hour is devoted to the program's staff working with one big group where parents and children interact. This arrangement ensures that the children can express their feelings and needs, however young they are (Rodrigo, 2016). Finally, another component of the program is that it is evidence based. An interdisciplinary team of researchers from the University of Barcelona, the University of Lleida, the University of La Laguna, and the University of Las Palmas de Gran Canaria carried out the implementation and evaluation process using funding from the La Caixa Foundation.

The program has undergone an evaluation process since the first year the local public administrations and nonprofit organizations implemented it (2011–2012). From 2011 until today, the researchers have evaluated all 980 groups that the program created in Spain linked to the Social Integration Branch of the La Caixa Foundation's *Proinfancia* program (Amorós et al., 2016; Rodrigo et al., 2013). The evaluation attempts to gather evidence of the experiences of children and parents after participating in the program. It analyzes the conditions that make the program effective and sustainable.

CPS utilizes evidence-based programs, and the government is currently expanding the development of evidence-based group programs supporting parental education (Rodrigo et al., 2010, 2013). Rodrigo (2016) defines evidence-based programs like this: "those which are theoretically based, with their contents fully described and structured in a manual, their effectiveness evaluated according to standards of evidence, and the factors that influence the implementation process identified and taken into account to explore variations in program results" (p. 65). There has been some debate about using evidence-based program evaluation in social work practice and education because of the nature and interpretation of concepts that contradict the socio-educational intervention principle of individualization (Plath, 2014). The restrictive viewpoints of evidence-based program evaluation, which interpret the interventions by assessing standardized practices, clash with contextualized socio-educational interventions. The adaptation of the socio-educational intervention seeks a balance between the use of standardized programs and individualized interventions. Continuous evaluation involves the professionals who implement the programs. It requires a redefinition of the programs and the conditions under which they were implemented based on the evidence obtained from the evaluations. Together, these elements provide this balance (Plath, 2014).

We have used a kind of evaluation that exceeds the lineal model of the usual phases involved in evidence-based evaluations. The evaluation we employ encourages more individualized responses. One of the most significant characteristics of our approach is to include young children's experiences and opinions in the evaluation. There is little research including children under 8 years old in program evaluation (Holland, 2009). This lack of research is associated with a perspective that does not consider children as important knowledge carriers. It is also due to the methodological difficulties of including children when designing evaluation research (Winter, 2006). Archard and Skivenes (2009) assert that children should be seen as primary service users and considered experts of their own experiences. In the context of the evaluations of programs that serve children and their families, this child-centric viewpoint implies that children's views are essential for service evaluations.

Development of Arts-Based Research Methods With Children

There are many challenges with capturing children's voices in program evaluation, especially when working with children younger than 8 years. We will show that ABR can help address these challenges. It allows for presenting research findings through children's voices and provides valuable knowledge for practitioners. ABR blends qualitative and quantitative methods to evaluate Learning Together, Growing as a Family. The development of the qualitative methods used in ABR involved a learning process. Based on our experiences, we integrated ABR as a methodological innovation in the evaluation design of Learning Together, Growing as a Family (Amorós et al., 2011, 2015) from 2015 to 2016. Initially, we conducted discussion groups with children, parents, and professionals. These discussion groups gave children, parents, and professionals the opportunity to share their opinions, examine subjects in-depth, and generate an easygoing dialogue between the adult participants. However, the information we were able to obtain from younger children in the groups was limited. Therefore, it was difficult to assess the impact the program had on the younger children. After 3 years of using these discussion groups, we had to look for new methodological approaches to improve children's participation in the evaluation of the program. We then developed a new research project to adapt our evaluation methods to children's needs and experiences. We created a methodological design that would allow us to capture children's voices and experiences in the program.

As we were trying to find a new research method to facilitate group dialogue between children in the program evaluation, we explored using children's drawings to use multiple symbolic representations in research (Coiduras et al., 2016). Research indicates that drawing is an effective way to facilitate communication with children about their experiences. Drawing allows children to express their emotional state and personal experiences, which might otherwise be difficult to do with words (Weber & Mitchell, 1996). ABR gives voice to children through drawing.

There are several benefits of using art in research to hear children's authentic voices about their experiences, perspectives, and opinions. The drawings promote children's communication by allowing them to share their views in a more accessible and personalized way, thus increasing the variety and quality of the information they provide. Allowing children to respond through their art keeps the (adult) researchers from influencing children's answers. The quality of the drawing does not matter; what is essential is the meaning the children want to give it. The meaning of the drawings is created through children's dialogue with the adults. In the conversation, the children comment on the drawings and clarify their meaning. This process keeps the researchers from misinterpreting the meaning of a drawing. In this way, the drawing is a form of "text" that the children can read and explain to the researchers conducting the program evaluation. The adults do not interpret the drawing; it is the children who explain their drawings (Weber & Mitchell, 1996). This approach is equivalent to a level of children's participation on the fifth rank (consulted and informed) of Hart's (1992) well-known ladder of children's participation, or the second level (hearing) in the model proposed by Bouma et al. (2018).

Ethical Aspects and Implementation Process

We applied the ABR method with groups of between three and five children because the literature suggests that small discussion groups are the best way to interview children from 5 to 6 years of age, especially when inquiring about their knowledge of or satisfaction with an experience (Mauthner, 1997; Leitch & Mitchell, 2007). Eighteen discussion groups were formed with a purposeful sample of 86 children from the children participating in the 256 groups in the program between 2016 and 2018. The sample included 53.2% boys and 46.8% girls with an average age of 8.92 (SD 1.84) years. Over one third of the participants (39.35% of the children) were of migrant background. All children spoke Spanish or Catalan in the discussion groups. The sample included participants from each of the different cities participating in the La Caixa Proinfancia Network: Barcelona, Bilbao, Córdoba, Gijón, Las Palmas de Gran Canaria, Lleida, Málaga, Murcia, Palma de Mallorca, Santa Cruz de Tenerife, Sevilla, Santiago de Compostela, Tarragona, Valencia, Vigo, and Zaragoza. The study was commissioned by the La Caixa Foundation Proinfancia program, which reviewed and approved the study design.

Once we selected the evaluation participants, we invited them to participate. When asking children to participate in research, it is important to discuss the status of children as individuals who require protection when they convey their consent to participating in the study (Rodríguez, 2017). In our evaluation, the caseworkers and the parents invited the children to participate in the research. (The parents also participated in the evaluation.) We obtained consent from the parents or guardians. We asked the children for their oral *assent* to participate in the research, thus establishing a partnership between the parents, children, and researchers as recommended by Lambert and Glacken (2011). Lambert and Glacken provide useful, practical examples of the negotiation process in seeking informed consent that is responsive to the ethical conditions required of research studies with children. We followed Lambert and Glacken's six recommendations for the negotiation of informed assent from children. The recommendations for assent include:

A: Assess child's capacity/readiness to assent and engage with child to build rapport

S: Supply child with adequate and comprehensible verbal and written information

S: Search for signs of refusal (subtle or obvious) and ensure no pressure is applied

E: Evaluate evidence of the child's understanding through questions and feedback

N: Negotiate assent continuously

T: Time is allocated for the child to think about whether to participate, or not. (Lambert & Glacken, 2011, p. 787)

We also followed the principles proposed by Neill (2005) by telling the children that confidentiality and anonymity of the information obtained in the research were guaranteed. We also informed them that we could not guarantee confidentiality regarding information about risks to themselves or others that emerged during the study.

The context in which researchers gather information, including aspects such as the level of confidentiality children perceive, the presence of other children or adults, or space, can significantly influence an investigation (Hill, 2006; Rodríguez, 2017). Other elements that affect children's involvement in research have to do with issues such as time control (Hill, 2006). We tried to attend to these issues and held discussion groups with children at the educational centers where the children participated in the program's sessions with their parents. The caseworkers who ran the program did not participate in the ABR interviews with the children, giving them the chance to express their opinions freely. The researchers provided no incentives because they did not want to influence children's willingness to participate. The small number of participants per group enabled individualized attention and clarification of doubts. We told the children how long the interviews would last while seeking their assent. The group interviews lasted 50 minutes on average.

We developed guidelines and recommendations for the interviewers to help create a safe atmosphere for the children. The interviewers included four researchers: one young woman (younger than 26), two middle-aged women, and one middle-aged man. We instructed the interviewers to ask questions following the objectives of the evaluation. These questions invited the children to create drawings about what they thought they had learned and which changes in themselves, their parents, and the family they perceived after participating in the program. The interview begins with the interviewers instructing the children to pay particular attention to creating a pleasant and comfortable environment. For example, an interviewer might create a friendly atmosphere by introducing the research like this: "We have gathered you here to know and share the experiences you have had in the Learning Together, Growing as a Family program. Do you remember what you have done in this program? Each time we meet, we will talk about different topics. Look at these drawings. [The interviewer shows drawings of the program.] They will help us remember all the activities we did. [The interviewer shows an image of each program module and reviews what was done in each module.]"

The interviewers seek to motivate the children and playfully conduct the activities. They try to encourage the children to draw by explaining that all kinds of drawings are valid and that they do not have to create a picture; their creation could be a combination of colors about how they feel about a question. When writing the interview guide, we tried to avoid ambiguous questions and aimed for straightforward questions about what the art meant to the children.

The interviews consist of two parts: In the first part, we explore what children have taken away from the program intellectually, attitudinally, and behaviorally. First, the interviewer asks the children to make a drawing based on the statement "Could you draw for me what you have liked most out of all the things that you have learned in this program (on the days that you have attended)?" This question lets the interviewer collect information about what the children learned and which group sessions were most impactful. The person who conducts the group interview gives children a chance to comment on their art after completing their drawing. The interviewer probes and inquires what the child wanted to express without interpreting the drawing. To achieve this, the interviewer encourages each child to explain what their drawing represents. For example, the interviewer might say, "What takeaway did you want to represent here?" There is no need to ask why unless the child explains it for themselves.

In the second part of the interview, the interviewer follows the same procedure as in the first part. The interviewer might say, "Please think of all the changes that have occurred with you or in your family." After that, the interviewer might ask the children to draw the most critical change or what they liked the most. The interviewer might inquire what children would draw if they had to explain to one of their friends what has changed in their home since they attended the program. The purpose of this question is to capture the changes that may have occurred in parenting and family dynamics after children and parents participated in the program. When the children have finished drawing, the interviewer uses the same process of analyzing the drawings as in the first part; for example, the interviewer might say, "Ask yourselves, which change have you drawn here?" If the child has only drawn one change, then the interviewer asks, "Can you please explain other changes that you may have noticed since you started in the program?"

During the interview, the children might remain silent or not feel like drawing. This did not happen frequently but raised the question of how researchers should handle silences when developing an interviewer's skills. In these situations, the interviewer could explain to the children that it is acceptable if they do not know how to or do not want to respond. The interviewer can then move on to the next question to avoid making the child feel uneasy about the interviewer searching for a response. The interview ends when the children decide it is over. This gives prominence to the children and protects their voices from being limited by the interviewer's agenda.

Finally, it is important to note that the interviewers recorded the ABR interviews with the children's agreement. These conversations about the drawings were transcribed for analysis. In addition, the interviewers collected the children's art, but if they preferred, the children could keep the pictures, and the researcher took a photo of them.

Data Analysis and Presentation of Results

The researchers transcribed the 18 interviews so they could systematically analyze their contents. The researchers used the data analysis software Atlas.ti 6.2 to analyze the interviews, which facilitated the analysis of a large volume of qualitative data. A previous study of the literature on promoting positive parenting allowed us to develop some of the preliminary categories that we thought might be important in the analysis. We had these categories in the back of our minds but did not use them in the first stage of analyzing the transcripts. In this phase, we analyzed the transcripts from the bottom up or grounded in the data (Glaser & Strauss, 1999): we read all the transcripts and selected significant quotes. The second stage of our analysis was conceptual. We tried to arrive at a higher level of abstraction, where we created codes and categories, related them to each other, and then redefined them (Glaser & Strauss, 1999). The two stages were in a continuous relationship throughout the analysis to determine the data's significant themes. This analysis allowed us to identify themes that overlapped in the children's narratives.

Examples of Children's Drawings and Voices

We presented the evaluation results in a report for child protection professionals (Amorós et al., 2017; Fuentes-Peláez et al., 2018). The report sought to describe cases that conveyed a general picture rather than individual and unique circumstances. It discusses the results using essential quotes by the children and drawings that illustrate the themes that emerged from our research. The children expressed similar things with different illustrations. Table 9.1 provides some examples of the results of parental skills training. It shows the kinds of drawings and the conclusion about them in the report (Amorós et al., 2017; Fuentes-Peláez et al., 2018). We have not used the children's names to ensure their anonymity. Children's quotes in Table 9.1 reinforce the idea of the drawings done by other children, which you can see on the left. In the third drawing, the child's explanation corresponds to the drawing.

The following is the excerpt that relates to children's illustrations and writing:

> The changes in the family context that the children detected mainly refer to parents' acquisition of proactive skills (skills that allow parents to act before problems appear) that influence the development of parental skills. The results of the evaluation show how the active role of children in the relationship with parents and in family coexistence promotes changes in parental skills related to expressing their emotions, communication, family organization and shared family leisure time. Children could assess

Table 9.1. Examples of Drawings and Quotes From the Report

Children's Drawings	Explanation of Children
 Boy, 7 years, Barcelona	"I have drawn the theme of communication at home, how to tell my mother more things that used to always silence me." Group interview, boy, 7 years, Galicia
 Girl, 6 years, Palma de Mallorca	"I have changed, and I respect my sister more." Group interview, boy, 8 years, Tenerife
 Boy, 11 years, Vigo	"I made some blue and green spots, which are the cold colors, and then yellow and red. These are warmer, to express the change of the environment at home, from more serious to getting along better and communicating better." Group interview, boy 11 years old, Vigo
 Girl, 11 years, Palma de Mallorca	"Affection for me is very important, because that way your parents show that you are important to them, and of course, not only do parents give you love, but you can also give them love." Group interview, girl, 10 years, Málaga

Source: Amorós et al. (2017, pp. 59–65).

how the methodology of the program favors this feedback effect between parents and children. They discussed experiencing greater autonomy with the acquisition of habits and routines of structured environments that, above all, was reflected in their greater collaboration in (age-appropriate) household tasks, such as making their bed, putting away the groceries, or throwing away the garbage. On the other hand, also in the family context, it was observed how there are participants who emphasize changes in their relationships with siblings, as well as an increase in their participation in different aspects of daily family life. . . . On the other hand, with respect to coexistence and family communication, children identified changes in both their parents, mothers, and them that indicate signs of the ability to express emotions and other assertive communication skills that move away from aggressive communication styles. (Fuentes-Peláez et al., 2017–2018, p. 58, translation ours)

Discussion and Conclusion

Article 12 of the United Nations Convention on the Rights of the Child sparked the moral imperative of "capturing children's voices" (Lewis, 2010). However, how we hear children's voices and include them in evidence-based evaluations (of child protection programs like Learning Together, Growing as a Family) still requires dedication and effort. This chapter discussed the role that young children could play in research processes that listen to their voices from an open, critical, and reflexive position. Researchers have gradually overcome initial skepticism about the validity and reliability of the information provided by children (Lewis, 2010). Our research demonstrated that children have different views from adults on the same issue. Their perceptions of their improvements and their interpretation of changes in parents' roles could be a valuable source for evaluation programs. An analysis of both viewpoints helps construct a more holistic view of a social service program that children participate in (Holland, 2009).

In the debate about the inclusion of children in research and evaluations of child protection programs, we must include study participants' age in the methodological discussion. One of the assumptions that has motivated the exploration of new methodologies is that children's cognitive development affects how we design research methodologies and instruments (Rodríguez, 2017). Children's cognitive development was the driving force behind the methodological changes to program evaluation that we reported here. Our work confirmed that cognitive development is not a unique issue related to age and is more flexible than expected in research endeavors. Platt (2016) helped us reflect on the need to interpret age not exclusively as a synonym for maturity but as a concept linked to personal development that depends on the person and their abilities and contexts. Our research experience has taught us that maturity and age are not the only aspects to consider in research design. Other elements affect researchers' methodological choices, for example, the context in which the research takes place, the researchers' competencies, and their views of children's participation in research and ethical dimensions of research.

We want to highlight two takeaways. The first takeaway concerns the state of childhood in terms of children's protection and respect for privacy. We think these cannot cancel out the possibility of including children in research (Rodríguez, 2017). In terms of research ethics, tensions have arisen between children's participation in research and their protection. Lambert and Glacken (2011) have provided theoretical and practical elements for negotiating informed consent to allow researchers to resolve these tensions. In our research, we resolved it by seeking informed consent from parents and guardians and verbal assent from the children. We clarified the information about confidentiality to children. Although the issue may seem more critical when children are in out-of-home care, the same guidelines apply.

The second takeaway concerns analyzing the drawings that children created with ABR. A potential risk of problems in operationalizing children's voices could arise (see Lewis, 2010). Cruddas (2007) warns of the danger of researchers reproducing a binary distinction between adults and children and reinforcing the "conventional" constructions of childhood. To avoid it, she suggests a dialogue between children and adults and achieving "engaged voices" (Cruddas, 2007, p. 479). For this reason, we emphasized the need to establish a genuine conversation between interviewers and children when implementing ABR. ABR allows the children to explain what they mean by what they have drawn. In our research we have not, however, explored how shared meanings between children and adults, as suggested by Dixon et al. (2019), can be constructed in a way that conceptualizes children as equal participants at the level of analysis. This is a question that future research must address. In summary, it is vital for researchers to critically assess the conditions under which they gather information from children and interpret the data. Researchers need to be mindful of how ethical procedures are applied in evaluation research with children to avoid the danger of silencing them (see Lewis, 2010).

To conclude, ABR is not a method; it is a methodology or way of capturing the meaning of children's experiences in a child-centric way. The results of our evaluation research by using children's drawings as an ABR method confirmed that the results of the evaluation are reliable and constitute an authentic way of accessing children's opinions about the impact of the program on them, their parents, and their families. Children are valid informants (Platt, 2016), and it is vital to hear them when evaluating the interventions that affect them (Archard & Skivenes, 2009; Lange & Mierendorff, 2009). It might help researchers' attitude toward children's participation in research to keep in mind that "it is the instruments that seem problematic, not the children" (Rodríguez, 2017, p. 3). This view could place children, not the method, at the center of evaluation research. The latest legislative reform in Spain created an opportunity for children to express their opinions in ways other than through words. We hope that this reform will be an entry point into innovative, more inclusive methods of communication for children.

Reflection Questions

(1) What kind of barriers do you think may limit children's participation in your research or program/service evaluation?
(2) How do you think you can overcome them?
(3) How can you promote the "engaged voices" concept in research or program evaluation?
(4) According to Lewis (2010), silence is not neutral or empty. How can we listen better and even include "hearing silence"?
(5) How do children benefit after they participate in research or program evaluation?

Notes

1. Article 2 reads: "Superior interest of the child . . . b) Consideration of the wishes, feelings, and opinions of the child, as well as their right to participate progressively,

depending on their age, maturity, personal development, and evolution, in the process of determination of their superior interest" (translation ours).
2. Article 9 reads: "The right to be heard and listened to. 1. The child has the right to be heard and listened to without discrimination of their age, disability, or any other circumstance, both within the family and in any administrative or legal process or mediation in which they are involved and that leads to a decision affecting them personally, socially or within their family, paying attention to their opinions depending on their age and maturity. Towards this end, children must receive the information that allows them to carry out this right in understandable language, accessible formats and adapted to their circumstances. . . . 2. It is guaranteed that children, when they are mature enough, will be able to exercise this right themselves or through a person designated to represent them. The maturity must be evaluated by a specialist, bearing in mind the development of the child and their capacity to understand and assess the specific issue in each case. In any case, the child is considered to be mature enough at twelve years of age. To guarantee that the child can exercise this right, they will be assisted by interpreters. *The child may express their opinions verbally or through nonverbal methods of communication* [emphasis ours]. However, when it is not possible or it is not in the child's interest, the child's opinion may be expressed through legal representatives if they do not have conflicting interests, or through another person who, due to their profession or special relationship of trust with the child, can transmit their opinions objectively" (translation ours).

References

Amorós, P., Byrne, S., Mateos, A., Vaquero, E., & Mundet, A. (2016). "Learning together, growing with family": The implementation and evaluation of a family support programme. *Psychosocial Intervention, 25*, 87–93.

Amorós, P., Fuentes-Peláez, N., Mateos, A., Pastor, C., Mundet, A., Rodrigo, Mª. J., Byrne, S., Balsells, Mª A., Vaquero, E., & Martín, J. C. (2017). *Programa "Aprender juntos, crecer en familia": Informe de evaluación 2016–2017* [Learning together, growing as a family. Evaluation report 2016–2017]. Fundación "la Caixa" and Universidad de Barcelona.

Amorós, P., Fuentes-Peláez, N., Mateos, A., Pastor, C., Rodrigo, M. J., Byrne, S., Balsells, M. À., Martín, J. C., & Guerra, M. (2011, 2015). *Aprender juntos crecer en familia*. Obra social Fundació.

Archard, D., & Skivenes, M. (2009). Hearing the child. *Child & Family Social Work, 14*, 391–399. https://doi.org/10.1111/j.1365-2206.2008.00606.x

Balsells, M. À., Fuentes-Peláez, N., & Pastor, C. (2017). Listening to the voices of children in decision-making: A challenge for the child protection system in Spain. *Children and Youth Services Review, 79*, 418–425. https://doi.org/10.1016/j.childyouth.2017.06.055

Bouma, H., López López, M., Knorth, E., & Grietens, H. (2018). Meaningful participation for children in the Dutch child protection system: A critical analysis of relevant provisions in policy documents. *Child Abuse & Neglect, 79*, 279–292.

Coiduras, J., Balsells, M. À., Alsinet, C., & Urrea, A. (2016). La participación del alumnado en la vida del centro: una aproximación desde la comunidad educativa

[Student participation in the life of a center: An approach from the educational community]. *Revista Complutense de Educación, 27*, 437–456. https://doi.org/10.5209/rev_RCED.2016.v27.n2.46353

Council of Europe. (2006). *Recommendation Rec(2006)19 of the Committee of Ministers to member states on policy to support positive parenting.* https://search.coe.int/cm/Pages/result_details.aspx?ObjectId=09000016805d6dda

Cruddas, L. (2007). Engaged voices—Dialogic interaction and the construction of shared social meanings. *Educational Action Research, 15*(3), 479–488. https://doi.org/10.1080/09650790701514937

Dixon, J., Ward, J., & Blower, S. (2019). "They sat and actually listened to what we think about the care system": The use of participation, consultation, peer research and co-production to raise the voices of young people in and leaving care in England. *Child Care in Practice, 25*(1), 6–21. https://doi.org/ 10.1080/13575279.2018.1521380

Fargion, S. (2014). Synergies and tensions in child protection and parent support: Policy lines and practitioners cultures. *Child and Family Social Work, 19*(1), 24–33. https://doi.org/10.1111/j.1365-2206.2012.00877.x

Fuentes-Peláez, N., Mateos, A., Pastor, C., Mundet, A., Rodrigo, Mª. J., Byrne, S., Balsells, Mª. A., Vaquero, E., & Martín, J. C. (2018). *Programa "Aprender juntos, crecer en familia": Informe de evaluación 2017–2018* [Learning together, growing as a family: Evaluation report 2017–2018]. Fundación "la Caixa" and Universidad de Barcelona.

Glaser, B. G., & Strauss, A. L. (1999). *Discovery of grounded theory: Strategies for qualitative research.* Routledge.

Hart, R. (1992). *Children's participation: From tokenism to citizenship.* Earthscan/UNICEF.

Hill, M. (2006). Children's voices on ways of having a voice: Children's and young people's perspectives on methods used in research and consultation. *Childhood, 13*(1), 69–89. https://doi.org/10.1177/0907568206059972

Holland, S. (2009). Listening to children in care: A review of methodological and theoretical approaches to understanding looked after children's perspectives. *Children & Society, 23*(3), 226–235. https://doi.org/10.1111/j.1099-0860.2008.00213.x

Lambert, V., & Glacken, M. (2011). Engaging with children in research: Theoretical and practical implications of negotiating informed consent/assent. *Nursing Ethics, 18*(6), 781–801. https://doi.org/10.1177/0969733011401122

Lange, A., & Mierendorff, J. (2009). Method and methodology in childhood research. In J. Qvortrup, W. A. Corsaro, M.-S. Honig (Eds.), *The Palgrave handbook of childhood studies* (pp. 79–93). Palgrave-McMillan.

Leitch, R., & Mitchell, S. J. (2007). Caged birds and cloning machines: How student imagery "speaks" to us about cultures of schooling and student participation. *Improving Schools, 10*(1), 53–71.

Lewis, A. (2010). Silence in the context of "child voice." *Children and Society, 24*(1), 14–23. https://doi.org/10.1111/j.1099-0860.2008.00200.x

López Peláez, A., & Segado Sánchez-Cabezudo, S. (2015). Child welfare systems and immigrant families. The case of Spain. In M. Skivenes, R. Barn, K. Križ, & T. Pösö (Eds.), *Child welfare systems and migrant children: A cross country study of policies and practices* (pp. 109–133). Oxford University Press.

Mauthner, M. (1997). Methodological aspects of collecting data from children: Lessons from three research projects. *Children and Society, 11*(1), 16–28.

Ministry of Health, Consumption, and Welfare. (2020). *Boletín de datos estadísticos de medidas de protección a la infancia, nº 22* [Statistical data bulletin on child protection measures]. Retrieved on August 3, 2021, from https://observatoriodelainfancia.vpsocial.gob.es/estadisticas/estadisticas/home.htm

Montserrat, C., Casas, F., Sisteró, C., Baena, M., Català, C., Fité, M., & Barrientos, A. (2016). *Les Intervencions psicosocioeducatives en famílies amb infants en risc en el marc dels Serveis Socials Bàsics* [Psychosocioeducational interventions in families with children at risk in the framework of basic social services]. Ajuntament de Barcelona. Benestar Social.

Neill, S. J. (2015). Research with children: A critical review of the guidelines. *Journal of Child and Health Care, 9*(1), 46–58. https://doi.org/10.1177/1367493505049646

Plath, D. (2014). Implementing evidence-based practice: An organisational perspective. *British Journal of Social Work, 44*, 905–923. https://doi.org/10.1093/bjsw/bcs169

Platt, L. (2016). *METHOD GUIDE 5: Conducting qualitative and quantitative research with children of different ages*. http://www.globalkidsonline.net/platt

Rodrigo, M. J. (2016). Psychosocial intervention. *Psychosocial Intervention, 25*(2), 63–68. https://doi.org/10.1016/j.psi.2016.02.004

Rodrigo, M. J., Máiquez, M. L., & Martín, J. C. (2010). *La educación parental como recurso psicoeducativo para promover la parentalidad positiva* [Parental education as a psychoeducational resource to promote positive parenting]. Federación Española de Municipios y Provincias (FEMP).

Rodrigo, M. J., Martín Quintana, J. C., Mateos, A., & Pastor, C. (2013). Impact of the "Learning Together, Growing in Family" programme on the professionals and attention to families services. *Revista de Cercetare Si Interventie Sociala, 42*, 145–165.

Rodríguez, I. (2017). La participación de la población infantil en el ámbito de los métodos cuantitativos de investigación [The participation of the child population method in quantitative research methods]. *Sociedad e Infancias, 1*, 283–298. https://doi.org/10.5209/soci.55895

Pösö, T. (2022). Children's consent to child welfare services: Some explorative remarks. *Children & Society, 11*(1), 52–65. https://doi.org/10.1111/chso.12483

Weber, S., & Mitchell, C. (1996). Drawing ourselves into teaching: Studying the images that shape and distort teacher education. *Teaching and Teacher Education, 12*(3), 303–313.

Winter, K. (2006). Widening our knowledge concerning young looked after children: The case for research using sociological models of childhood. *Child & Family Social Work, 11*(1), 55–64. https://doi.org/10.1111/j.1365-2206.2006.00385

10
The "Making My Story" Project in Brazil

Monica Vidiz, Lara Naddeo, and Debora Vigevani

Introduction

This chapter explores the potential for change and limitations of the "Making My Story" project (*programa Fazendo Minha História*) in children's participation. The project aims to ensure that children and adolescents in out-of-home care possess the means to express themselves through knowing and owning their past, present, and future stories. It seeks to improve children's involvement in decisions about their lives in the context of group and residential and foster care.[1] We will describe our experiences as professionals involved in the project and discuss its theoretical underpinnings, which are derived from psychology and psychoanalysis (Dolto, 1989; Marin, 1999; Safra, 2005; Winnicott, 1975, 2005a, 2005b) and the sociology of childhood (Alanen, 2001; Mayall, 2015; Qvortrup et al., 2009). We will examine important aspects of children's involvement in decisions about their lives with the help of case vignettes related to Lundy's (2007) model of participation.

We chose to examine these aspects because we perceived them as relevant based on our experience in the project and the literature on children's participation. These aspects include intergenerational emotional bonds (Gallagher et al., 2012; ten Brummelaar et al., 2018; Van Bijleveld et al., 2015). We also draw on a view of children as active participants from a very young age, which involves listening to more than children's words (Alderson, 2004; Alderson & Morrow, 2011; Eliacheff, 1995; Gallagher et al., 2012), and children's actual influence on decision-making (Gallagher et al., 2012; Lundy, 2007). We will argue that the Making My Story approach contributes to children's participation in a way that involves their voice, space for children to be heard, and an audience (see also Lundy, 2007). We will suggest that children's ownership of their life stories is fundamental to their participation. However, children's influence is still constrained by the social dynamics that assign them a powerless position in decision-making.

Monica Vidiz, Lara Naddeo, and Debora Vigevani, *The "Making My Story" Project in Brazil* In: *Children and Young People's Participation in Child Protection*. Edited by: Katrin Križ and Mimi Petersen, Oxford University Press.
© Oxford University Press 2023. DOI: 10.1093/oso/9780197622322.003.0010

For this chapter, we have adopted the definition of participation used by the United Nations Committee on the Rights of the Child (UNCRC, 2009). According to the UNCRC (2009), participation is understood as "ongoing processes which include information sharing and dialogue between children and adults based on mutual respect, and in which children can learn how their views and those of adults are taken into account and shape the outcome of such processes" (p. 5). We use Lundy's (2007) model of children's participation as our theoretical underpinning. This model distinguishes between four elements involved in participation processes: space, voice, audience, and influence. The term "space" refers to environments that children trust where they have opportunities to develop and express their views. The element of voice relates to adults giving children appropriate information and the opportunity to communicate their perspectives. The audience element refers to those who are interacting with children during participation processes. In Lundy's words: "The voice [of children] must be listened to." The last element— influence—refers to the actual impact that children's perspectives have on decision-making or the extent to which their opinions are taken into consideration and used to shape the outcomes of decision-making processes (Lundy, 2007). Lundy acknowledges that participation processes are dynamic and that these stages are interrelated.

We would like to note that this chapter focuses on children's engagement in the micro processes of decision-making because the project has proven to be especially valuable for these processes. At the same time, we understand that children's participation involves both interactional and structural aspects of children's lives—the micro and macro spheres. We have also chosen this focus because prior research indicates multiple challenges in children's meaningful participation in the residential care context (see, e.g., ten Brummelaar et al., 2018).

Child Protection, Out-of-Home Care, and Children's Participation in Brazil

Brazil is the fifth largest country in the world in terms of both area and population. Its population is very diverse due to massive migrations in the 19th and 20th centuries. Although Brazilian society has historically been considered a "racial democracy" (Freyre, 1956), it is nonetheless marked by racism and classism, following slavery and Brazil's colonial legacy. Racism, classism, and colonialism have influenced children's place in Brazil's history. The history of children's out-of-home care dates to the colonial period, when institutional care focused on the state spreading Christian values and Eurocentric culture. After being a Portuguese colony from (what is commonly called) the country's "discovery" in the 1500s until its independence in 1822, Brazil experienced a 20-year-long military dictatorship and became a democratic federal republic in 1988. When slavery was abolished in 1888, social policies hardly existed, and the number of formerly enslaved people and impoverished children and teenagers living in the streets increased. In 1927, the government issued a legal code that stipulated the state's responsibility for children and adolescents in so-called irregular situations, such as children living on the streets. This code aimed to control abandoned and delinquent children and isolate them to protect society (Rizzini & Rizzini, 2009).

At that time, out-of-home care services consisted of large institutions far from city centers and were enclosed by fences. Health services, academic education, and recreational activities took place in these institutions, allowing little interaction between the children and their communities. Children in care were raised in these rigid and controlling institutions, fueled by the perception that they were hoodlums or victims. Following the UNCRC and strong social pressure, the government enacted the Statute of the Child and Adolescent in 1990 (Brasil, Presidência da República, 1990). This statute is the most important basis of children's rights in Brazil today. It considers children and adolescents citizens entitled to rights and who deserve protection (instead of punishment; Rizzini & Rizzini, 2009).

The statute establishes that children's development and reunification with their families are central goals for care services. Out-of-home care is a temporary protection measure for children and adolescents who are at risk of or suffer from the violation of their rights. The decision about care is taken by the so-called child and youth court and involves a judiciary process, which may result in children being in the state's care. The official guidance documents accompanying the statute indicate that out-of-home care services should simulate a family life experience, even though they must be run professionally. This should be achieved with the help of smaller group and residential homes that resemble private homes. (No more than 20 children and adolescents live there.) Brazilian regulation establishes three different types of care placements (Brasil et al., 2009): There are foster families (placement of one child or a few children in the home of a family) and "home-like residences" or *casa-lar*. These are group homes for up to 10 children and a professional resident care provider. There are also larger group homes that care for up to 20 children, with about 10 professional care providers working alternate shifts. Children in group and residential care homes range from 0 to 18 years old. The distribution of these age groups is quite balanced, as well as their gender (CNJ, 2020). Since the enactment of the statute, residential care institutions have gradually become more integrated, promote transitions for children and teenagers in and out of care, and increase their engagement with the community (Rizzini & Rizzini, 2009).

There are 34,157 children and adolescents in out-of-home care in Brazil (CNJ, 2020). This is a small number in proportion to the total child population and compared to other countries. Children represent almost one third of the Brazilian people, accounting for 65 million people (Abrinq Foundation, 2019), but children in care represent less than 0.001% of the total child population. They are members of economically and socially marginalized families, and 64.3% of them are Afro-Brazilians (so-called *negras* or *pardas*; CNJ, 2020).

The main reasons children enter care are neglect and parental drug or alcohol abuse, domestic violence, and homelessness (CNJ, 2020). Poverty is still considered a direct or indirect reason for children entering care, even though legally, poverty is not an acceptable reason for removing children from their families, given that the state can provide social assistance and protective measures. Data about the number of children in care in Brazil is not consistent. We know that 96% of children in care are in residential care homes in groups of up to 20 children and teenagers, and only 4% of children live with foster families—a type of service that is increasing very slowly (CNJ, 2020).

Brazilian legislation mirrors the principles of the UNCRC, which established children's rights to opinion, expression, and participation (Article 16 in Brasil, Presidência da República, 1990). In out-of-home care, the statute guarantees the right of children to be informed and "be heard and participate in the actions and the definition of the measure of protection . . ., and having their opinion considered by the judiciary authority" (Brasil, Presidência da República, 1990, translation ours). However, child protection in Brazil faces significant challenges in conceptualizing and putting children's participation into practice. The term "participation" has an expansive meaning in child protection and can relate to different spheres of children's social engagement. This broad definition is one of the challenges of implementing participation, as suggested by Woodhead (2010). The Brazilian children's rights system focuses on children's provision and protection rights, which it views as more relevant than participation. This focus reflects the system's welfare-based (or *assistencialista*) tradition concerning impoverished children and is shaped by social constructions of children and families in poverty as recipients of charitable intervention (Rizzini & Rizzini, 2009).

As noted by childhood studies scholars (Qvortrup et al., 2009), children's vulnerability and focus on their "becoming" (a view of children as adults in the making) emphasize adults' position as responsible for protecting children's present and future. This understanding of children assumes that adults are responsible for determining what children's "best interests" are, even though children may have their views considered. This perception of children constrains participation and enhances paternalism. When it comes to children in care, adults' biases toward children's families of origin support paternalism: impoverished and vulnerable families are considered "dysfunctional" and "undesirable" (Rizzini et al., 2007, p. 18). The tension between participation and protection is thus reinforced by an underlying intent by the system to "civilize" these children or "save" them from their origins and prevent them from facing their destinies as impoverished individuals, criminals, or vagabonds. We employ Taft's (2015) understanding of the intersection between participation and identity here: "Participation involves not only being able to speak but also to having one's identity, status and opinion recognized as worthy of respect and serious consideration" (p. 462). Participation can hardly be considered as implemented if children's origins and points of view are not recognized and valued by the adults charged with their care.

It is essential to highlight the practical issues that hinder children's participation in residential care services. These services have mainly been developed by nonprofit organizations that receive insufficient funding from the municipalities. Professional teams are often overwhelmed with practical tasks and lack the time and ability to implement children's involvement. The low wages of group home professionals often result in high levels of staff turnover, which impedes the creation of lasting bonds between professionals and children and hinders a productive work environment (Furlan & Souza, 2013; Siqueira & Dell'Aglio, 2006). Court professionals oversee a high number of cases and are not able to meet each child with the adequate time and frequency needed: only 12% of the court teams are exclusively in charge of child and youth cases, whereas 88% concurrently respond to criminal, civil, and family cases (D'Agostino, 2014).

The "Making My Story" Project

The Making My Story project was created in 2002, a few years before the foundation of the Making History Institute (*Instituto Fazendo História* or IFH, at https://www.fazendohistoria.org.br/). The project was developed by Claudia Vidigal, a psychologist who was one of the founders of the institute. She conceived the project when out-of-home care services still consisted of large institutions enclosed by fences, where children and adolescents did not receive personalized care. While she was completing her bachelor's degree, Claudia was volunteering at an institution that cared for 400 children. The professionals of these large group homes rarely knew children's basic information, such as their names or ages. The young children spent most of their day alone in their cribs. Claudia's job involved providing stimulation for Natalie, an 11-month-old child, whom she met weekly. Claudia Vidigal said:

> I remember I walked into a big room with a lot of children and many diapers to be changed. [There were] too many children and too little history. That was my concern: who is this child? Sometimes one educator didn't know a child's name and had to ask another one.... It lacked individuality. When Natalie left, I got the feeling that everything I had experienced with her there would be forgotten, too. Who could tell her what had happened? How would she know that she only walked for the first time when she was two years old because she was afraid to put her foot down on the floor since she spent too much time in the crib? Then I thought: every child is unique. You need to have your story guaranteed. And this is how the project was born. (IFH, n.d., p. 10, translation ours)

In 2005, Claudia and three other psychologists, who also worked in out-of-home care services, decided to join forces and establish the institute. All of them practiced with methodologies that complemented each other and aimed at improving the quality of care for children and adolescents. The mission of the Making History Institute is to contribute to the development of children and teenagers living in care and support them to take ownership of their lives and transform their stories. Since its creation, the institute has reached different states of Brazil and has worked with approximately 12,000 children and young people living in care. Making My Story works with an average of 25 out-of-home care services as official partners per year. In addition, about 20 group and residential homes develop the methodology themselves each year. In 2020, the project reached 628 children and adolescents. The project has been implemented with a proportionally small number of children and adolescents who are in care services in Brazil. Although the official national guidance for care services mentioned the methodology (Brasil et al., 2009), its implementation is not mandated by law. The project's reach is limited because its use demands human and financial resources, especially when developed through a formal partnership with the institute, which includes intensive training and support.

The institute is funded through a variety of sources to ensure its operations and sustainability. It receives donations from people and companies and funding through grants and public calls, either from private foundations or the government. In addition, a significant part of the budget comes from our work through the training and supervision services contracted by care services and municipalities (IFH, 2020).

Making My Story and other projects developed by the institute are open methodologies. This means that any organization can produce them, either with the close supervision and support of the institute through a formal partnership (funded by the institute's resources or paid for by the organization) or autonomously through a wide range of educational and supportive material provided at no cost.

The Making My Story team is responsible for training, selecting, and supervising collaborators who work with children and teenagers. Collaboration happens through group meetings, which take place systematically. The team is involved in organizing and disseminating the project methodology and in training and supporting other professionals to conduct these activities. For example, we provide training and arrange meetings with the group home professionals to guide them through the challenges faced in implementing the project. All three authors developed this role in the project for several years (from 2007 to the present time), and one of us has become the project coordinator.

Most organizations that have developed a formal partnership with the institute are in São Paulo, the same city as the institute. The Making My Story methodology is well known in several regions of Brazil. Care services in many areas of Brazil develop their methods independently once their teams participate in the trainings we provide or because they were inspired by the educational resources available on the institute's website. Many organizations that develop the methodologies themselves stay in contact with our team and rely on our support to exchange experiences, clarify doubts, and obtain guidance, thus maintaining an informal partnership.

Among other strategies developed by the institute, the Making My Story project aims at ensuring a means of expression so that every child and adolescent in care knows and owns their past, present, and future story. The project originated from the need to help children understand more about their stories, families, and situation in care (Marin, 1999; Dolto, 1989). The genuine respect for children's life stories, families, and the right to truth is at the core of its approach. Children's understanding of their past and present help them develop their opinions and express their life possibilities. It enables them to create awareness about their life projects, thus empowering them and affecting their future, since providing information is a crucial aspect of participation (Cashmore, 2002; Lundy, 2007).

Rationale

The project originates in the understanding that life in care is a sensitive period for children. In this period, it is especially valuable for children to develop close relationships with adults and experience a trusting environment where they can talk about and understand their life stories. Children's right to know their history and become involved in decisions about their lives is fundamental to Making My Story. An appreciation of children's literature as a valuable cultural asset and a means for children to get in touch with and talk about their life stories was an important starting point for creating the project. The reading intervention—the act of adults reading aloud to children, young people, or adults, literate or not, freely, and pleasurably—was adopted as a strategy in the project, based on scholarship that studied the relationship between children's literature and their emotional development (Bettelheim, 2011; Coelho, 2002; Freire, 2011; Petit, 2009a, 2009b; Reyes, 2010). According to Coelho (2002), "In the encounter with literature, people have the opportunity to enlarge, transform or enrich their existence of life in degree and intensity not equaled to any other activity" (p. 29, translation ours).

Reading fictitious stories is a great way to encourage children to talk about themselves because it makes it easier for them to realize and understand what they have experienced. Books are an invitation to the fantasy world and offer another door into lived experiences. When we encounter a story, we can access our feelings, thoughts, and internal conflicts through the eyes of a character. This process allows us to name feelings that we had not acknowledged. We can see new possibilities, recharge our hopes, dream, and build future projects. According to anthropologist Petit (2009a, 2009b), reading fictional stories provides children with knowledge, words, stories, and images that give them something to hold on to in moments when they feel lost and scared. Narratives provide children with continuity and order, even when breakdowns in care have characterized their lives.

Transition to care typically involves many changes in children's routine, daily practices, and social environment. Children are away from their homes, friends, and neighbors and usually attend a new school. For children, the routine of a residential home or a foster family is different from before. The rules are different, and the adults they encounter are strangers at the beginning. In this initial period, it is usual that children are not sufficiently informed about the reasons leading to the separation from their families and their future perspectives. As suggested by the literature (Marin, 2010), our team noticed that this commonly leads to children's superficial or imaginative understanding of the situation, increasing feelings of loss, loneliness, displacement, fear, and anger, and possibly hampering their adaptation to the new routine. Children sometimes experience a lack of information and conversations with professionals longer than the initial stage.

Out-of-home care must be a period in which children and young people feel protected and create trustful relationships that support their sense of belonging, autonomy, and participation. Receiving adequate information about their family context, the child protection measure, different alternatives, and their consequences is a right and essential for children's well-being. As the elements of space and voice in Lundy's (2007) model suggest, information is crucial for a child to form and give an opinion. The right to information is intrinsic to the right to participation. Children can express and elaborate on their views about their life story only in a safe environment, with adults whom children trust. Our professional experience in the Making My Story project confirms research that indicates the importance of at least one person who is close to the child. This person listens to the child's views and facilitates their communication with the adults responsible for decision-making. This is especially important considering that decisions about children's lives are usually made by adults who may not have close bonds with them, such as social workers, lawyers, psychologists, and judges (Gallagher et al., 2012; ten Brummelaar et al., 2018).

In the Making My Story project, one (and always the same) adult meets weekly and individually with a child or adolescent for as long as the child protection measure lasts. This adult is trained and supported by a psychologist or social worker from the institute's team of professionals and is usually a volunteer. However, it can be a professional who works at the residential care home or a foster parent. This adult is referred to as a "collaborator" by the project team. During the weekly encounters, the adult and child (or adolescent) play, talk, read books, and build a life storybook with photos, drawings, paintings, texts, and stories narrated by the child or adolescent.

The general goal of Making My Story is to offer a means of expression for each child and adolescent to elaborate and appreciate their past and present story. The three specific goals of the project are to encourage children and adolescents to read more and with greater pleasure; to allow each child and adolescent to recognize the value of their story and have it recorded in an album (the life storybook); and to promote warm, loving conversations about life stories between adults, children, and adolescents.

Each participating residential home counts on a collection of at least 150 children's books, which can be read and used during these encounters. The library consists of various books that encompass universal themes, such as friendship, loss, family, emotions, and so on. Upon starting the project, each child will receive a blank life storybook to fill out in a way they want, for example, a graphical and textual representation of the various aspects of their life. This book is their own, and children will take it with them when they leave care. The project guidelines state that participation in Making My Story must be voluntarily chosen by the child, never forced. The project team instructs the professionals of the residential care home to talk with children to explain the project and invite them to participate. They tell them to respect children's willingness to participate and train them to make it clear to children that they have the choice to not participate in the project or withdraw from it at any time. In the first meeting with the child, the collaborators read an agreement that explains what the project is about, how it will work, how frequently they are going to meet with the child, and for how long. Both the collaborator and the child sign this contract and usually put it on the first page of the storybook.

With the weekly support of the collaborator, the storybook becomes a place for children to record and preserve their journey, with important information about their identity, family, time in care, friends, school, perspectives, and dreams for the future. The book is created with the active participation of children and adolescents. They are the ones who choose the themes of each page, written content, colors, and graphics. Even when the children are not literate, their words and ways of telling stories are used by the collaborators, who write down what the child says.

The meetings between the collaborators and children take place in the residential home or the foster home. The room must provide privacy and enable the children to address topics at their own pace. Themes concerning the past, present, and future can be addressed. It is common that issues related to the current time are easiest to access at the beginning of the relationship. The bond between the collaborator and the child, the constant presence of the collaborator, and respect and trust help the child understand the conditions that led them into care and speak about it freely in a safe space.

The methodology is flexible and can be adapted to the child's age, cultural context, and preferences. Collaborators must use tools that coincide with each child's universe. These tools can be different kinds of books, toys, games, and activities. Play and fun are essential to engaging the children and creating a bond between children and collaborators. Alternative resources such as photography and video creation may also be used. These tools have proven to be especially useful with adolescents. With a camera or mobile phone, they can record relevant aspects of their daily life and history. In our experience, we have seen the importance of offering various resources to children to express themselves. Some may not feel comfortable with writing, for example, so that drawing can be a better option. In this way, we respect each child and try to adjust to their moment of life, interests, and abilities, based on the importance of using different techniques appropriate to each child's needs, age, and moment in life (Gallagher et al., 2012; Healy & Darlington, 2009; Winter, 2010).

The following quote by a teenager who participated in the project illustrates some of its outcomes:

I came to the residential center two days after my sixteenth birthday.... I couldn't stand that place, but gradually things started getting better. One thing that caught my attention was the life storybook of "Making My Story" that all children and adolescents made. For this reason, I told the center's social worker that I also wanted to do my life storybook.... When I first saw Ana [the collaborator], I was a little surprised. I had imagined a different appearance because I didn't know any volunteer, and like any human being, I had my pre-judgment. It may not be ethical to say what I thought about her in our first meetings. . . . I thought she was just a preppy woman, that she had no job and that she was trying to spend her time with a poor girl. I felt like an object, but still, the longer I stayed with her, the more I liked her. . . . Over time, everything changed, and finally, I realized that I was totally wrong! I changed my perception and opened myself to Ana. To her, I could speak about my fears, my mistakes, my passions, anyway, everything. (Account of Patricia, in IFH, 2013, translation ours)

The institute has adopted several strategies over time to evaluate the project's results by measuring the outcomes related to its three goals. The concept of participation was never directly explored in the evaluations. However, we have assessed this aspect by using reports of volunteers and professionals at the residential homes and the direct experience of our team. We have undertaken the annual evaluation of the project with the help of focus groups with children; questionnaires answered by children, volunteers, and professionals at the care homes; direct observations by the project team; and reports by volunteers and professionals of the care services collected by the project team. Currently, we are using questionnaires that the children and adolescents answer with the help of their volunteers.[2]

These evaluation strategies that the institute has used do not adopt scientific standards. An evaluation (Tiwari et al., 2017) undertaken by a research team from the University of East London (UEL) in 2017 was informed by Oxfam's framework for assessing developmental impacts (Green, 2012). This unpublished evaluation provided an external perspective on the Making My Story project. It assessed the impact of the project methodology on children and adolescents who participated in a specific version of the project. Secondly, it assessed the long-term impact of the project methodology on children and young people who have participated in several versions of the project since its creation in 2002. The university team drew interesting conclusions in the report:

In terms of impact, the FMH project is an important counter-cultural tool in promoting equity, by reflecting on stories of shared humanity and where one stands within the wider structures of society. Although not stable places, shelters are a mechanism for social sustainability in which children are removed from harm, assisted in developing autonomy over their lives. The FMH approach equips children to adapt and deal with uncertainties in the future, such as adult attention, relationships, their hopes and dreams. IFH and FMH give children and young people voice within the judicial system, which bears down on all aspects of their lives. The project can be a positive influence on the employment and aspirational prospects of young people in the face of high levels of social inequality and prejudices against the poor in the society. (Tiwari et al., 2017, p. 3)

Additionally, the evaluation conducted by the project staff in 2018 showed that among children and adolescents participating in the project, 75% participate in reading activities regularly. Eighty-one percent like to read and listen to stories, 75% have at least one favorite book, and 75% talk about their daily lives with someone. Eighty-one percent know the reason for their placement in out-of-home care, 100% possess a life storybook with records of people and remarkable moments of their lives, and 94% actively participate in constructing their life storybook. One hundred percent like their life storybook, and 88% take care of it (IFH, 2018). All these factors are considered positive indicators for the goals set by the project.

Lessons From "Making My Story"

This section presents three case vignettes to illustrate the main aspects of the Making My Story project that influence children's participation in decision-making. These cases were selected by the authors and refer to our experiences, observations, notes, and reports. The criteria we used for the selection of the vignettes were their relevance to the topic of participation and enough information about the cases that allowed us to present and reflect on them. (In many cases, our team does not have close interaction with children, the collaborators, or professionals involved, so it was essential to choose cases that we had ample information about.) The children's names are pseudonyms to maintain confidentiality, and any content that could disclose a child's identity was changed. Each case refers to a particular situation, which we think allows us to make valuable observations when conceptualizing and implementing children's participation in other settings beyond the Making My Story project.

Space and Audience: The Importance of Emotional Bonds

The following case vignette describes a situation that reveals the dynamic aspect of life stories and relationships in creating them. It aims to demonstrate that a close and trusting relationship often provides a positive environment for participation. To accomplish the first step toward participation, children and adolescents must feel that they can share their concerns, doubts, feelings, and thoughts with a person who is listening attentively. Participation is enabled if the hierarchical bond between adults and children is challenged. Challenging this bond allows for a horizontal relation from which adults and children can cooperate to search for answers, decisions, and resolutions that are a better fit for their situation.

Case Vignette 1: Lucas

Lucas spent his early childhood with his mom and was then placed in a residential care home at 2 years due to neglect. Lucas lived in the residential home for 12 years, during which he had no contact with his mother or father. He had lost touch with his mother and had no contact with his father until he was 14, when his father was found. After a short, tentative period living with his father, Lucas returned to care and was then placed in another group home. When he was 15, Lucas started to participate in the Making My Story project. Lucas and his collaborator Tania formed a close bond and had several conversations about him and his present, future, and past. Lucas expressed the desire to visit his mother and siblings and some of his previous caregivers. Tania accompanied Lucas to a party in an earlier home, where he met previous caregivers and shared memories of his childhood. This meeting sparked Lucas's interest in his past. Tania was moved by his sudden curiosity in finding out more and helped him search for his relatives on the Internet. They found an older sister and managed to get in touch with her and Lucas's mother. The family started to visit him and told Lucas that they had tried to find him for a long time, but the court and the first residential care home had informed them that he was living with his father.

In Making My Story, the bond between collaborator and child is the first and foremost priority, without which the aims of the project cannot be achieved. Therefore, collaborators are encouraged to focus on the relationship with the child or adolescent, gain their trust, be open with them, have fun together, and maintain confidentiality (whenever this does not imply a risk for the child). Collaborators' involvement with many aspects of the child's life is also encouraged. In this way, collaborators can build a rapport with the children. The individual approach may create situations in which the collaborators act alongside the children to pursue specific changes in their life stories, as the case of Lucas and his collaborator illustrates. Making My Story is, of course, not the only path through which close, trusting bonds can be established in out-of-home care. Still, the accounts of many children, collaborators, and staff from residential care homes have shown that for many children, their bond with the collaborator is one of the few individualized, close, and lasting bonds that they established with adults in the home. The fact that this adult is an outsider is positive because it allows for an innovative and authentic approach with each specific child. This goes hand in hand with research that found that children value informal processes and closer, personal relationships supporting participation (e.g., Furlan & Souza, 2013; Siqueira & Dell'Aglio, 2006). Cashmore's (2002) and Munro's (2001) findings suggest that the high level of staff turnover and other flaws in the child protection system hinder the creation of these relationships: a lack of time and professionals' prioritization of bureaucratic and practical duties rather than the bond with the child impede these relationships. Our observations are echoed by Brazilian authors like Furlan and Souza (2013) and Siqueira and Dell'Aglio (2006). Our experience confirmed the research findings of these authors: the collaborator often fulfills the role of a confidante or advocate. Both these roles might not exist in the relationship between children and the residential care home service team, including psychologists and social workers.

The bond between children and collaborators generates a different, trustful space from which new ideas, feelings, and questions emerge. Tania's genuine interest in and attention to Lucas's life story seemed to be an opportunity for him to recognize his wish to know more about his past and family. In Lundy's (2007) terms, Lucas's relationship with Tania gave him both space and the audience he needed to participate. It seems that in other relationships, Lucas was not able to access this amount of interest. Possibly due to the horizontal aspect of the relationship proposed in the Making My Story project, the collaborator was not in a position of knowledge or control over Lucas's life. Tania's role was that of someone who was there to share in the uncertainties and accompany him through them. It is safe to assume that previous caregivers and professionals from the court thought on behalf of Lucas (rather than alongside him) about his life story and the decisions about his life. Based on their protective roles, they seemed to position Lucas as someone to be protected rather than heard. His family was seen as just absent or neglectful due to his history. On the other hand, the collaborator embraced a different perspective as a volunteer who kept a horizontal relationship with Lucas. Although she was an adult, she positioned herself as equally incomplete, accepting the mysterious aspects of the situation. This position enabled a participatory environment in which Lucas felt that his opinions, views, and concerns were recognized and valued.

In this situation, the collaborator challenged the social construction of children as vulnerable, immature, and inexperienced "becomings." Tania faced a condition in which there were no clear answers, trusting that Lucas could cope with it. Adults often prefer to avoid this kind of situation, considering it harmful or too stressful for the child (Van Bijleveld et al., 2015). Still, Tania was available to support and accompany Lucas throughout this experience.

Voice: Listening to More Than Words

Throughout our years of working in out-of-home care, we have experienced that adults' ideas about children's development, particularly infants, emphasize that young children cannot understand and actively participate in their care. Early childhood strongly triggers a sense of protection in adults. Adults tend to deprive young children of participating in and knowing about the decisions about their life because they aim to protect them. Nevertheless, even the youngest children are affected by life experiences and family breakdowns and often express their suffering in various ways (Eliacheff, 1995). The case of Julia illustrates how an early childhood characterized by instability of care and a lack of information and understanding of what was happening made Julia very suspicious, confused, and constantly fearful of a new breakdown in care.

> Case Vignette 2: Julia
> Julia's story is full of care breakdowns and separations. After she was removed from her biological mother when she was a few months old, Julia lived in an institution for more than 2 years. She lived her first years without knowing much about why she was taken away from her mother

and with little knowledge about her future perspectives. When Julia was almost 3, a couple adopted her. We know little about the time she spent with this family and the circumstances that led to the breakdown of this placement. When Julia, once again, entered care, she was placed in a foster family. Since the beginning, Julia demonstrated confusion about what was happening to her: she was shy, cried, and seemed lost in her new home and talked only when necessary. Mario and Isabella, Julia's foster family and collaborators, started creating her life storybook, which reconstructed Julia's life trajectory since birth. (She was 3 years old when she began participating in the project.) With their help, Julia learned about her biological mother, why her mother could not take care of her, her life in the residential home, her relationship with the prior adoptive family, and the reasons for the breakdown of the adoption placement. Julia needed to hear that she was not to blame for the breakdown. Little by little, Julia's story was reorganized visually and chronologically, with photos and drawings that helped her feel safe and cared for. Her storybook was an object she would often look at, and her foster family would show it to her when they thought she needed it. Sometimes she appeared sad and quieter, while at other times she seemed nervous and anxious. She started to talk more freely about her story, remembered some scenes, and showed her book to people she trusted. She began to engage in dramatic play pretending to be a mother or a daughter and said her biological mother's name. She explained that she was born in her mother's belly. After some months in her foster family and constant conversations that helped Julia understand what had happened to her, she appeared calmer and expressed her feelings more assertively.

Once placed in a foster family, Julia had the opportunity to understand her life story and why she had experienced so many changes. Julia gradually started to understand her story and what had happened to her. The photos, drawings, and playtime were essential for her to learn about her life story and her present life. Her foster parents perceived her need to understand her situation better and trusted that Julia would deal with the information.

The storybook appeared to be an essential element in this process because Julia's forms of communication were related to playing and visual and sensory aspects. The method of constructing the storybook helped the adults widen their understanding of Julia's ways of communicating her perspectives. They could hear and understand her through her play and behavior and not only through her words. This case exemplifies what Lundy (2007) calls "voice" in her model of children's participation.

Influence: Recognizing Children's Lives

The case of two teenage siblings, Maria and Daniel, illustrates how children's participation, as established by the Statute of the Child and Adolescent (Brasil, Presidência da República, 1990), is not fully implemented. In many instances, professionals ignore children's right to information and participation in out-of-home care. In this case, the children's violations within the family and the way the child welfare services removed them from their home violated the children's right to be heard and informed.

> **Case Vignette 3: Maria and Daniel**
> Maria (15) and Daniel (14) arrived at the residential care home without understanding what was happening. A child welfare worker had gone to their house and put them in a car, saying that they would return home soon. The official reason given for their removal from home was neglect. They had a hard time understanding the protection measure. They saw no reason for it and suffered from the decision. Despite all the violations and suffering they had experienced, the siblings felt they were strong and capable of dealing with the family difficulties. They did not deny that their father had attacked them in the past, but they said that they could avoid their father's aggression at present.
>   This is the situation in which they began to participate in the project. In weekly meetings with their collaborators, they got the chance to understand their feelings. The literature books encouraged them to speak about their stories, and gradually, the siblings realized that they had a space to comprehend what was going on. Maria and Daniel talked with affection about their paternal uncle, who was willing to take custody of them. The uncle visited them weekly while preparing his home to receive them. However, for some reason we are unaware of, the court had doubts about this possibility. Daniel and Maria felt powerless because they had no active role in the judicial process. It took 2 months for their hearing to happen. The collaborators suggested to Daniel and Maria that they could write a letter to the judge to tell their version of the facts.

> In the letters, written with the support of the collaborators, the teenagers described how they suffered because they were living far from their community and family. They explained that they had a great affection for their uncle. Once the court received these letters, the court moved up the hearing. The siblings prepared to talk to the judge by constructing pages about their wishes and plans in their life storybooks.
>
> When Maria and Daniel met the judge in the official hearing, they expressed how disturbed they had been by the way they had been removed from the home. The judge apologized and acknowledged the disrespect with which they had been treated. At the hearing, the judge determined that the uncle would take custody of Maria and Daniel.

In Maria and Daniel's case, none of the four elements of children's participation proposed by Lundy (2007) occurred. Under national regulations (Brasil, Presidência da República, 1990; Brasil et al., 2009), the first measure to be taken when a risk has been identified is assessing the family's situation and verifying the need for out-of-home care. If the authorities had conducted an assessment and Maria, Daniel, and the rest of the family had been listened to and actively participated in the process, this protection measure might not have been necessary. The uncle could have been identified as a family member able to obtain custody of the teenagers before their placement in a group home.

The residential care home service team and the project collaborators somehow broke the cycle of the siblings' exclusion when they tried to repair the situation by explaining to them what was happening, stated their rights, and legitimized their feelings. By suggesting that they write a letter, the volunteers showed that Maria and Daniel's anger was understandable and had to be considered by the authorities. Maria and Daniel's thoughts and feelings had value and deserved recognition. The judge, in this case, was also an audience, listening to the teenagers' perspectives and understanding their views. This case thus evidenced what Lundy (2007) understands as voice and audience.

Hearings with a judge tend to be short and frequently uncomfortable for children. Children and adolescents do not feel free to express what they think directly to someone older and in a position of power whom they do not know. For this reason, it is necessary to prepare children for this meeting. The collaborators eased this discomfort by helping the children create pages in the album that they could use to obtain more clarity with what they wanted to express. This process appears to have helped Maria and Daniel to feel confident and safe during the hearing. They could express their views and actively participate in the decisions affecting their future. This case ended up reaching the last element of Lundy's (2007) model of participation: influence. This is the stage where adults take children's views into consideration in the decision-making process.

Conclusion

In this chapter, we presented the aspects of the Making My Story project that contribute to children's participation: intergenerational emotional bonds, understanding children as active participants, listening beyond children's words, and influence. We aimed to illustrate how these aspects occur, how they improve participation, and how they correspond to different parts of Lundy's (2007) model of children's participation. It is important to consider our approach to participation as multifaceted. It does not only occur at the moment when children express their views. It is an ongoing process that happens in diverse spheres. From this perspective, it is likely that the Making My Story project contributes to deeper layers of the elements of space, voice, and audience offered to children rather than the formal moment of decision-making in court, which concerns the aspect of influence. These aspects relate intrinsically to children getting in touch with their personal and family stories. They take ownership of them by being informed, posing questions, and developing and expressing their views.

Participation is not static and does not only occur in meetings between professionals and children about their cases. It is a process that changes over time and is created daily in residential care homes and foster families. Collaborators and project staff generate many reflections about what the children want to say to the residential home care team. The children express their attitudes, feelings, and thoughts. This process adds value and importance to what the children express. This individualized and sensitive approach considers the particularities of every child and adolescent and can influence the understanding that the care team has about them. The construction of new visions can affect the reports written by professionals and support the judge's decision-making process. To summarize, the Making My Story project appears to have salient outcomes regarding the appreciation of children's perspectives in decision-making processes.

Our experience shows that the process of constructing a life storybook can also help children prepare for moments in which they need to talk with judges in front of audiences and interviews with social workers. The book creates a channel of communication between children and the professionals involved in the case. It serves as a subtle and careful way to support children and adults when approaching complex subjects and communicating about them.

Children gain opportunities to form an emotional bond with an adult, are heard through their actions and play, and get in touch with their life stories. These are important steps that may contribute to creating children's participation. Nevertheless, the Making My Story project faces significant limitations regarding children's participation. These relate to different layers of power involved in the implementation. The outcomes in the decisions by the judicial authorities depend on the importance assigned to children's perspectives and experiences by the professionals in charge of the care measure—workers in out-of-home care services and the court.

In our experience, we have heard of only a few instances in which professionals of the care services or the child and youth court considered the content of the life storybook as a listening tool and as facilitating children's expressions of their views. There are a few residential care homes that bring the books along to meetings at the court. A few times, collaborators of the project who have a strong bond with children and adolescents are asked to participate in meetings and discussions to support the judge's decisions. Maria and Daniel's case, in which the life storybook proved to be very helpful for participation and influenced the judge's decision, remains a rare exception. In this exceptional case, children could speak for themselves and had their views heard. However, in most instances, collaborators tend to enable a space for children's expression, and then they assume the role of communicating on behalf of the child. Therefore, the child's position is still a powerless one. In a context where children do not always find the voice, audience, and influence to position themselves as agents, this strategy can be powerful to facilitate processes of indirect participation. Nevertheless, even though the support of an adult throughout the whole process is valuable, at times, it is the adult's, not the child's, voice and influence that turn out to be crucial to promote children's participation. Hopefully, children and adolescents may hold more power to speak and to take a stand for themselves in the near future.

It is not only children who find themselves in a powerless position in decision-making. In many instances, even the Making My Story team feels powerless when the court or care team makes decisions that overlook the opinion and requests of children and adolescents. The project staff and collaborators are not in a position of relevance in the child protection system; they do not have much space to represent what children and adolescents think and feel.

Even though implementing children's participation was not the primary goal in creating the Making My Story project, it has unfolded as an unexpected and positive outcome in several cases. From a perspective that focuses on the process of participation, the project contributes to the early and primary stages of participation, with information sharing, dialogue, respect, and collaboration between children and adults. Participation supports children in appropriating their life story, expressing their thoughts and feelings, and positioning themselves toward decisions about their lives. In various contexts in child protection, these are fundamental stages in establishing and achieving children's participation. However, we have also pointed out that the structural dynamics that assign children a powerless social position are significant barriers to adults valuing children's perspectives and the de facto influence they can wield in decision-making processes.

Reflection Questions

(1) To what extent do children in care build close, trusting bonds with adults? How do these relationships foster children's participation?
(2) In what ways do caregivers understand young children as active participants and listen to children beyond their words?
(3) Which opportunities do children find to understand and get appropriative of their life stories and have them recognized? How does that constrain or enable their participation in decision-making?
(4) Which aspects of Making My Story highlighted throughout this chapter are valuable and can be implemented in your specific context? How could this be accomplished?

Notes

1. Of the children and adolescents in out-of-home care in Brazil, 4% live with foster families and 96% live in group and residential care homes (CNJ, 2020). Similarly to this

national trend, only 62 among the 628 children who participated in the project in 2020 were in foster families (IFH, 2020).
2. As Making My Story embraces an open methodology, with support materials and publications available on the institute's website free of charge, many out-of-home care providers develop this project on their own and do not necessarily inform the institute and thus are not counted in the figures annually gathered by the institute.

References

Abrinq Foundation. (2019). *Population*. Retrieved August 9, 2019, from https://observatoriocrianca.org.br/cenario-infancia/temas/populacao

Alanen, L. (2001). Explorations in generational analysis. In L. Alanen & B. Mayall (Eds.), *Conceptualizing child-adult relations* (pp. 11–22). Routledge/Falmer.

Alderson, P. (2004). Ethics. In S. Fraser, V. Lewis, S. Ding, M. Kellett, & C. Robinson (Eds.), *Doing research with children and young people* (pp. 97–113). Sage.

Alderson, P., & Morrow, V. (2011). *The ethics of research with children and young people: A practical handbook*. Sage.

Bettelheim, B. (2011). *A psicanálise nos contos de fada* [Psychoanalysis in fairy tales]. Paz e Terra.

Brasil, Presidência da República [Presidency of the Republic of Brazil]. (1990). *Lei 8069 - Estatuto da Criança e do Adolescente* [Law 8069 - Child and Adolescent Statute]. 1990-07-13. http://www.planalto.gov.br/ccivil_03/LEIS/L8069.htm

Brasil, Presidência da República, MDS, & SDH. (2009). *Orientações técnicas: serviços de acolhimento para crianças e adolescentes* [Technical guidance: Out-of-home care services for children and adolescence]. https://www.mds.gov.br/cnas/noticias/orientacoes_tecnicas_final.pdf

Cashmore, J. (2002). Promoting the participation of children and young people in care. *Child Abuse and Neglect*, *26*(8), 837–847. https://doi.org/10.1016/S0145-2134(02)00353-8

CNJ. (2020). *Diagnóstico sobre o Sistema Nacional de Adoção e Acolhimento* [National adoption register]. https://www.cnj.jus.br/wpcontent/uploads/2020/05/relat_diagnosticoSNA2020_25052020.pdf

Coelho, N. N. (2002). *Literatura infantil: Teoria, análise, didática* [Children's literature: Theory, analysis and didactics] (7th ed.). Moderna.

D'Agostino, R. (2014, May 25). *Só 12% das varas da infância no país são exclusivas, segundo CNJ* [Only 12% of youth courts in the country are exclusive, according to CNJ]. G1.

Dolto, F. (1989). *Dialogando sobre crianças e adolescents* [Dialogue about children and teenagers]. Papirus.

Eliacheff, C. (1995). *Corpos que gritam: A psicanálise com bebês* [Screaming bodies: Psychoanalysis with babies]. Editora Ática.

Freire, P. (2011). *A importância do ato de ler* [The importance of the act of reading] (51st ed.). Cortez.

Freyre, G. (1956). *The masters and the slaves (Casa grande e Senzala): A study in the development of Brazilian civilization* (S. Putnam, Trans.) (2nd ed.). Alfred A. Knopf.

Furlan, V., & Souza, T. de P. (2013). Exclusão/inclusão social: Políticas públicas de acolhimento institucional dirigidas à infância e juventude [Social inclusion/

exclusion: Public policies for institutional care aimed at children and youth]. *Diálogo*, 23, 35–48. https://doi.org/10.18316/909

Gallagher, M., Smith, M., Hardy, M., & Wilkinson, H. (2012). Children and families' involvement in social work decision making. *Children and Society, 26*(1), 74–85. https://doi.org/10.1111/j.1099-0860.2011.00409.x

Green, D. (2012). *From poverty to power*. Practical Action Publishing.

Healy, K., & Darlington, Y. (2009). Service user participation in diverse child protection contexts: Principles for practice. *Child & Family Social Work, 14*, 420–430.

IFH. (n.d.). *Fazendo Minha História: Guia de ação para colaboradores* [Making My Story: Guidelines for collaborators]. Instituto Fazendo História. https://static1.squarespace.com/static/56b10ce8746fb97c2d267b79/t/56bcc5567da24f4faa269479/1455211873350/guiafmh.pdf

IFH. (2013). *Esta é nossa história* [This is our story] (C. Vidigal, F. Ferraz, L. Sion, & M. Vidiz, Eds.). Editora Alaúde.

IFH. (2018). *Relatório Anual 2018* [2018 Annual Report]. Instituto Fazendo História. https://static1.squarespace.com/static/56b10ce8746fb97c2d267b79/t/5c938d74971a1866cb5f7066/1553173974247/RELATÓRIO+ANUAL+IFH+2018+FINAL+web+curvas.pdf

IFH. (2020). *Relatório Anual 2020* [2020 Annual Report]. Instituto Fazendo História. https://static1.squarespace.com/static/56b10ce8746fb97c2d267b79/t/6082b73835d08840b1ae773f/1619179363774/IFH_Relatorio+2021_Arquivo+Final_WEB_paginadupla.pdf

Lundy, L. (2007). "Voice" is not enough: Conceptualising Article 12 of the United Nations Convention on the Rights of the Child. *British Educational Research Journal, 33*(6), 927–942. https://doi.org/10.1080/01411920701657033

Marin, I. S. K. (2010). *Febem, família e identidade* [Febem juvenile detention centers, family and identity]. Editora Escuta.

Mayall, B. (2015). Intergenerational relations: Embodiment over time. In L. Alanen, L. Brooker, & B. Mayall (Eds.), *Childhood with Bourdieu* (pp. 13–33). Palgrave Macmillan.

Munro, E. (2001). Empowering looked-after children. *Child and Family Social Work, 6*(2), 129–137.

Petit, M. (2009a). *A arte de ler ou como resistir a adversidade* [The art of reading or how to resist adversity]. Editora 34.

Petit, M. (2009b). *Os jovens e a leitura* [Young people and reading]. Editora 34.

Qvortrup, J., Corsaro, W. A., & Honig, M.-S. (2009). *The Palgrave handbook of childhood studies*. Palgrave Macmillan.

Reyes, Y. (2010). *A casa imaginária: leitura e literatura na primeira infância* [The imaginary house: Reading and literature in early childhood]. Global.

Rizzini, I., & Rizzini, I. (2009). Children and youth institutionalized care in Brazil: Historical perspectives and current overview. In M. E. Courtney & D. Iwaniec (Eds.), *Residential care of children: Comparative perspectives* (pp. 154–172). Oxford University Press Scholarship Online.

Rizzini, I., Naiff, L., & Batista, R. (2007). *Acolhendo crianças e adolescentes: Experiências de promoção de direito à convivência familiar e comunitária no Brasil* [Fostering children and adolescents: Experiences in promoting the right to family and community life in Brazil]. Cortez.

Safra, G. (2005). *Curando com histórias* [Healing with stories]. Edições Sobornost.

Siqueira, A. C., & Dell'Aglio, D. D. (2006). O impacto da instituticionalização na infância e na adolescência: uma revisão da literature [The impact of institutionalization on childhood and adolescence: A literature review]. *Psicologia e Sociedade, 18*(1), 71–80. https://doi.org/10.1590/S0102-71822006000100010

Taft, J. K. (2015). "Adults talk too much": Intergenerational dialogue and power in the Peruvian movement of working children. *Childhood, 22*(4), 460–473. https://doi.org/10.1177/0907568214555148

Ten Brummelaar, M. D. C., Harder, A. T., Kalverboer, M. E., Post, W. J., & Knorth, E. J. (2018). Participation of youth in decision-making procedures during residential care: A narrative review. *Child and Family Social Work, 23*(1), 33–44. https://doi.org/10.1111/cfs.12381

Tiwari, M., Pickering-Saqqa, S., & Kraft, K. (2017). *Lessons-learned evaluation* (Unpublished manuscript, University of East London).

United Nations Committee on the Rights of the Child (UNCRC). (2009, July 29). *General comment No. 12: The right of the child to be heard*. CRC/C/GC/12. https://www.refworld.org/docid/4ae562c52.html

Van Bijleveld, G. G., Dedding, C. W. M., & Bunders-Aelen, J. F. G. (2015). Children's and young people's participation within child welfare and child protection services: A state-of-the-art review. *Child and Family Social Work, 20*(2), 129–138. https://doi.org/10.1111/cfs.12082

Winnicott, D. (1975). *O brincar e a realidade* [Play and reality]. Imago Editora.

Winnicott, D. (2005a). *A família e o desenvolvimento individual* [The family and individual development]. Martins Fontes.

Winnicott, D. (2005b). *Tudo começa em casa* [It all starts at home]. Martins Fontes.

Winter, K. (2010). The perspectives of young children in care about their circumstances and implications for social work practice. *Child & Family Social Work, 15*, 186–195.

Woodhead, M. (2010). Foreword. In B. Percy-Smith & N. Thomas (Eds.), *A handbook of children and young people's participation* (pp. xix–xxii). Routledge.

PART III
CONCLUDING REMARKS

11
Concluding Remarks

Katrin Križ and Mimi Petersen

Introduction

We began the adventure that became this book when we met at the European Scientific Association on Residential and Family Care for Children and Adolescents (EUSARF) conference for child welfare practitioners and researchers in Portugal in the summer of 2018. We felt inspired by the many thought-provoking presentations on children and youth's participation in social change activism and child protection research and practice. We worked with and studied young people's participation for many years, Mimi Petersen as an educator, researcher, and social work practitioner, and Katrin Križ as an educator and researcher. We sensed that we were living through an exciting cultural and social momentum empowering children and young people by facilitating their participation in child protection. We edited this book to contribute to promoting this momentum further. We found great joy in collaborating with our colleagues on this volume, despite the challenges to collaboration created by the global coronavirus pandemic. We overcame these challenges thanks to our colleagues' steadfast commitment to children's participation and technological innovation.

We included many examples of children and young people as agents of social change, children's experiences with child protection organizations, and child protection professionals' approaches to facilitating participation. Our goal was to inspire children and youth, children's rights activists, child protection and international development practitioners, students, scholars, and public policymakers in child protection to participate in what Rodrigo González Álvarez, Mijntje ten Brummelaar, Kevin R. O. van Mierlo, Gerald P. Mallon, and Mónica López López have called "the children's participation movement" in Chapter 6 of this book.

Katrin Križ and Mimi Petersen, *Concluding Remarks* In: *Children and Young People's Participation in Child Protection*. Edited by: Katrin Križ and Mimi Petersen, Oxford University Press. © Oxford University Press 2023. DOI: 10.1093/oso/9780197622322.003.0011

In these concluding remarks, we will summarize what we learned from the individual chapters about pathways to children and young people's participation in child protection. We will discuss social change actions led by children and youth and describe professional approaches to children and young people's involvement in child protection. We will analyze the conditions in which participation can flourish, which we call "participation generators." We will present the effects of children and youth participation on children and young people, social work education and practice, policy development, and children and young people's collective action against violence toward children.

Children and Young People as Agents of Change

Children and young people act as social change agents in many ways. They advocate for changes in and design child protection policy, conduct research leading to changes in the child protection system, develop social work models, participate in decisions about their lives, and engage in collective action against violence toward children. "Experts by experience" are children and young people who have experience with the child protection system. In several countries, experts by experience have become actively involved in educating future child protection professionals and changing the law, policy, and practice approaches to professional social work based on collaborative actions and research with adults. They have initiated and implemented changes in child welfare, education, mental health services, and the criminal justice system.

The chapters described how youth-led change could be transformative for children and young people and lead to change in social work training and practice and to community and societal change: children and youth experience a shift in consciousness by gaining competencies, self-confidence, and self-worth. They increase their efficacy, resilience, empowerment, and trust in democratic political processes. They gain a sense of belonging to a group by collaborating with other youth. At the same time, the chapters showed that children and young people's participation could raise ethical concerns about children and youths' privacy and consent to participate in research and social change. It may lead to ambivalence and resistance from adults, who find that youth-led action may retraumatize children and youth or create an additional burden for the adults who must change their ways. Children and youth may find participating stressful and overwhelming, and interactions with adults intimidating. Financial and logistical resources and consistent and trusting relationships with professionals who safeguard against these risks and other issues may help avoid these experiences.

The chapters illustrated that the "participation generators" or contexts facilitating youth-led change included institutional (cultural, legal, policy, and organizational) and individual supports for young people. The "participatory capital" encouraging youth-led change and promoting genuine participation of children and youth who encounter public child protection agencies encompasses several resources. These are facilitatory and transformative legal, policy, and practice contexts and emotional, financial, time, and logistical supports. They involve the capacity building of children, youth, and adults. They encompass children and youth's creativity, capacities, strengths, and skills; their alliances and cooperation with other children and youth; and their partnerships with adults working in nongovernmental organizations, public agencies, and government entities. The chapters demonstrated that children and young people's participatory capital varies depending on age, ethnicity, gender, nationality, and so on.

Methods and Outcomes

The PROs of the Change Factory, experts by experience in Norway, have trained future child welfare workers at the university level by providing pedagogical tools and changing the curriculum of child welfare education in Norway. The Change Factory's work rests on the idea that children and youth can develop and initiate systemic change based on their experience within the systems they seek to change. The "My Life Education" project described by Roar Sundby aims to improve social work students' relational and collaborative skills. The project has led to an open and genuine exchange between the PROs and social work students at the university level. Sundby showed that the PROs experienced positive interactions with the students: They gained self-confidence and mentioned that telling their stories had a healing effect. They were satisfied that sharing their stories might change the experiences of other children in the child welfare system in the future. The social work students became more aware of their personal experiences and histories, enjoyed an increased sense of community among themselves, gained relational and collaborative skills, and felt more confident in their ability to practice with children and youth collaboratively.

In Israel, care leavers have successfully shaped child protection law and policy by participating as advocates on the Israeli Council for the Child in Care youth advisory board and assisting the Ministry of Social Services and Social Affairs in designing the first ombudsperson agency for children in care. The youth advisory board aimed to influence the services operated by the Council for the Child in Care and other child welfare agencies and affect national child welfare policy.

Talia Meital Schwartz-Tayri and Hadas Lotan described in their chapter on Israel how the youths collaborated with the Israeli parliament and created a program for graduates of independent living programs. They negotiated with lawmakers who deliberated on a new foster care law and lobbied for new legislation in the Knesset (the Israeli parliament) for children leaving care. They created several new programs for children graduating from independent living programs, including a youth-to-youth mentorship program for youth transitioning out of care. The young people on the advisory board had a positive experience overall. They felt satisfied with their interactions with Council in Care managers and policymakers. They gained self-esteem, strength, and a sense of their abilities. They developed a strong sense of belonging and group spirit, which motivated them to continue helping other youth transitioning out of care. The young people noted that advocacy takes time and financial resources (e.g., to cover transportation to meetings). Participation could be difficult because of the youth's lack of self-confidence and presentation skills. Some of the adults they worked with disregarded the young people as participants. The youth had approached their work in parliament with a mistrust of politicians. Still, they gained trust, efficacy, and communication skills because of their involvement in the policymaking process. They described their experience as empowering and life changing.

In the "Roskilde Project," experts by experience in Denmark shaped child welfare practice by evaluating and developing new methods with children and youth. This model moves social work practice from child centric to child directed, as Mimi Petersen's chapter described. In "Project Bella," youth from marginalized immigrant backgrounds engaged in community organizing to present the experiences and concerns of their local community to others. They worked with researchers and professionals, participated in workshops and conferences, took a trip to Iceland, and contributed to a documentary about their community. The youth created and led guided tours of their housing project to residents, the mayor, and international social work students and presented their work at a local and international conference.

Most young people started attending school regularly because they participated in the project. The young people reported gaining self-esteem, new skills, and knowledge of social workers' and teachers' roles and responsibilities. The adults learned to have more faith in youths' capabilities and how to collaborate with them. The project created a better understanding and dialogue between young people and professionals (teachers, social workers, community workers, etc.). The young people felt very motivated to continue leading change in the community.

In the coffee-growing zone in Nicaragua, children and young people took collective action to promote and defend children's rights in their communities, as described by Harry Shier. They did so through *protagonismo infantil*—children's leadership in developing and implementing social change through collective action to empower children. Unlike the other examples in this part of the book, the children in Nicaragua do not evaluate or develop public services for children and young people. They are community activists who have raised consciousness and sought societal changes to protect children from violence. Shier described many social change actions organized, led, and run by children, including youth theater against violence in the home, festivals against violence toward children, and a weekly radio show. Children engaged in transformative research by gathering and analyzing data on violence against children on coffee plantations and increasing children's understanding of sex and sexuality. Children created a dragon of violence that they marched through the streets. They formed learning and action groups to teach gender equality, women's rights, and masculinities. They developed child protection policy guidelines to protect children from risks they face when they travel to school. Transformations also happened at the personal level when children and youth gained self-esteem, motivation, critical thinking, initiative, perseverance, and solidarity.

Generators of Child- and Youth-Led Change

The contexts in which child- and youth-led change occurs vary considerably. In Nicaragua, protagonismo infantil grew out of the exploitation and poverty of children working on coffee plantations in remote mountain communities. Local schoolteachers founded the Nicaraguan nongovernmental organization (NGO) CESESMA to make education more relevant for working children in rural communities. The NGO developed a child's rights approach to assist rural children and youth in promoting their rights, including their right to protection from violence. The adults working for the NGO accompanied and facilitated youth-led actions for social change. As Shier and the other chapters also highlight, adults can play a prominent role in youth-led transformation. Adults can support children and youth's capacity building, analyze the risks of children and youth's actions, and provide rules and safeguards for children and youth engaged in transformative research, practice, and organizational and social change. Shier emphasized that adults must be upskilled and motivated to act as duty bearers to protect children's rights to protection and participation. They need to inform children and recognize them as rights holders and active citizens.

In Norway, children enjoy a high social status, and the state has actively supported youth-led changes in child welfare for many years. The My Life Education project described by Roar Sundby has enjoyed cultural, financial, and organizational support from public entities in Norway. The Norwegian Directorate for Children, Youth, and Family Affairs financed the project, a cooperation between the Change Factory and two Norwegian universities. Children's participation rights are strongly protected in Norwegian law. Public entities (including municipalities, universities, and parliament) have cooperated with the Change Factory to develop public services for children that champion their rights as developers and participants in public services. The Norwegian government recognized the Change Factory as a National Knowledge Center in 2018. The Norwegian Directorate for Children, Youth, and Family Affairs produced national guidelines stipulating that children's knowledge is as valuable as knowledge from the practice field and evidence-based scientific knowledge. The guidelines aimed to include children and youth as experts by experience to train future child welfare workers in collaborative skills. The adults who work with the PROs ensure that their stories and suggestions are never interpreted or altered by adults. The PROs are paired with adults they know and trust when meeting with social work students. The Change Factory prepares them for meetings and conferences and debriefs them if their interactions with university students are challenging or uncomfortable.

Israeli law and policy have championed children's participation rights for over two decades. The 2008 child welfare reform established procedures regulating how local communities should weigh children's voices in decisions about their lives. Children and youth's participation in school decision-making is well supported by the law but less so in other areas. The youths on the youth advisory board received payment for their participation in each meeting and travel expenses. Two social workers facilitated the youths' meetings and the seminar. The Ministry of Social Services and Social Affairs invited the young people to collaborate to design the first ombudsman agency for children in care. The young people reported that they appreciated the adults not judging them.

In Denmark, Mimi Petersen and her colleagues provided capacity building and logistical and emotional support when collaborating with experts by experience in child welfare research and policy design. The youth involved in Project Bella learned to plan and run meetings and conduct research in their community to effect positive local change. The project, which a Danish foundation funded, paid them as if it were a part-time, after-school job. The adults helped organize a weekend trip, a trip to Iceland, and conference participation. The consistent relationship between the youth and adults was characterized by trust, respect, and a willingness to collaborate.

Generators of Participatory Professional Practices

The chapters in the book's second part show that participatory professional practices involve professional attitudes, relationships, and practice approaches, creating environments for all children and youth to participate regardless of age, ability, ethnicity, gender identity, migrant background, sexuality, and so on. Participatory attitudes toward children are nurturing and free of biases, labeling, and stigmatizing children and youth. Caring, consistent, respectful, and nonhierarchical relationships between children, youth, and adults encourage participation. Creative practice methods that combine playful visual and nonverbal modes of expression with verbal communication allow for the involvement of younger children. The chapters suggest that research and practice need to play a more proactive role in finding means to make babies, toddlers, and younger children visible in professional decision-making in child protection.

While the Dutch child protection system has paid increasing attention to children's participation in child protection–related processes, there is no coherent national policy. The implementation varies by children's age, case context, and municipality. The interviews with LGBTQIA+ young people in the Audre project showed that an affirmative and supportive environment is a prerequisite for participation, as Rodrigo González Álvarez, Mijntje ten Brummelaar, Kevin R. O. van Mierlo, Gerald P. Mallon, and Mónica López López showed. Capacity building and training are needed for foster carers, current and future child protection professionals, and other children and youth. Foster care and school settings need to be caring and supportive of LGBTQIA+ children and youth for participation. A nurturing and consistent, enduring relationship with caseworkers is vital: caseworkers need to take their time to get to know LGBTQIA+ children and young people, hear and "see" them, and advocate for them. Children and young people need to be informed and prepared, especially for transitioning to a (new) foster family or other placement and transitioning out of care. Caseworkers need to give LGBTQIA+ children and youth the space to disclose personal information and the timing of disclosure.

German law regulates children's participation rights from disadvantaged families, and professional practice supports children's participation. Children have gained more power in decision-making at the social level. However, German child protection remains protective and paternalistic. Daniela Reimer's biographical research with children and youth in foster care in Germany showed that professionals need to be open to children and young people's participation for participation to occur. This professional attitude involves adults refraining from using language and placing labels on children that stigmatize their mental health and other diagnoses, family, and status as a foster child. Professionals must avoid embracing a bureaucratic mindset, where focusing on rules and processes outweighs listening to children. A professional focus on problem-solving impedes participation. Adults need to listen to children in a child-friendly environment, value and inform children, and ensure that children and youth can be partners in decisions and make decisions themselves. They must seek forgiveness and retroactive consent if they decide against children's wishes. Child protection caseworkers need to take children's wishes seriously and support them, prepare children for visitation meetings with family, and evaluate their self-image and the perspective of children, and they need time and skills to implement participation. Research on children and child welfare practices can promote children and youth's involvement in child protection.

In the United States, children do not enjoy as solid legal participation rights as in many other countries presented in this volume. The United States is the only United Nations member state that has not ratified the

United Nations Convention on the Rights of the Child. However, practice approaches such as family group conferences that involve children, family members, and professionals involved with the child show a great potential for facilitating the participation of children older than 10 years and children who can express themselves verbally. These family team conferences are called team decision-making (TDM) meetings in the Californian public child protection agencies studied by Megan Canfield, Jenna Gaudette, Emma Frushell, and Katrin Križ. The chapter on the United States showed how child protection caseworkers' attitudes toward children can significantly promote participation. Similarly to the chapter on Germany, Canfield and colleagues' interviews with child protection caseworkers suggest that caseworkers should refrain from placing negative labels on children. Workers' views of children as capable, strong, and powerful promote participation. Perceptions of incompetence and moral failure impede it.

Child protection caseworkers perceive babies and toddlers as nonparticipants because they lack verbal communication skills. This perception needs to change. Child protection agencies could achieve this change with the help of systemic transformations that allow very young children's wishes to be heard. They could hire independent spokespersons who represent young children's best interests in family team meetings in inclusive, nonoppressive ways. They could also accomplish this change with the help of creative approaches involving young children. These methods could include practice approaches such as the arts-based research (ABR) described by Nuria Fuentes-Peláez, Ainoa Mateos, M. Àngels Balsells, and María José Rodrigo, or the methods of the "Making My Story" project that Monica Vidiz, Lara Naddeo, and Debora Vigevani described in this book. Social work training needs to teach future child welfare workers about age- and ability-related biases in facilitating children's participation and how to address them. Research on babies and young children's participatory experiences and needs plays a pivotal role in finding effective methods to make these groups of children more visible and present in decisions about their lives.

In Spain, the law has only recently protected children's participation rights. The ABR presented by Fuentes-Peláez and colleagues is an innovative participatory practice approach allowing children younger than 8 to evaluate child welfare programs designed for them. Young children evaluated a parenting program called "Learning Together, Growing as a Family." Local public administrations and nonprofit organizations implemented the program with the help of the Social Integration Branch of the La Caixa Foundation.

Researchers from several universities in Spain evaluated the program by asking vulnerable children to draw their experiences in the family and discuss the drawings in small groups of children in a familiar environment. The researchers wrote a carefully crafted interview protocol that kept the interviews straightforward, playful, and encouraging. The researchers sought informed verbal assent from children to participate in the evaluation and informed consent from their parents. Children's participation in the assessment contributed to their feelings of empowerment.

The Making My Story project by the nonprofit organization Making History Institute in Brazil also draws on creative ways to involve children in out-of-home care in decisions that affect their lives. Monica Vidiz and colleagues discussed how children and young people create a storybook about their lives so they know, understand, and own their past, present, and future stories. This understanding helps children develop their opinions and express what they want for their lives. In Brazil, national law stipulates that children in out-of-home care are heard and involved in the decisions about protection measures. However, the (nonprofit and public) agencies providing out-of-home care services for children have difficulties implementing children's participation rights in practice because of a lack of financial resources, time, and ability and a focus on service provision and protection. The institute receives funding from private donors, companies, private foundations, and the government. Funds are also acquired with the help of training and supervision services to care services and municipalities.

In the Making My Story project, adult collaborators recruited and supervised by the institute implement the project in different regions of Brazil. The volunteers, social workers at group homes, or foster parents become allies to children and youth by collaborating with them on creating their stories. The adults play with the children, read books, create videos, encourage dramatic play, write letters to the court, and create a life storybook containing photos, drawings, paintings, texts, and the child's stories in a warm and caring atmosphere. Children do not have to be literate to create a book. It is pivotal that children use forms of expression other than words because it allows adults to understand younger children's experiences and hear their opinions. The life storybook the children create belongs to them. They take it with them when leaving care. The methodology is flexible and adapted to each child. The adults listen to children's stories and views and facilitate communication with the adults responsible for decision-making, such as social workers and judges. Like other chapter authors, Vidiz and colleagues emphasize the saliency of emotional bonds and horizontal relations between children and their adult allies.

We hope that the examples presented in the book's chapters will inspire children and young people, children's rights activists, child protection and international development practitioners, social work students, scholars, and public policymakers. We want to conclude this book by expressing our profound appreciation of the children and young people who are charting paths forward in children and young people's individual and collective participation in child protection.

Afterword

Nigel Patrick Thomas

Children's participation in child protection is an area of theory and practice that is full of tensions and contradictions. Those tensions and contradictions are clearly visible in this volume. Foremost among those is a perceived contradiction between a child's right to be heard and adults' responsibility to keep children safe from harm.

This is an international book, with contributions from very different contexts across Europe and the Americas. The social and economic contexts are very different, as are the policy contexts and even the terminology; for example, in the United Kingdom, child protection tends to have a more specialized meaning related to actual abuse, while in other places, it embraces what we in the United Kingdom would call child care. And yet, by bringing these contributions together in one volume, we can see that there is a great deal we have in common in terms of what we are trying to achieve, what is being achieved and how, and what obstacles lie in the way. My congratulations to the editors on what will be a really useful contribution to the international literature in this field.

My own doctoral research looked at children's participation in decisions when they are in state care (Thomas, 2000). So what has changed since then?

On the evidence of this book, there is a greater theoretical sophistication to discussions of participation and protection. The work of authors included here or cited here, such as Harry Shier or Laura Lundy, has provided tools for thinking more clearly about what participation is and how to promote it, as well as tools for practice. Engagement with social theorists such as Axel Honneth has also enabled a firmer theoretical foundation than a simple reliance on the United Nations Convention, with all its limitations.

In terms of what the book can tell us about the state of practice, the opportunities for children's *collective* involvement in shaping policies and services appear to be flourishing, here and there. The initiatives described in the first part of the book are all exciting and encouraging in their different ways, whether that be young people helping to train professionals in Norway (Chapter 2), contributing to the development of local services in Denmark (Chapter 3), engaging in dialogue with policymakers at a national level in Israel (Chapter 4), or as activists taking the initiative themselves in tackling violence against children in Nicaragua (Chapter 5). The question remains how pervasive these are and how they can be extended and built on to benefit the many thousands of children in public care, or in need of protection, in our different countries.

As for children's involvement in *individual* decision-making about their own lives, I confess that I find it hard to see much sign of real progress. As Daniela Reimer sums it up (Chapter 7), "children frequently feel that they do not participate, only participate to a small extent, and participation is only possible when they act out." Or as Mimi Petersen notes (Chapter 3): "None of the children ... felt they were involved as active subjects when the child welfare authorities made decisions about their well-being."

True, there are innovative programs pioneering creative ways to engage with children in discussing their own care and protection, of which there are examples in this book. However, there were similar programs 20 or 30 years ago. For instance, the project in Brazil described in Chapter 10 reminds me very much of the "life storybook" approach being promoted by the British Association for Adoption and Fostering in the 1980s (Ryan & Walker, 1993; later edition cited in Chapter 2). When Monica Vidiz and colleagues write that "Participation is not static and does not only occur in meetings between professionals and children about their cases. It is a process that changes over time and is created daily in residential care homes and foster families," or when Mimi Petersen finds that "trust, feeling safe, and clarity" are essential prerequisites for participation, it all sounds very familiar.

So why have such approaches not become common practice now? Why is it that children's participation in really important decisions about their safety and well-being, their care and education, is so often absent—or, when it happens at all, is superficial or tokenistic? The answer does not appear to be an absence of policy, for the policy framework is clearly there in many jurisdictions, supported by the widespread acceptance of the United Nations Convention on the Rights of the Child. Indeed, the most profound and radical examples of children's participation in these chapters come from Nicaragua, where the policy and service framework is probably the weakest. However, an explicit policy can be undermined in all sorts of ways by other imperatives. My own experience (as a practitioner, educator, and researcher) in the United Kingdom is that whatever law and guidance say, and have said for many years now, about listening to children and taking account of their wishes and feelings, the louder message from senior managers, politicians, and indeed the media is "play it safe, and on your head be it if anything goes wrong." This, of course, leads practitioners to be cautious and practice to be procedural rather than relational.

Other explanations for the widespread failure to engage with children in meaningful ways and bring them fully into the decision-making process have to do with practitioners' confidence in their abilities and their attitudes and beliefs about children's capacity, level of understanding, and "vulnerability." Some of this is age related, and Chapter 8 offers a nicely nuanced account of how age intersects with other social characteristics in social workers' approaches to including children in dialogue. As Roar Sundby reports in Chapter 2, genuine participation demands real relationships based on equality, "professional distance" is a problem that gets in the way, and adult assumptions that they know children's "best interests" have to be challenged (something else that I explored many years ago: Thomas & O'Kane, 1998).

One reason why children's collective participation in policy and services appears to have a more robust track record than children's individual participation in decisions about their own care is precisely that the perceived contradiction I mentioned earlier, between a child's right to be heard and adults' responsibility to keep children safe from harm, is so much more present in the latter case. The obsession with our own responsibility to protect children, and to "know" what is best for them, can blind us to the fact that they know a great deal about their own lives and even at a young age can help us to understand what is best for them. At bottom there should be no contradiction between a child's right to respect and an adult's duty to care for, protect, and nurture them.

Mimi Petersen refers in her chapter to Axel Honneth's (1995) concept of recognition. What I find particularly useful in Honneth's theoretical framework is his articulation of three distinct modes of recognition: "love, rights, and solidarity" (or "love, respect, and esteem"). The children in our care, or whom we work with, need to be loved and cared for as unique individuals; they are entitled to respect for their human rights as persons, and they deserve esteem for what they can contribute to our shared aims and values. Without all that, there can be no real participation (see Thomas, 2012). With interpersonal relationships founded on mutual recognition and organizational structures and cultures based on the same principles (in other words, institutions that give children recognition in those three ways), so much more can be achieved. There lies the challenge for us all.

References

Honneth, A. (1995). *The Struggle for Recognition: The Moral Grammar of Social Conflicts*. Polity Press.
Ryan, T., & Walker, R. (1993). *Life Story Work*. British Agencies for Adoption and Fostering.
Thomas, N. (2000). *Children, Family, and the State: Decision-Making and Child Participation*. Macmillan (Paperback edition 2002, Policy Press).
Thomas, N. (2012). Love, rights and solidarity: Studying children's participation using Honneth's theory of recognition. *Childhood*, *19*(4), 453–466.
Thomas, N., & O'Kane, C. (1998). When children's wishes and feelings clash with their 'best interests'. *International Journal of Children's Rights*, *6*(2), 137–154.

Index

For the benefit of digital users, indexed terms that span two pages (e.g., 52–53) may, on occasion, appear on only one of those pages.

Tables and figures are indicated by *t* and *f* following the page number

ABR. *See* arts-based research
active citizenship, 90, 96–97
adolescent's participation. *See* children's participation; older children's participation
adultism, xii–xiii
adults
    as duty bearers, 86, 88, 96
    role in youth-led transformation, 233–34
advisory boards. *See* care leavers' advisory boards
affirmative child welfare practice for LGBTQIA+ children and youth, 116–18
ageism, 176–77
agents of change, children and young people as, 6, 230–35. *See also* care leavers' advisory boards; Change Factory; child-directed child welfare; violence, children claiming right to live without
age-related participation boundaries. *See also* arts-based research
    babies and younger children's participation, 163–69, 164*t*
    general discussion, 175–78
    generators of participatory professional practices, 236–37
    older children's participation, 164*t*, 169–75
    overview, 156–57
    prior literature on, 159–61
    research methods, 161–62
    U.S. child protection system, 157–59
aging out of care. *See* care leavers' advisory boards

ambiguity of citizenship principle, 134–35
Antonvosky, A., 51–53
A. P. Møller Fund (Denmark), 46
Archard, D., 187
AROPE (At-Risk of Poverty and Exclusion) rate, Spain, 184–85
arts-based research (ABR)
    child protection in Spain, 184–85
    data analysis and presentation of results, 192–93
    development of research methods with children, 187–89
    ethical aspects and implementation process, 189–92
    examples of children's drawings and voices, 193–95, 194*t*
    general discussion, 195–97
    generators of participatory professional practices, 237–38
    Learning Together, Growing as a Family program, 183, 185–87
    overview, 7, 182–83
asexual youth and children. *See* LGBTQIA+ youth participation
assent, in arts-based research, 189–90
At-Risk of Poverty and Exclusion (AROPE) rate, Spain, 184–85
attitudes
    as criterion for empowerment, 54
    professional, closed to participatory practice, 145–48
audience
    in Lundy's model of children's participation, 202
    and Making My Story project, 214–16, 219, 220

246 INDEX

Audre project (Netherlands)
  generators of participatory professional practices, 235–36
  research findings, 115–21
  research methods, 113–15

babies, participation by, 161, 163–69, 164t, 237
Backe-Hansen, E., 134–35
Balsells, M. A., 7, 182, 237
Barth, R. P., xii–xiii
Bellahøj, Denmark. *See* Project Bella
Berrick, J. D., 160–61
Bessell, S., 136
biographical interviews, 136–38
biographies, participation in children's, 138–48
biological family, visitations with, 143–44, 150
bisexual youth and children. *See* LGBTQIA+ youth participation
bottom-up development of child protection guidelines, 94–95
Bouma, H., 188–89
Brazil, child protection and out-of-home care in, 202–5, 238. *See also* Making My Story project
Bridge to Independence program (Israeli Council for the Child in Care), 64–65, 67. *See also* care leavers' advisory boards
bureaucratic mindset, 146

California child protection system, 158–59, 160–62. *See also* age-related participation boundaries
Canfield, M., 6–7, 236–37
capability, as criterion for empowerment, 54
care leavers' advisory boards (Israel)
  challenges with participation, 74–75
  child and youth welfare services in Israel, 64–65
  experience of youths involved in, 71–76
  general discussion, 76–79, 232
  generators of child- and youth-led change, 234–35
  overview, 63

  research methods, 70–71
  young people's participation, 65–70
case support, token participation in, 143
Cashmore, J., 214–15
CESESMA NGO (Nicaragua), 89–95, 98, 99–100, 233–34. *See also* Nicaragua, children claiming right to live without violence in
change agents, children and young people as, 6, 230–35. *See also* care leavers' advisory boards; Change Factory; child-directed child welfare; violence, children claiming right to live without
Change Factory (Norway)
  awareness of students' personal histories, 23
  challenging the education system in child welfare, 19–20
  evaluations by students, pros, and teaching staff, 25–27
  framework and terminology, 18–19
  general discussion, 27–30, 231–32
  generators of child- and youth-led change, 234
  My Life Education project overview, 17–18
  overview, 13–17
  political and ethical reflections, 28–29
  PROs' messages to students, 23–24
  students' communication skills, 22–23
  students' relational understanding, 21–22
  ways of including PROs in social work education, 20–21
child-centered social work, 43–45, 44f
child-centric perspective, 3
child consultants investigating violence on coffee plantations, 91
child-directed child welfare
  case vignette, 58–59
  child welfare in Denmark, 35–36
  general discussion, 51–57, 232–33
  generators of child- and youth-led change, 235
  outcomes and lessons learned, 51–57
  overview, 34–35
  Project Bella, 45–51, 48f, 49f
  Roskilde Project, 37–45, 39t, 41t, 44f

INDEX 247

child equality perspective, 3, 18–19
CHILDPRO research project (Norwegian Research Council), 161–62
child protection systems (CPS)/child welfare services (CWS). *See also* arts-based research; Change Factory; child-directed child welfare; children's participation; Dutch child protection system
   in Brazil, 202–5
   children's participation movement results for, 108–9
   children's rights to participate in decision-making, xi–xiii, 1, 87, 131–33
   defined, 1–2
   in Denmark, 35–36
   in Israel, 64–65
   LGBTQIA+ youth experiences in, 109, 110–11, 121–23
   in Nicaragua, developing guidelines from bottom up for, 94–95
   in Norway, 13–15, 34–35
   in Spain, 182, 184–85
   in United States, 157–59, 236–37
Children and Adolescents' Voices Heard radio show (Nicaragua), 95
children as change agents, 6, 230–35. *See also* care leavers' advisory boards; Change Factory; child-directed child welfare; violence, children claiming right to live without
Children First law (Denmark), 36
children's participation
   aims of book, 1–2
   book organization, 6–7
   chapter selection criteria, 5
   children and young people as agents of change, 6, 230–35
   current status of, 240–43
   defined, 2–3, 52, 148–49, 156–57, 202
   generators of child- and youth-led change, 233–35
   generators of participatory professional practices, 235–39
   grounding concepts and questions, 2–4
   overview, 229–30
   results of movement for, 108–9
   rights to, xi–xiii, 1, 87, 131–33
   significance of scholarship on, 4–5
child welfare policy advocacy. *See* care leavers' advisory boards
citizenship, active, 90, 96–97
clients, labeling children as, 18–19
co-decisions, in Change Factory's values, 18
Coelho, N. N., 208
coffee plantations, child consultants investigating violence on, 91
cognitive development, and research methodologies, 195–96
cognitive readiness, role in children's participation, 168
coherence, 51–53
collaborators, in Making My Story project, 210–11, 214–16
collective involvement, opportunities for children's, 240–41
Collins, P. H., 3–4
communication skills, gaining in care leavers' advisory boards, 73–74
communication with children. *See also* arts-based research
   in child welfare education, 17–18
   in My Life Education project, 22–23
Comparative Perspectives on Social Work With Young People module (KP, Denmark), 49–50
competent actors, recognition of children and young people as, 51–57
comprehensibility, 52–53
conditions, as criterion for empowerment, 54
confidentiality, in arts-based research, 190
consent, in arts-based research, 189–90, 196
consultants investigating violence on coffee plantations, children as, 91
cooperation
   defined, 14
   in My Life Education project, 24
co-production
   defined, 14
   in My Life Education project, 19
Council for the Child in Care (Israel), 64–65, 67. *See also* care leavers' advisory boards

court decision, children taken into care without in Germany, 133
courtrooms, children's participation in, 171–73
CPS. *See* child protection systems/child welfare services
creativity, power of in prevention of violence, 98
Crenshaw, K., 56
Crowe, K. M., 14
Cruddas, L., 196–97
cultural change from within, 97–98
cultural frame related to families and parent-child relations, xii–xiii
cultural imperialism, 97
culture, family, 139–40
CWS. *See* child protection systems/child welfare services

decision-making, participation in. *See* children's participation
Dell'Aglio, D. D., 214–15
democracy, participation in, 134
Denmark, child-directed social work in
  case vignette, 58–59
  child welfare in Denmark, 35–36
  general discussion, 232–33
  generators of child- and youth-led change, 235
  outcomes and lessons learned, 51–57
  overview, 34–35
  Project Bella, 45–51, 48*f*, 49*f*
  Roskilde Project, 37–45, 39*t*, 41*t*, 44*f*
  Together on Bellahøj project, 45–46
diagnoses, applying to foster children, 147–48
Dickens, J., 160–61
dishonesty, caseworker perceptions of, 174–75
Dixon, J., 196–97
Dragon of Violence (Nicaragua), 92
drawings. *See* arts-based research
Dutch child protection system
  children's participation in, 111–12
  general discussion, 121–22
  LGBTQIA+ children and youth in, 109, 112–13

  research findings, 115–21
  research methods, 113–15
duty bearers, adults as, 86, 88, 96

Eberitzsch, S., 134
education in social work in Norway, 14–15. *See also* Change Factory
emotional bonds, importance of, 214–16
empowerment
  children claiming right to live without violence, 88
  lessons learned in Nicaragua, 95–96
  as rationale for more participation of foster children, 134–35
  understanding and approach to, 54
enlightened rationale, 134–35
equality, child, 3, 18–19
ethical reflections on My Life Education project, 28–29
ethical research
  arts-based research, 189–92
  in Roskilde Project, 37
  and silencing of children's voices, 99
European Scientific Association on Residential and Family Care for Children and Adolescents (EUSARF), 5
evidence-based knowledge in child welfare education, 19–20
evidence-based programs, 186–87
experts by experience, 230

families, cultural frame related to, xii–xiii
family, visitations with, 143–44, 150
family culture, 139–40
family group decision-making, 159
festivals against violence towards children (Nicaragua), 91
fictional stories, in Making My Story project, 208–9, 210
foster care, children's participation in, 134–36. *See also* German foster care system, children's participation in
"Friendly City for Children" programs (Israel), 66
Frushell, E., 6–7, 236–37
Fuentes-Peláez, N., 7, 237–38
Furlan, V., 214–15

Gal, T., 135
Gaudette, J., 6–7, 236–37
gay youth and children. *See* LGBTQIA+ youth participation
gender identity expression. *See* LGBTQIA+ youth participation
gender roles, and violence in Nicaragua, 92–93
genuine participation, 175–76
German foster care system, children's participation in
  children's participation rights in Germany, 131–33
  general discussion, 148–51
  generators of participatory professional practices, 236
  overview, 129–31
  participation in children's biographies, 138–48
  prior literature on children's participation in foster care, 134–36
  research methods, 136–38
Glacken, M., 189–90, 196
González Álvarez, R., 6–7, 235–36

Hart, R., 156–57, 188–89
histories, personal, in My Life Education project, 23
home, youth theater against violence in (Nicaragua), 90–91
honesty, caseworker perceptions of, 174–75
Honneth, A., 51–52, 240, 242–43
horizontal relationships, and Making My Story project, 214–16
human rights–based approach (HRBA) to keeping children safe, 86–89
humility, as Change Factory value, 18

IFSW (International Federation of Social Workers), 48, 49*f*
imagination, power of in prevention of violence, 98
immigrant children, in Denmark, 37–38
Independent Living Initiative (U.S.), 66–67
independent living programs (ILPs), 64–65, 172–73

individual decision-making, children's involvement in, 241
individualistic approach to children's participatory rights, 134–35
influence
  in Lundy's model of children's participation, 202
  and Making My Story project, 218–20
information
  as crucial for child participation, 209
  importance to LGBTQIA+ children and youth, 120
informed consent, in arts-based research, 189–90, 196
International Federation of Social Workers (IFSW), 48, 49*f*
intersectionality, 3–4, 34, 56–57, 176–77
intersex youth and children. *See* LGBTQIA+ youth participation
Israel, care leavers' advisory boards in
  challenges with participation, 74–75
  child and youth welfare services in Israel, 64–65
  experience of youths involved in, 71–76
  general discussion, 76–79, 232
  generators of child- and youth-led change, 234–35
  overview, 63
  research methods, 70–71
  young people's participation, 65–70
Israeli Council for the Child in Care, 64–65, 67

joint decision-making. *See* Project Bella

Kabeer, N., 54
Knowledge Centers (Norway), 16–17
knowledge from children, in child welfare education, 19–20
Københavns Professions Højskole (KP), Denmark, 49–50. *See also* Roskilde Project
Križ, K., xi, 6–7, 160, 161–62, 229, 236–37

ladder models of participation, 35, 134
Lambert, V., 189–90, 196
Lansdown, G., 156–57
Lareau, A., 77

Lavan, D., 90
Law on Social Services (Denmark), 35–36
Learning Together, Growing as a Family program (Spain), 183, 185–87, 237–38. *See also* arts-based research
lesbian youth and children. *See* LGBTQIA+ youth participation
LGBTQIA+ youth participation
    children's participation in Dutch CPS, 111–12
    experiences in child protection systems, 110–11
    experiences in Dutch CPS, 112–13
    general discussion, 121–23
    generators of participatory professional practices, 235–36
    overview, 6–7, 107–9
    research findings, 115–21
    research methods, 113–15
Liebel, M., 131
life storybook, in Making My Story project, 210–11, 213, 221
literature, in Making My Story project, 208–9, 210
lived experiences from children in child welfare education. *See* My Life Education project
local children's parliaments (Israel), 66
López López, M., 6–7, 235–36
Lotan, H., 6, 232
love, as Change Factory value, 18
Lundy, L., 177, 202

Making History Institute, 206–8, 238. *See also* Making My Story project
Making My Story project (Brazil), 241
    background, 206–8
    child protection, out-of-home care, and children's participation, 202–5
    general discussion, 220–22
    generators of participatory professional practices, 238–39
    lessons learned from, 213–20
    overview, 201–2
    rationale, 208–13
Mallon, G. P., 6–7, 235–36
manageability, 52–53

manipulation, caseworker perceptions of, 175
Mateos, A., 7, 237
maturity, role in children's participation, 165–67, 168, 169, 195–96
meaningfulness, 52–53
medical intervention, practitioners seeing profession as, 147–48
minority backgrounds, in Roskilde Project, 37–38
mistrust, care leavers' advisory board participation and, 72–73, 77
multidimensional approach to foster children's participation, 134–35
Münder, J., 133
Munro, E., 214–15
My Life Education project (Change Factory)
    awareness of students' personal histories, 23
    challenging the education system in child welfare, 19–20
    evaluations by students, pros, and teaching staff, 25–27
    framework and terminology, 18–19
    general discussion, 27–30, 231–32
    generators of child- and youth-led change, 234
    overview, 17–18
    political and ethical reflections, 28–29
    PROs' messages to students, 23–24
    students' communication skills, 22–23
    students' relational understanding, 21–22
    ways of including PROs in social work education, 20–21

Naddeo, L., 7, 238–39
National Festival Against Violence Towards Children (Nicaragua), 91
National Knowledge Centers (Norway), 16–17
Netherlands. *See* Dutch child protection system
new masculinities program (Nicaragua), 92–93
Nicaragua, children claiming right to live without violence in

general discussion, 233–34
overview, 85
rights-based approach to keeping children safe, 86–89
youth projects and processes, 89–95
normality, lack of, 147
Norway. *See also* Change Factory
age-related participation boundaries in, 160
child welfare services in, 13–15
generators of child- and youth-led change, 234
Norwegian Research Council, 161–62
Norwegian University of Science and Technology (NTNU). *See* My Life Education project

older children's participation, 159–61, 164*t*, 169–75
Olsen, A. N., xii–xiii
ongoing case support, token participation in, 143
open conversations, in My Life Education project, 22–23
openness, as Change Factory value, 18
opportunities, as criterion for empowerment, 54
outcomes for children and adults, as rationale for children's participation, 134–35
out-of-home care. *See also* care leavers' advisory boards; Change Factory; child protection systems/child welfare services; German foster care system, children's participation in; LGBTQIA+ youth participation; Roskilde Project
in Brazil, 202–5, 238
in Denmark, 35
literature on children's participation in foster care, 134–36
overview, 6
residential care facilities in Israel, 68–69
transition to, participation in, 141–43, 149–50

parental education programs. *See* Learning Together, Growing as a Family program

parental needs over children's participation, 139–40
parental pseudo-participation in Germany, 133
parent-child relations, cultural frame related to, xii–xiii
participation, children's
aims of book, 1–2
book organization, 6–7
chapter selection criteria, 5
children and young people as agents of change, 6, 230–35
current status of, 240–43
defined, 2–3, 52, 148–49, 156–57, 202
generators of child- and youth-led change, 233–35
generators of participatory professional practices, 235–39
grounding concepts and questions, 2–4
overview, 229–30
results of movement for, 108–9
rights to, xi–xiii, 1, 87, 131–33
significance of scholarship on, 4–5
participation generators
of child- and youth-led change, 233–35
overview, 231
of participatory professional practices, 235–39
participatory capital, 231
participatory professional practices, 6–7, 235–39. *See also* age-related participation boundaries; arts-based research; German foster care system, children's participation in; LGBTQIA+ youth participation; Making My Story project
paternalism, 205
pedagogical processes, participation in, 134
personal histories, in My Life Education project, 23
Petersen, M., xi, 6, 34, 35, 38, 41*t*, 229, 232–33, 235, 241
Petit, M., 208–9
Platt, L., 195–96
policymaking, youth engagement in. *See* care leavers' advisory boards
political arena, care leavers' engagement in, 68–70, 72–73, 76–78, 79

political reflections on My Life Education project, 28–29
positive connections with caseworkers, importance to LGBTQIA+ children and youth, 118–19
positive parenting, 185
postcolonial societies, cultural change in, 97
posttraumatic growth, 55–56
Practical Guide for Professionals and Foster Parents (Zwernemann), 147–48
practical resources, offering to older children, 173–74
practice knowledge, in child welfare education, 19–20
preparation, importance to LGBTQIA+ children and youth, 120
preteens. See older children's participation
preventative family preservation interventions. See Learning Together, Growing as a Family program
problem finders and solvers, professionals perceiving themselves as, 147–48
problem-solving approach. See child-directed child welfare
professional attitudes closed to participatory practice, 145–48
professionals in child welfare (PROs), Change Factory
  challenging education system in child welfare, 19–20
  evaluation of My Life Education project, 25–27
  generators of child- and youth-led change, 234
  messages to students, 23–24
  methods and outcomes, 231–32
  My Life Education project framework, 18–19
  overview, 13–16
  protection for, 20–21
  ways of including in social work education, 20–21
program evaluation. See arts-based research
Project Bella (Denmark)
  children's participation in, 46–50, 48*f*, 49*f*
  effect on young people involved in, 50–51
  general discussion, 232–33
  generators of child- and youth-led change, 235
  outcomes and lessons learned, 51–57
  overview, 34, 35, 45–46
  participants, 37–38, 41*t*
  roles and activities, 41*t*
PROs, Change Factory. See professionals in child welfare
protagonismo infantil, 54, 90, 233
protection from violence. See violence, children claiming right to live without

queer youth and children. See LGBTQIA+ youth participation
questioning youth and children. See LGBTQIA+ youth participation

reading intervention, Making My Story project, 208–9, 210
recognition, 51–57, 242–43
Reimer, D., 6–7, 236, 241
relational skills training, in My Life Education project, 21–22, 26
relationships
  with caseworkers, importance to LGBTQIA+ children and youth, 118–19
  and Making My Story project outcomes, 214–16
researchers, children as, 91, 93–94, 98–99
residential care facilities, in Israel, 68–69
resilience, 55–56
resistant capital, 55–56, 77–78
resourcefulness, dichotomy of vulnerability and, 55–56
resources, offering to older children, 173–74
responsible citizens, children as, 96–97
rights-based approach to keeping children safe, 86–89
rights holders, children as, 86, 88
rights to participation, children's, xi–xiii, 1, 87, 131–33

INDEX

right to live without violence. *See* violence, children claiming right to live without
Rodrigo, M. J., 7, 186–87, 237
Roskilde Project (Denmark)
    approaches to collecting children's perspectives, 38–41
    approach to children's participation, 43–45, 44f
    case vignette, 40–41, 58–59
    general discussion, 232–33
    methodological flexibility and creativity, 42–43
    outcomes and lessons learned, 51–57
    overview, 34, 35, 37
    parents' reluctance to involvement in, 42
    participants, 37–38, 39t
    roles and activities, 39t, 41–42, 41t
Rotlevi, S., 65

safety from violence, 85, 86–89. *See also* violence, children claiming right to live without
Safety Organized Practice (SPO), California, 159
safety plans. *See* Roskilde Project
Santa Martha Coffee Plantation (Nicaragua), 91
Save the Children, 91
school councils in Israel, 66
Schwartz-Tayri, T. M., 6, 232
self-awareness, in My Life Education project, 23
self-confidence, gaining in care leavers' advisory boards, 73–74
self-help groups, care leavers' advisory boards as, 72
service users, labeling children as, 18–19
sex and sexuality, children researching children's understanding of, 94
sexual orientation and gender identity expression (SOGIE). *See* LGBTQIA+ youth participation
shared family culture, 139–40
Shier, H., 5, 6, 14, 54, 88, 93, 156–57, 233–34
"Signs of Safety/Safety Plans" study (Petersen). *See* Roskilde Project

silencing of children's voices, 99–101
Siqueira, A. C., 214–15
Skelton, T., 99
Skivenes, M., xi–xiii, 3, 5, 6, 160, 161–62, 187
Skyscrapers at Bellahøj (documentary), 48–49
Social Assistance Act (Denmark), 35–36
social change, children and young people as agents of, 6, 230–35. *See also* care leavers' advisory boards; Change Factory; child-directed child welfare; violence, children claiming right to live without
social recognition, 51–52
social relations, in My Life Education project, 23
Social Security Act (U.S.), 158–59
Social Services Act (Denmark), 35–36
Social Services Code (SGB VIII), Germany, 132–33
social work. *See* child-directed child welfare; child protection systems/child welfare services
social work education in Norway, 14–15. *See also* Change Factory
socio-educational interventions, 186–87
SOGIE (sexual orientation and gender identity expression). *See* LGBTQIA+ youth participation
Souza, T. de P., 214–15
space
    importance to LGBTQIA+ children and youth, 121
    in Lundy's model of children's participation, 202
    and Making My Story project, 214–16, 220
Spain. *See also* arts-based research
    child protection in, 184–85
    Learning Together, Growing as a Family program, 183, 185–87, 237–38
    legislation on child protection in, 182
SPO (Safety Organized Practice), California, 159
Statute of the Child and Adolescent (Brazil), 203–5
stories, life. *See* Making My Story project

Strandbu, A., 3
stressful visitations with family, 143–44
students. *See also* Change Factory
    participation in Roskilde Project, 41–42
    Project Bella and social work education, 49–50
Sundby, R., 6, 231–32, 234, 242
support, care leavers' advisory boards as, 72
supportive child welfare practice for LGBTQIA+ children and youth, 116–18
symbolic age boundaries
    babies and younger children's participation, 163–69, 164*t*
    general discussion, 175–76
    older children's participation, 164*t*, 169–75
    overview, 157, 163

Taft, J. K., 90, 205
team decision-making (TDM), 159, 168, 169–71
teenagers. *See* older children's participation
ten Brummelaar, M., 6–7, 235–36
theater against violence in the home (Nicaragua), 90–91
Thomas, N., 5, 240
Together on Bellahøj project (Denmark), 45–46
token participation in ongoing case support, 143
Transformative Research by Children and Adolescents (TRCA), Nicaragua, 93
transition to care, participation in, 141–43, 149–50
trans youth and children. *See* LGBTQIA+ youth participation
trust
    care leavers' advisory board participation and, 72–73
    gaining in Project Bella, 50

United Nations Convention on the Rights of the Child (UNCRC), xi, 7, 51
    and age-related participation boundaries, 177

    and children's participation rights in Germany, 132
    definition of participation used by, 202
    Israel's ratification of, 65
    LGBTQIA+ youth participation and, 107–8
    and rights-based approach to keeping children safe, 86–89
    scope of participation, 1
    U.S. opposition to ratification of, 158–59
United States (U.S.). *See also* age-related participation boundaries
    care leavers' advisory boards in, 66–67, 78
    child protection system in, 157–59, 236–37
    Independent Living Initiative, 66–67
University College Copenhagen, 49–50. *See* Roskilde Project
University of East London (UEL), 212–13
University of South-Eastern Norway (USN). *See* My Life Education project

values, Change Factory, 18–19
van Mierlo, K. R. O., 6–7, 235–36
Vidigal, C., 206–7
Vidiz, M., 7, 237, 238–39, 241
Vigevani, D., 7, 238–39
violence, children claiming right to live without
    general discussion, 233–34
    overview, 85
    rights-based approach to keeping children safe, 86–89
    youth projects and processes, 89–95
visitations with family, 143–44, 150
voice
    in Lundy's model of children's participation, 202
    and Making My Story project, 216–18, 219, 220
voices of children. *See also* arts-based research
    capturing, 195
    silencing of, 99–101
vulnerability, dichotomy of resourcefulness and, 55–56

Woodhead, M., 204–5

Yosso, T. J., 55–56, 77–78
younger children's participation. *See also* arts-based research
    age-related participation boundaries, 160–61, 163–69, 164*t*, 237
    in Making My Story project, 216–18
young people as change agents, 6, 230–35. *See also* care leavers' advisory boards; Change Factory; child-directed child welfare; violence, children claiming right to live without
young people's participation. *See* children's participation
young women's groups (Nicaragua), 92
youth theater against violence in the home (Nicaragua), 90–91

Zwernemann, P., 147–48